D1032249

LARRY A. JACKSON LIBRARY
Lander College
Greenwood, S. C. 29646

**The Discovery of
the Third World**

The MIT Press

Cambridge, Massachusetts, and London, England

**The Discovery of
the Third World**

Ignacy Sachs

220425

LARRY A. JACKSON LIBRARY
Lander College
Greenwood, S. C. 29646

Copyright © 1976 by The Massachusetts Institute of
Technology.

Originally published in French under the title *La
Découverte du Tiers Monde* by Flammarion, Paris.

Translated by Michael Fineberg

All rights reserved. No part of this book may be reproduced in any form or by any means, electronic or
mechanical, including photocopying, recording, or by
any information storage and retrieval system, without
permission in writing from the publisher.

This book was set in IBM Composer Univers by
Margaret Hayman, and printed and bound by
Lithocrafters, Inc. in the United States of
America.

Library of Congress Cataloging in Publication Data

Sachs, Ignacy.
    The discovery of the Third World.

    Translation of La découverte du Tiers monde.
    Includes bibliographical references.
    1. Underdeveloped areas.   2. Ethnocentrism.
I. Title.
HC59.7.S24913   309.1'172'4   76-27676
ISBN 0-262-19145-8

To my friends
in Poland

Introduction: The Chicken Coop, or Optimism

The discovery of the Third World[1] marks a caesura in the intellectual history of our generation. Postulated by some immediately after the Russian Revolution of 1917, anticipated by others during the Second World War, that discovery took shape in the popular mind of Europe and North America between 1949 and 1955, that is to say between the winning of the Chinese Revolution and the conference of Asian and African countries at Bandoeng. The image of a world inhabited by a minority of men and a vast majority of natives,[2] a product of the "Vasco da Gama era," collapsed beneath the wave of emancipation which swept the three continents where colonialism flourished, and with it collapsed the hierarchical structure by which it was justified, made up of a civilized central authority and a subjugated, barbaric periphery. Europocentrism, with its convenient certainties sustained by racial stereotypes, pretended geographical determinism, and faith in a pre-established harmony underlying the international division of labor, has had its day.

Today we are faced with the soul-searching task of revising our *Weltanschauung*; over and above political contingencies, our habits of thought and modes of action are being challenged. In short, we must reinvent the world,[3] reinterpret it with the help of genuinely universal values. But the way to do this is through self-examination, made possible and more productive by our confrontation with the Third World. Outgrowing Europocentrism is the exclusive concern of Europeans, and in that sense this essay will be profoundly Europocentric.

At first glance one is tempted to draw a parallel with the discovery of America. The sudden widening of the geographic horizon and, above all, the new contact with peoples whose existence had not even been suspected, upset the *Weltanschauung* of fifteenth- and sixteenth-century Europeans. But the discovery of America was an encounter between worlds until then completely separate,[4] whereas that of the Third World is taking place within a global economic and political system marked by a deep-seated and steadily increasing asymmetry and a cause-and-effect relationship between underdevelopment of some nations and the overdevelopment of others.[5] Recent scientific and technological progress has been only one factor in the aggravation of this disequilibrium. In fact, the breakdown of this system is at the origin of the Third World's emergence. In these circumstances, confrontation tends to become conflict.

In the culminating scene of Dürrenmatt's *Romulus the Great,* Odoacer, the victorious chief of the Germans, comes upon the Roman Emperor in his palace, where he has remained too weary to flee the enemy. The two get to talking. Romulus expresses surprise at the trousers which the Germans wear and above all at their human appearance: ". . . Tacitus describes you as beings with blue eyes aglint with arrogance, red hair, and enormous, barbaric bodies; but seeing you, I have the feeling that I am talking to a Byzantine botanist from Byzantium in disguise. . . ."[6] Odoacer has a sip of wine and finds it quite horrid in comparison with beer. Still, he admires a statue of Venus, which he attributes to Praxiteles. Briefly then, two men meet, willing to reconsider their prejudices, in spite of the attachment which one feels for the toga and wine and the other for trousers and beer. But they enter into genuine communication and sympathy with each other only when a hen crosses the stage; they both confess that they are dedicated poultry-breeders.

Dürrenmatt had it much too easy here: his two heroes, in spite of being, by profession, heads of state, were, in their own ways, humanists. And yet, to provide some support for his optimism, he deemed it necessary to bring in the hen and to contrive for them an area where they could get along together—which turned out to be the chicken coop. Will we be able likewise to find a point at which our interests converge and thus discover a common language for us and the Third World? For this, at least two preliminary steps are necessary. First of all, we must demystify the image of the other while seeking to see ourselves reflected in his eyes; next, we must refine our analytical tools and divest them of their Europocentric content. Only subsequently will we be free to venture into the chicken coop; when that happens, we will need an operational approach to the accelerated socioeconomic development of the Third World.

Notes

1. The term Third World first appeared around 1955 and owes its acceptance to its ambiguity and to our confusion in the face of a set of problems which cannot be reduced to a simple capitalist-socialist dichotomy at the level of an analysis of sociopolitical structures, nor to the confrontation of two antagonistic blocs at the level of international politics.

2. The expression is Jean-Paul Sartre's (from the preface to Frantz Fanon, *Les damnés de la terre*; Paris, 1961). For a definition of the "Vasco da Gama era," see K. M. Panikkar, *Asia and Western Dominance* (London, 1959).

3. Albert Bettex's history of discoveries and inventions, supported by superb documentary evidence, is significantly entitled *L'invention du monde* (The invention of the world; Paris, 1960).

4. As Fernand Braudel says, "Mankind began to become *one* (although has not yet succeeded) only at the end of the fifteenth century. Until then, and more and more so as we go back through the centuries, it was divided up into different spheres, each of them accommodating one particular civilization or culture with its own distinguishing features and its own long-term choices." *Civilisation matérielle et capitalisme* (Paris, 1967), p. 435.

5. See in this connection Witold Kula's excellent essay, "Sottosviluppo economico nella prospettiva storica," in *Annali della Fondazione Einaudi* (Turin), 3 (1969), 23-36.

6. Based on the Polish translation of Dürrenmatt's play, which appeared in the review *Dialog* (Warsaw), no. 1 (1959), p. 89.

**The Discovery of
the Third World**

The Image of the Other

They are called savages; they are rude,
honest folk, and the men of our country
are sophisticated rogues.
—Voltaire, *L'Ingénu*

Ethnocentrism: From Primitive Peoples to Modern Nations

"I am at the Center of the World!" This cry of the Kwakiutl neophyte should, according to Mircea Eliade, be seen in the context of a basic religious experience: the division of the homogeneity of space into sacred space and secular space and the founding of the world, which becomes possible only once the "still point"—the *Axis Mundi*—has been located, in relation to which the course of the universe will be determined and which, since it must pass through the Center of the World, links up and organizes the three levels of the Cosmos—in the sky, the earth, and the different kinds of hell. The religious man naturally aspires to live at the Center of the World—of the Cosmos as opposed to the chaos which envelops it—and this desire would appear to be common to all traditional societies. "What characterizes traditional societies is the implicit opposition which they see between their inhabited territory and the unknown and undetermined space which surrounds it: the former is the 'World' (more accurately, 'our world'), the Cosmos; the rest is no longer a Cosmos but a sort of 'other world,' an alien, chaotic space peopled by ghosts, demons, and 'aliens' (who themselves are likened, moreover, to demons and ghosts)."[1] Mircea Eliade backs up his demonstration with numerous examples drawn from the symbology of the Center of the World and derived from different religions. He concludes from these that the need felt by men in traditional societies to live in a total and organized world can be seen both at the level of his house and at the level of his village, his town, or his country. It is in this way that man in premodern societies knows that "his country is in fact situated in the middle of the Earth, that his town is the navel of the Universe, and, above all, that the Temple or the Palace are true Centers of the World; but he also wants his own house to be situated at the Center and to be an *imago mundi*."[2]

It is not necessary in my opinion to go all the way with Eliade in the philosophical construction he imposes on the existential religious fact in order to accord a central place to the ethnocentric system of reference in the explanation of cultures and, *a fortiori*, in the history of relationships between societies.

The Negroes, both men and women, all flocked to see me as towards some great marvel, for it seemed to them to be a great thing to set their eyes on a Christian, this being unheard of in their experience. They were no less astonished at my whiteness than at my clothes which aroused a great admiration in them for they were in the Spanish style. Some of them touched my hands and arms which, putting their saliva on them, they rubbed in order to see if my whiteness was a result of make-up or dye or whether it was flesh. Recognizing that it was flesh, they remained dumfounded.[3]

Five centuries after the voyage of the Venetian Ca da Mosto to Guinea, the American anthropologist Turnbull noted that the Pygmies were moved to pity on seeing him because he was big, therefore clumsy, and his hairy legs and arms made him look like an ape.[4]

It is a well known fact that an honest man can be recognized by the way he wears his hair. The Celts were barbaric in the eyes of the Roman *togati* because they were hairy *(comati)* and wore trousers *(bracati)*.[5] The Vikings called the first Indians they saw on the coast of America "Skraelings," that is to say, contemptible savages, for "these swarthy and ugly men arranged their hair in an unpleasant fashion."[6] Furthermore, they did not hesitate to barter with them according to the principle of nonequivalence, to borrow a euphemism from contemporary economics; taking advantage of the fact that the American Indians were unfamiliar with cattle breeding, they exchanged milk for furs: "Karlsefni forbade his men to sell arms. Then he hit on the idea of telling the women to carry milk out to the Skraelings, and when the Skraelings saw the milk they wanted to buy nothing else. And so the outcome of this trading expedition was that the Skraelings carried their purchases away in their bellies, and left their packs and furs with Karlsefni and his men."[7]

Reading this passage one cannot help thinking of the trafficking that was later to take place during the period of colonial expansion. Paul Valéry was right when he said: "Unhappily for the human race, it is in the nature of things that relationships between peoples always begin with contacts established by individuals who are least fitted to seek out common roots and to discover, before anything else, a correspondence of sensibilities. Peoples always come into contact first through their most callous and greediest men; or else through those most determined to impose their doctrines and to give without receiving, which distinguishes them from the former. Neither type is in any way concerned with equal exchange, and their roles do not consist in the slightest in respecting the peace, freedom, beliefs, or property of others. Their energy, their talents, their reason, and their devotion are applied to creating or exploiting inequality. They exert themselves and often sacrifice themselves in their endeavor to do to others what they would not like to have done to themselves. They are bound to regard people with contempt, sometimes even unconsciously, in order to apply themselves to reducing or seducing them. In the beginning is contempt: there exists no easier form of reciprocity nor any quicker to establish itself."[8]

But these observations do not give the whole picture. Contempt is not always the only thing that comes into play. First there is often an exaggerated feeling of wonder; the shock of the unexpected results in inflated reactions. One thinks of Cristopher Columbus's diary and of its eulogy of the remarkable savages of the Caribbean islands[9]—which in no way prevented the Spanish from later massacring so many of the native population of Mexico. Later, the conquerors were greatly interested in the question of whether the Caribbean Indians had souls. As for the Caribs, they hoped to ascertain, by drowning Europeans, whether their corpses decomposed in the same way as their own.[10]

The dialectic of the civilized and the barbaric obeys laws which as yet have not been given sufficient study, in which predominates a relativism all of whose consequences we are far from having grasped. The Europeans discovered the world, crossed its oceans, described its surface, gave names to most of its geographical features, and explained the workings of the planetary system. But what in fact is a discovery? "I have never been able to understand how lands inhabited by men can be discovered. From what it appears, Siemion Drejniew discovered the straits between Asia and America. And what about us? And what about the Eskimoes? Our ancestors after all knew very well that the straits were there. It's as though I were to go to Yakutsk and to announce that I had discovered that town. The Yakuts would be grieved to hear it." So the Chukot* hero of an autobiographical novel declares to his school-teacher.[11]

It is my opinion that the systematic study of the image of the other deserves to be given priority by UNESCO, in view of the intrinsic interest of the subject, of the rare opportunity it affords of organizing multi-disciplinary international collaboration, and in consideration, finally, of its political implications. Ethnocentrism influences the contemporary international scene to a dangerous extent, constituting, in fact, one of its chief characteristics.

According to the classic definition of William Graham Sumner, ethnocentrism is seeing things as though the group to which one belongs is the center of everything, all other groups being classified and rated in relation to it.[12] It does not mean, then, becoming entrenched in an isolated system of values in which self-sufficiency might be ensured, as was the case with the inhabitants of Easter Island. They had a name for each bay and each rock on their island but, being isolated and, to all intents and purposes, alone in the world, felt no need to name the island;[13] the Cosmos does not have to be named.

And if we compare ourselves with others, it is in order to judge them according to our own standards. Not satisfied with professing the excellence of the group to which we belong and of its system of values, we get into deeper waters demonstrating its superiority. Now, the easiest way of sustaining a feeling of superiority is to show that others are inferior by attributing to them all the vices and shortcomings imaginable and by condemning them to chaos if not to hell itself. The worse things are in reality, the more one tries to embellish one's feeling of superiority, feeding it on ethnocentric beliefs and propaganda.

*Siberian ethnic group. (Trans.)

But it is obvious that against the ethnocentrism of one group is set the ethnocentrism of the other, opposite group, with the result that each side accuses the other of inferiority and that each becomes convinced of its own superiority. When hatred escalates in this way it can lead pretty far. H. Rap Brown has stated that hatred and violence, inspired by the hatred of whites, are necessary to the black revolutionary movement.[14]

The concept of ethnocentrism, as I see it, therefore goes beyond tribal society and encompasses the intellectual attitudes of all human groups, who are set against other groups according to variable criteria: affiliation with a race, a civilization or cultural area, a nation, a religion, or a caste. Racism, Europocentrism, and the Europophobic Asiocentrism and Afrocentrism that are the reaction to it, chauvinism, religious intolerance, and discrimination against "untouchables" are then simply manifestations and particular cases of ethnocentrism. But I must emphasize the asymmetry inherent in the concept of ethnocentrism, which, through the implicit comparison and opposition of "superiors" and "inferiors," creates an artificial and arbitrary hierarchy. In principle, patriotism does not enter into my definition, nor does libertarian nationalism, although, as we shall see subsequently, the demarcation line between "positive" nationalism and "chauvinistic" nationalism is not always easy to establish, and the most noble sentiments may degenerate into the most abject form of racist ideology. At all events, to be convinced of the excellence of one's own country and to love it, without wronging or hating one's neighbors, is not ethnocentrism. This definition is, consequently, both narrower and more subtle than that proposed by G. P. Murdock.[15]

In particular, it seems to me that the attitudes of Europeans toward the Third World and those of the Third World toward Europe ("Europe" being understood as a symbol for all of 'Western" civilization[16]) are, in both cases, imbued with a specific ethnocentrism which in fact subsumes and includes various "standard" types, such as racism, xenophobic forms of nationalism, and religious intolerance, and increasingly gives way to a new conceptual dichotomy—a misconception, to my mind—opposing the north and the south.

No one takes too seriously Spengler's jeremiads and his apocalyptic vision of a decline of the West brought about by the colored world's revenge against the white, made possible by the foolhardy dissemination of European technological knowledge which should have been jealously guarded. "The intangible privileges of the white races have been thrown to the winds, squandered, given away. The uninitiated have caught up with their initiators. Perhaps they have even overtaken them, combining the guile of the 'native' with the great atavistic intellectual maturity of their very ancient civilizations. . . . The exploited world bids fair to take its revenge on its overlords. The countless multitudes of the colored races—at least as capable, but far less demanding—will destroy the economic organization of the whites right down to its very foundations."[17] But there are a thousand other more underhand ways of promoting racial prejudice against the Third World, by using mass communication, advertising, and, sad to say, school textbooks—and this is a second level on which the systematic study of the manifestations of ethnocentrism should focus. Let me give an example. In the homeland of the Encyclopaedists, schoolchildren in the second grade are introduced to social psychology through extracts from a piece of writing by Paul Claudel entitled "Features of the Chinese Character," which runs as follows:

The Chinese develops more slowly, thinks, learns, and acts more slowly than does the European. It is far easier for him than for us to remain in a state of indifference and inertia. . . . From the point of view of physical strength and productivity (his) value is lower than that of the European. . . . The Chinese spends longer at his work, but he lounges about much more, he sleeps, he chats with his friends, he drinks a cup of hot water, he smokes a little pipe, he is very rarely capable of putting his back into whatever he is doing. . . .

Having described these physical characteristics, we can endeavor to put the finishing touches on a sort of psychological portrait. . . . As cold and calculating as he may be in ordinary life . . . , the Chinese will never hesitate to let matters of self-esteem come before all others, to the detriment of his most urgent and most valuable interests. . . . Never will [he] admit, never will he sincerely admit to himself a fault, a mistake, or any form of inferiority . . . , never will he humiliate himself. . . . After pride, the most powerful feeling to enter the heart of the Chinese is love of gain. . . . He is ruthless about property and money. Long-range considerations are absolutely foreign to him. He will demolish a bridge in order to make himself a wheelbarrow. . . . He is supreme amongst wasters and destroyers. . . . Everything has a value for him. . . .

But he is above all a "money-grubber," a tradesman who always seeks to give as little as possible for as much as possible. If, in order to earn money, he has to work, he will work, but if he can live without working or by working less, he will do his best to attain this ideal. . . . More than a workman, he is a tradesman, more than a tradesman, he is an unbridled speculator and gambler.[18]

The commentaries which the authors of this textbook place before and after this passage serve only to reinforce the impression which it creates. We learn, by way of introduction, that this psychological portrait of the Chinese retains its interest in spite of a revolution in the Chinese life-style since the last war and that in other writings Claudel praises the Chinese—a people he claims to have loved dearly. Two conclusions are proposed to the children, which undoubtedly are meant to be urged upon them by way of the exercises and the ensuing discussion: One should take care not to make hasty generalizations and one should beware of prejudices; nevertheless, "a faithful observer such as Claudel considers it possible to make out the following features in the Chinese character (which perhaps have something to do with the Chinese nervous system):

—their love of gain: they are tradesmen, speculators, gamblers;
—their pride: "never do they consent to lose face."
And finally: "It is useful to be familiar with their racial characteristics when one deals with them."

Ethnocentric stereotypes generally die hard. Once set in circulation, they display an astonishing propensity to be reincarnated in the most diverse forms. An example of this is the fear of the "yellow peril," in which vague memories of the Mongolian invasions and the defeat inflicted on the Russians by the Japanese in 1904 merge in people's minds with the hostility inspired by the winning of the Chinese revolution. In 1966, having put on a program on Warsaw television devoted to the problems of the Third World, I received from one of the viewers (a workman or a farmer to judge by the style and the spelling) the following letter, which speaks volumes on the state of mind of a part of the public in the countries of Eastern Europe:

"I listened with great interest to your television program on 1st April. You spoke in a very learned and interesting manner, but why should we bother about the economic problems of the backward countries? Who was concerned about our fate when we were prisoners and under the occupation and when the occupying forces and the invaders took away from us the best things we had and treated our country as a source of supply for food and labor? Who thought of Poland then? Tell us what we should do to make things better in our country and so that we can be rich and affluent. I would be glad to listen to a program about the problems of our country and ways of managing our economy well and wisely because we are suffering from a great number of economic mistakes and defects. Tell us what we should do to make ourselves and our country rich more quickly. Where should we invest? What should we avoid? How should we live and work to attain well-being? Let's concern ourselves with ourselves and with our economy instead of with remote acquaintances, because they did not give a thought to us when we were in a bad way and suffering hardships and just the same now they would not give a thought to Poland and the Poles. Do you remember how, after the war, only America came to the aid of Poland through the UNRRA? We should therefore turn our attention to the economy of our own country and not to the problems of the Eskimoes and the Papuans because that won't bring us any more bread and, at the most, it will give us rivals and enemies as we see for instance in the case of Communist China; the Russians helped them, built up their industries and fed them and now [the Chinese] are reaching for Siberia, using the slogan "Asia for the Asians." Fortunately, their grasp is still weak, but what would happen if they were to strangle Russia? They would reach us too and we would become slaves of the Chinks or the blacks, which I ask you kindly not to forget and to bring up this problem before a larger audience, before the Central Committee and the Cabinet."

Which just goes to show that "Cartierism"* and racism are not to be met with solely in Western societies.

Notes to Chapter 1

1. Mircea Eliade, *Le sacré et le profane* (Paris, 1965), p. 28.

2. *Ibid.,* p. 40.

3. A. Ca da Mosto, "Relation de voyages à la côte occidentale d'Afrique," in *La découverte de l'Afrique,* introduced by Catherine Coquery (Paris, 1965), p. 103.

4. Colin M. Turnbull, *The Forest People* (New York, 1961). Consulted in the Polish edition, *Lesni Ludzie* (Warsaw, 1967), p. 238.

5. See A. N. Sherwin-White, *Racial Prejudice in Imperial Rome* (Cambridge, England, 1967).

6. Gwyn Jones, ed., *Eirik the Red and Other Icelandic Sagas* (New York, 1961), p. 151.

7. *The Vinland Sagas: The Norse Discovery of America,* tr. Magnus Magnusson and Hermann Palsson (New York, 1965), p. 65. The passage quoted is taken from the *Graenlendinga Saga.*

8. Paul Valéry, *Regards sur le monde actuel* (Paris, 1945), pp. 185-186.

9. A long quotation from this diary, of which only a summary is known, is reproduced in *Historia del S.D. Fernando Colombo* (Venice, 1571). Consulted in the Polish translation, *Dzieje Zywota i Znamienitych Spraw Admirala don Krysztofa Kolumba przez jego syna Hernanda Colona* (Warsaw, 1965), p. 157.

10. See Claude Lévi-Strauss, *Race et histoire* (Paris, 1953).

*Policy of refusing aid to Third World countries. (Trans.)

11. Juryj Rytchen, *Ajvanhu,* translated from the Russian into Polish by W. Bienkowska (Warsaw, 1966), p. 109.

12. W. G. Sumner, *Folkways* (Boston, 1906), p. 13.

13. See A. Métraux, *L'île de Pâques* (Paris, 1965), p. 50.

14. Interview published in *Le Nouvel Observateur,* no. 148 (1968), p. 20.

15. "Ethnocentrism," in *Encyclopaedia of the Social Sciences* (New York, 1949), vol. 5, p. 613.

16. According to George Young, "in North America the earliest epoch of Europeanization by extermination so simplified matters that North America is more European than Europe." ("Europeanization," in *Encyclopaedia of the Social Sciences,* vol. 5, p. 628).

17. Oswald Spengler, *L'homme et la technique* (Paris, 1958), pp. 175-176. (French translation of *Der Mensch und die Technik: Beitrag zu einer Philosophie des Lebens.*)

18. J. Beaugrand and M. Cournault, *Le Français par les textes,* classe de 5e (Classiques Hachette, Paris, 1963), pp. 314-315. This is an extract from *Sous le signe du Dragon,* published in 1908.

2

Europocentrism: From Its Origins to the Discovery of the Third World

"For the three or four hundred years that the people of Europe have been swarming all over the world and constantly publishing new accounts of their travels and dealings, I am convinced that we have known no men other than Europeans."[1] This passage from Rousseau, written two hundred years ago, echoes the famous *History of the Gorgias,* which were kingdoms discovered by Rabelais between Pantagruel's teeth, causing him to exclaim: "And I started to think that what is said is quite true—that one half of the world does not know how the other half lives."[2]

Rousseau complained that this state of affairs arose because there were only four categories of people who traveled: sailors, merchants, soldiers, and missionaries. Since then we have added to this list airline employees, politicians, tourists, and sportsmen. Be that as it may be, is it possible for us to say that the words of Rabelais and Rousseau have lost any of their relevance? Europocentrism continues to dominate our way of thinking and, having been projected worldwide by colonialism and the expansion of capitalism, it casts contemporary culture in its mold, placing blinders over the eyes of some and forcing itself on others by deculturation. Although I do not intend to do a systematic historical analysis, I shall attempt to outline the main features of its history: for this, there is no lack of material.[3]

Several authors, such as René Grousset;[4] the Italian historian Federico Chabod;[5] and the Dutch historian Baudet, author of an important essay entitled *Paradise on Earth—Some Thoughts on European Images of Non-European Man,*[6] see Europocentrism as deriving from the Greek-barbarian antinomy.

Certainly, this primary antinomy set different cultures in opposition with each other even in its time. In a passage which is admirable for its sense of historical relativity, Thucydides notes a clear sign of barbarism in the fact that the Persians, in contrast to the Greeks, do not appear naked when taking part in the games, but he immediately adds that the Greeks formerly did not either and that the present state of Persian culture affords, in fact, an image of Greek culture in earlier days.[7] A few observations by Herodotus and a celebrated passage by Aristotle[8] have served as a basis for a superficial theory contrasting the Europeans' taste for democracy with the submission of Asians to despotism, a theory which today still finds commentators eager to exaggerate its significance and to forget the multiple links which have bound all the cultures of the Mediterranean and of Asia Minor together. Of course, the geographic features of this pre-Europe differed from that to which we are now accustomed.[9] According to Tacitus, living conditions in Germany were too harsh for people from Asia, Africa or Italy to want to visit it.[10] And *Heart of Darkness,* by Joseph Conrad, opens with an amazing reconstruction of the terror which the Roman legionnaires must have felt on being confronted by the dense forests surrounding London. ("And this also . . . has been one of the dark places of the earth.")

In the Middle Ages the civilized-barbarian antinomy took on a religious dimension: it set the Christian against the infidel, more particularly against the Moslem and, less violently, Europe against Byzantium.

The relations between Christendom and Islam are not strictly symmetrical, as Islam was perhaps somewhat less intolerant, whereas on the other side Mahomet was placed in Dante's Inferno with the schismatics, *"seminator di scandalo e de scisma."*[11] It would be worthwhile to do a systematic analysis of Arabic writings inspired by the Crusades in order to see what sort of image of the Franks emerges from them. Sometimes there are mingled in them hostility and a certain curiosity and a feeling of ironic and condescending superiority toward the European barbarians, to go by a few delightful passages from the autobiography of Usanna ibn Munquidh and, in particular, the satire on European medicine.[12] Moreover, it is to be noted that, even on the European side, there was not always an attitude of uncompromising condemnation. For instance, in a twelfth-century romance, *Floire et Blanceflor,* we find the good Babylonian emir who represents a curious protoplast of the Oriental sages of Enlightenment literature.[13]

As for the opposition between Europe and Byzantium, historians are in disagreement as to the extent of the rift. For Ullmann, the concept of Europe implied the exclusion of the Greeks from Byzantium, a fact which Byzantium recognized.[14] At the other extreme, Barraclough rejects the very concept of a European culture and denies the existence of frontiers between Europe, Asia, and Africa.[15] Without wishing to take a dogmatic stand in this controversy, I shall merely point to a text which speaks volumes on the image of barbaric Europe which emerged in Byzantium. In the *Alexiad,* a splendid chronicle written by Anna Comnena around the middle of the twelfth century in memory of her father, the Emperor Alexis, the author rails against barbarians of Asia Minor and expresses her horror of Islam. But her harshest words are aimed at the Latin barbarians, in particular Pope Gregory VII. I refer the reader to the description of the tortures that this "abominable Pope" inflicted on the envoys of the German Emperor Henry IV after the latter had threatened to depose him: "To begin with, he (Gregory VII) outraged them savagely, then cut their hair and beards, the one with scissors, the other with a razor, and finally he did something else to them which was quite improper, going beyond the insolent behavior one expects from barbarians, and then sent them away. I would have given a name to the outrage, but as I am a woman and a princess, modesty forbids me. What was done on his orders was not only unworthy of a high priest, but of any man at all who bears the name of Christian."[16] It was not until the end of the fourteenth century that some Byzantines, such as Demetrius Cydones, became aware of the cultural and technological advances achieved by the Latin barbarians.[17]

There exists a certain historiography of Catholic inspiration—I refer by way of example to the works of Christopher Dawson[18] or Génicot[19] —which sets out to prove that, on the threefold foundation of the Greco-Roman tradition, the Church, and the Empire, a European consciousness came into being in the Middle Ages. This interpretation, which is doubtless extreme and must be seen as part of the golden

legend of the Middle Ages, has been challenged on two levels. Barraclough, in the polemic he shares with Dawson, insists on the power of
anti-Catholic currents of thought during the Middle Ages and on the
fact of their repression.[20] The twelfth century was indeed a time of
secularization—and not merely the century of cathedrals. Against the
mirage of a society marked by the splendor of its cathedrals, Jacques
Le Goff sets the image of a society dominated by fear and anxiety and
always on the verge of famine.[21]

In this society, which was more heterogeneous and less brilliant than
the authors of the Lives of the Saints would admit, the Far East—and
not only Egypt and Mesopotamia, which already figured in Romance
symbolism[22]—played an important role (albeit hardly noticed), and for
two reasons: people admired and lusted after material culture, as we
would say today, and the legendary splendor of the East; while at the
same time the Gothic inferno was inhabited by Oriental monsters.[23]

Thus in the thirteenth century large guilds of "Saracen tapestry
makers" and "makers of Saracen alms-purses" worked in Paris,[24] because the trade in Oriental luxury goods, although at times very extensive, was not sufficient to meet the requirements of the market.[25]
The extremely rare accounts of voyages merely served to reinforce the
desirability of the riches of the East,[26] while at the same time support-
ing rather than discouraging various legends about the fantastic fauna
and the various semihuman monsters commonly held to live in India or
in Ethiopia.[27]

On the other hand, it was at this time that the Tatar became the
Tartar, the Antichrist, that the Emperor Frederick II, in his letter to
the King of England dated 31 July 1241, expressed the hope that with
the grace of God "the Tartars will be hurled into the Tartarus."[28] The
terror to which Europe had been prey during the Mongol invasions was
expressed in the language of sculpture and then in that of painting.
Demons with bat's wings,[29] divinities with several arms, demons with
women's breasts, with long ears, with a single horn, with elephants'
trunks, men with dogs' heads, a complete sinister iconography the Asian

origins of which have been convincingly demonstrated by Baltrusaitis, emanates an atmosphere of gloom. But in the second half of the thirteenth century Europeans and Mongols drew closer together, doubtless as a result of their hope of forming an alliance against their common enemy—Islam. Popes sent off missions to the Far East and, in 1248, the first Mongol embassy arrived in Rome.[30] Terror was replaced by "wonder imbued with anxiety";[31] the serene gods and the Buddhist spirits, along with a whole array of haloes, crystal globes, and colorful objects took the same path as the demons. Chinese influence is visible in Italian painting of the fourteenth century,[32] and Bosch's many, albeit puzzling, ties with both the iconography and the philosophy of the Far East (by way of the Kabbala) cannot be doubted.[33]

In short, two contradictory attitudes coexisted during the Middle Ages toward anything clearly not European, which happened in this case to be the Far East: certain values were accepted, others symbolized the other world.[34] But these attitudes were more latent than manifest; Europe had not yet really come to terms with the problem of its definition in relation to the external world. It was only in the sixteenth century, following the discovery of America, that the question was posed with all its implications.

Once again I must stress here the extent of the difference, the force of the surprise: suddenly Europe found itself confronted by remarkable cultures, not even dreamed of. The problem was to occupy the great minds of the Renaissance.

Let there be no misunderstanding: I say "the great minds." The memoirs of average citizens of the period bear witness to a world in which America still does not figure. By way of example I might mention the journal of Maître Nicolas Versoris, Counsel at the Parlement of Paris[35] and that of Pierre de L'Estoile.[36] In his preface to the first of these volumes, P. Joutard raises the question: "Of that intellectual, spiritual, and moral ferment to which Rabelais bears such eloquent witness, what impresses itself on the mind of our worthy citizen? Very little." At all events, in these memoirs, there is nothing about discoveries and voyages. De L'Estoile seems scarcely more interested by America. This deep-seated lack of interest in continents beyond the seas was to persist right up to the eighteenth century,[37] though doubtless seaports were an exception. Thus, in 1550, the town of Rouen, to celebrate the joyful entry of King Henry II, put on a lavish show of an ethnographic character presenting scenes from the life of the Tupinamba Indians with the collaboration of fifty Indians and two hundred and fifty sailors from Normandy who spoke Tupi and, for the occasion, dispensed with their clothes.[38] Celebrations of the same kind took place a century later at Gdansk to mark the visit of the Polish royal family.[39]

Central and Eastern Europe took even longer to grasp the importance of Columbus's discovery. It is true that pamphlets written in Czech were circulated as early as 1504. In Poland, starting in 1506, the discovery was mentioned in several Latin publications where, moreover, the name of Columbus was replaced by that of Vespucci; but it was not until 1551 that Marcin Bielski, in his *Chronicle of the World,* reported on the discovery of America in the Polish language. It is to be noted in passing that this chronicle reports the most fantastic information about the remote countries of Asia and Africa, information which had taken root in medieval tradition and often had sources as old as the *Naturalis Historia* of Pliny the Elder.[40] All the same, it was to enjoy great popularity in other Slavic countries and subsequently to be repeated in numerous almanacs. The first mention of the New World in the Russian language dates from approximately 1530 and is to be found in a manuscript of the monk Maximus the Greek. The name "America" did not appear until the Russian translation of Bielski's *Chronicle* was published some fifty years later.[41] So when, in 1598, the Polish poet Sebastian Klonowicz dedicated a few stanzas to the great voyages, including that of Magellan, his observation that the entire country was familiar with these exploits is to be attributed to poetic license and to the fact that he was highly cultured!

Those who were enthusiastic about the discoveries formed in fact a restricted circle—adventurers, tradesmen, politicians, and intellectuals.

One cannot help subscribing to the opinion of Robin Hallett, who writes of the eighteenth century (and this applies *a fortiori* to the previous period): "To a French peasant, a German artisan, or an English farm-laborer, Africa would mean as little as Europe to a Fulani cowherd, a Bambara farmer or a Yoruba craftsman."[42] But this did not stand in the way of a profound change of attitude toward the external world. The two latent trends, mentioned earlier, came to the surface and became more pronounced, but at the same time underwent changes. Admiration and fear gave way to greed and a feeling of superiority, the foundation of which lay in fantasies of brutal heroism. At the same time, contact with the new cultures gave rise to anthropological speculation which was in tune with humanism, then at the peak of its development. The noble savage made his appearance in the intellectual life of Europeans and assisted them in their first gropings toward cultural relativism. As a result two basically opposed theories began to take shape. According to Gilbert Chinard, "One considered the inhabitants of the New World as being scarcely superior to animals, the other saw them as beings who were happier, more virtuous and more reasonable than the Europeans."[43] R. Romano has shown how the two negative stereotypes of the Indian come into being: when he resists he is accused of cannibalism; when he submits he is described as lazy in order to justify unbridled exploitation.[44]

Let us now look more closely at the second theory, the one which sets Europe in opposition to that which is not Europe by turning the roles round, for, as Chabod wisely put it, "La figura dei barbari, dei veri barbari, la fanno qui gli Europei."[45] In fact, as Baudet points out, we are faced with two distinct conceptions: primitivism mourning the past ("no more") and utopianism looking toward the future ("not yet").[46] Both belong to the mainstream of European ideas. They are not aimed at action, in contrast with theories of religious, racial, and cultural superiority, which seek to justify—at the ideological level—the brutality of conquest.

But the violent acts and crimes of the conquerors provoke reactions which do not result in a general cultural pluralism either, but in a program of action based on tolerance. We think of Las Casas, that precursor of relativistic anthropology, whose controversy with Sepulveda is that of a humanist coming up against racism disguised as a moral and legal doctrine teaching that barbarians must submit to civilized peoples as a law of nature.[47] But we also think of Montaigne who, in the essay "Des Coches," deplores the fact that America has not fallen "into hands which would have gently polished and reclaimed that which was wild there, and fortified and promoted the good seeds produced there by nature"—in which, at first glance, he echoes the chronicler of the expedition of Cabral: "They are good people of an admirable simplicity. They could easily be moulded in the required direction, since the Lord has endowed them with fine bodies and fine faces, like worthy people."[48] This disturbing insistence of Caminha on the malleability of the natives was, however, a sign of the intolerant colonization that was to come. Montaigne, on the other hand, drew up a veritable indictment of colonization: "How easy it would have been to profit from such new souls, so eager for learning, showing proof for the most part of such fine natural beginnings. Instead, we availed ourselves of their ignorance and their inexperience in order to bend them more easily towards treachery, lechery, avarice and towards all sorts of inhumanity and cruelty, in keeping with and on the model of our own ways. How could such a price be set on the promotion of profiteering and trade? So many towns razed to the ground, so many natives exterminated, so many millions of peoples put to the sword, and the richest and most beautiful part of the world overthrown for the sake of commerce in pearls and pepper: hollow victories."[49]

After the discoveries of other lands, then, Europe became more conscious of the problem of its identity in relation to the non-European territories and reacted in a variety of often contradictory ways. All of the ambivalent complexity of these reactions is reflected in Shakespeare's *The Tempest.*

Caliban, the natural son of a witch, repugnant in his ugliness, is undoubtedly cast in the same image as the demons that the Puritans saw lurking behind each tree in the American forests. The wise Prospero starts off by establishing with him a relationship of trust, for he feels forsaken on the island. But Caliban tries to assault Miranda. Is this enough to explain why Prospero, acting as an outraged father, has reduced Caliban to slavery? Caliban is ugly and brutish and has just learned to speak, but he speaks the purest language of poetry, and the island resounds with sweet music for him. It is through his mouth that Shakespeare lets the savage speak his desire for freedom. In the end Caliban regains possession of the island, but not before he has submitted once again to Prospero.

The story of Caliban is that of the denaturalization of man and may be seen as an anticipation of Rousseau. In his essays on Shakespeare, the Polish critic Jan Kott sees in *The Tempest* a synthesis of the history of the world.[50] I prefer a narrower interpretation: has not Shakespeare invited us to a dress rehearsal of the "Vasco da Gama era"? Kott rightly observes that Caliban, an anagram of Montaigne's noble cannibals, is not a noble savage. But I cannot agree with him when he says that, on the island where *The Tempest* takes place, there is no place for utopia and that there the history of the world is to be stripped of all illusions. For, in act 3, Gonzalo in fact describes a government of just men. Utopia does indeed enter into Shakespeare's play.

In the meantime, the Third World (as we would say today) was rapidly becoming more familiar. Thus, in 1450, the Europeans knew less about Africa than was known in antiquity; in 1550, the Portuguese voyages around the world already belonged to the past; in 1650, the main countries of Western Europe and the Atlantic coast of Africa were united by a flourishing trade. Tales of travel enjoyed wide circulation, and the number of readers increased thanks to the advance of printing. G. Atkinson has done a study of approximately 550 works on Asia, Latin America and Africa which appeared in France before 1610.[51] In the seventeenth and eighteenth centuries, tales and descriptions of the manners and customs of the savages were to be found in great numbers, and in the eighteenth there also appeared geographical, botanical, and zoological treatises. Let me repeat Métraux's observation, while retaining the distinction that he makes between "travelers and missionaries who described the manners and customs of the savages and those who used their observations to create a science of man,[52] that, in a few specifics, ethnology as we know it was being born. But it should not be forgotten that a great deal of space was still being devoted to the most fantastic information and to speculations which make one smile. Marco Polo's account of his travels enjoyed its greatest success in the second half of the sixteenth century. Father Lafitaux, in his *Moeurs des Sauvages Américains comparées aux moeurs des premiers temps,* which appeared in 1724, speaks of the headless creatures of South America, while Buffon relates, not without some misgivings, it is true, the accounts of travelers who claimed to have seen in the Philippines human creatures with tails four to five inches long. It is again Buffon who ingeniously explains that the Lapps' custom of offering their women to foreigners may stem from the fact "that they recognize their own deformity and the ugliness of their women; they apparently find less ugly those that have not been spurned by foreigners."[53] This theory must have roots which go a long way back, since Anastas Nikitin, the merchant from Tver who visited India during the second half of the fifteenth century, relates that the inhabitants, who were "very black," wanted their offspring to become whiter, and that the visitors who contribute to this cause receive presents.[54] As for tales of travel proper, Atkinson's observation is relevant: on the one hand great similarities exist between accounts brought back from entirely different countries and, on the other, men of different outlooks may make contradictory observations in the same country,[55] encouraged in this by the scarcity of information and the ignorance of their readers.

But inevitably the increasing importance of commercial traffic resulted in the creation of a genuine world economy. The philosophers of the eighteenth century were perfectly aware that "the effect of the discovery of America was to link Asia and Africa to Europe."[56] In

L'Essai sur les moeurs, Voltaire notes how products from overseas had come to take a place in everyday life: "Henri IV breakfasted on a glass of wine and white bread; he took neither tea, nor coffee, nor chocolate; he did not avail himself of tobacco; his wife and his mistresses possessed very few precious stones; they did not wear cloths from Persia, China, or India. When one thinks about it, today a burgher's wife wears on her ears more beautiful diamonds than Catherine de' Medici; Martinique, Mocha and China provide a servant-girl with her breakfast. . . ."[57]

In a quite different connection, the military superiority of the Europeans became more pronounced, despite the Turkish advances into Austria. The period when the Portuguese confronted the Africans with lances was no more.[58] The Italian historian, Carlo M. Cipolla, sees European superiority in terms of ships and guns as providing the key to any explanation of the Vasco da Gama era. This amounts to asking the reasons for the nonreceptivity of certain countries, such as China, to technological innovations of the modern age, to asking why it is that they are incapable of becoming industrialized. This is a question that the Chinese themselves have raised in the twentieth century, as is shown by this quotation from Feng Kuei-jen: "Why are they small and yet strong? Why are we large and yet weak? . . . We have one thing to learn from the barbarians: solid ships and heavy guns."[59]

It was, however, the crisis of the European feudal system which, more than any other factor, was to spotlight the countries belonging today to the Third World. Against the political realities of the ancient régime, its critics set the idealized image of other cultures—or they showed the ills of Europe through the eyes of imaginary and disingenuous travelers from Asia and America. Historical and ethnographic fables with a highly European moral to them[60] came very much into vogue. "The Chinese are wise and are familiar with fables, although they live a long way away," wrote Bishop Ignacy Krasicki, one of the leading minds of the eighteenth century in Poland, in a poem entitled "The Chinese Emperor and his Son."[61] Similarly, I might mention the importance of the dispute over ritual practices and, more generally, of

China in the crisis of European conscousness;[62] the infatuation with Chinoiserie which was its artistic adjunct, and the questions raised by eighteenth-century economists, already halfway between fable and the beginnings of a theory of development.[63]

As B. Baczko pointed out in his perceptive monograph on Rousseau: "The century of the Enlightenment, rather than directing itself toward a confrontation with other cultures, looks at itself in them as in a mirror, wishing to find there, and indeed finding there, those enduring factors of human nature and those possibilities for human reason that it sees in itself, in its own age."[64] It may be observed in passing that Orientalism does not always serve progress and that, in a country like Poland, two quite distinct trends are to be made out in the eighteenth century: "Sarmatism," of a clearly conservative character, appealing to spurious national tradition, looking for decorative arts and dress, to the East, whence the Sarmatians were supposed to have come, and progressive ideas originating in the West, decked out in Oriental costume.[65] Nowhere, except in medieval Spain, has the artistic culture of Islam exercised such an influence over the tastes of a most Catholic society.[66] Moreover, popular interest in America and the Indians was first stimulated in Poland by anti-Jesuit polemics; in the eighteenth and nineteenth centuries it acquired a new dimension when the problem of independence arose.[67]

But the train of thought set in motion by increasingly active trade with non-European cultures was not limited to the critique of feudalism, which remained in the very mainstream of European ideas.

First, going a step beyond cultural pluralism, a principle of action was sketched out by Rousseau, for whom it seemed that the natural man should be interpreted as a theoretical model of unachieved potentialities.[68] Claude Lévi-Strauss recounts this in his essay, "Jean-Jacques, Founder of the Sciences of Man":[69] Rousseau, "the most ethnographic of philosophers,"[70] ready to grant everyone his chance, wondered whether the great apes of Africa and Asia, ineptly described by travelers, "might not in fact be real wild men, whose race, dispersed in the forest in early times, did not have the opportunity to develop any of its potential faculties, did not acquire any degree of perfection, and still existed in the primitive state of nature."[71] I do not think that Diderot's position was basically different. In the *Supplément au voyage de Bougainville,* Oron says to the Almoner: "But you won't show the mores of Europe by those of Tahiti, nor consequently the mores of Tahiti by those of your country."[72]

Then, in Voltaire, and particularly in the *Essai sur les moeurs,* is to be found "an attempt to depart from customary Europocentrism and to embrace the history of all the peoples of the world,"[73] which does not prevent him, in *Le Siècle de Louis XIV,* from overlooking, as did Bossuet, Islam, India, and China, and deliberately situating the four "great centuries" of the human era solely within the context of European history.[74] For Voltaire, at the same time that he postulates a universal history, remains convinced of the progress of Europe since the Middle Ages[75] and of the superiority of the Europeans in relation to the newly discovered peoples: "Our Western peoples have caused to shine forth in all these discoveries a great superiority of mind and courage over the Oriental nations. We have established ourselves amongst them, and very often in spite of their resistance. We have learned their languages, we have taught them some of our arts."[76]

This feeling of superiority often goes hand in hand, in the century of the Enlightenment, with a fairly clear idea of the unity of Europe, *"ein bewunderwurdiges Ganze,"* as Adelung puts it.[77] In a curious passage Gibbon expresses an idea which was common in his time, when he grants the philosopher the right to consider Europe "as one great republic whose various inhabitants have attained almost the same level of refinement and cultivation."[78] This Europe, according to him, no longer has to fear a Tartar invasion because guns and fortifications set an insurmountable barrier in the way of the barbarians who, in order to vanquish Europe, would have to adopt the same techniques of war. They would then cease being barbarians. Even if worst came to worst—I am still summarizing Gibbon—and the hardy peasants of

Russia, the numerous armies of Germany, the gallant noblemen of France, and the intrepid citizens of Great Britain succumbed one after the other, there would still be a solution: put the rest of civilized society on board ten thousand boats and let them cross the Atlantic Ocean so that Europe may revive and flourish on the American continent!

From Europocentrism we come to racism, which developed in response to the very requirements of colonial conquest. Some researchers, such as Panikkar,[79] declare that relations with the Asian peoples did not display this characteristic until later and that in the eighteenth century there still was no color prejudice among the Europeans in China and India. According to this thesis, it was a supremely political phenomenon, as would be proved by the simple fact that racism never developed to any great extent in countries which remained independent, such as Thailand or Japan. Did not one of the first Spanish descriptions of Japan, based on Pero Diez's stay there in 1544, describe its inhabitants as white?[80] The Brazilian sociologist, Gilberto Freyre, has insisted on the Portuguese tendency toward miscegenation and on the absence of racial prejudice in their colonization—which is explained by the strong Arabic and African influences to which medieval Portugal was exposed.[81] Freyre considers these influences to underlie the Portuguese faculty of adapting European values and techniques to tropical conditions.[82] K. L. Little, the author of an interesting study published by UNESCO, comes to the conclusion that there was "a virtual lack of racial relations, as we define them, before the period of the expansion and exploration of overseas territories by the Europeans."[83]

This thesis cannot, however, be accepted without reservations. Though Little claims that Moslems are traditionally blind to skin color, certain texts of Arabic geographers of the Middle Ages use clearly racist stereotypes to describe the populations in the south of the Sahara: blacks are portrayed as flighty by nature and lacking intelligence—the differenciation of races being attributed to climate.[84] A. N. Sherwin-

White has shown that, contrary to the commonly accepted opinion on the total absence of racial prejudice in the ancient world, in Rome, in fact, at the very least "cultural prejudice" against the barbarians of the North, and above all against the Greeks and the Jews was in fact far from negligible in Rome.[85] As for the thesis brilliantly defended by Freyre and supported by the Portuguese historian, Armando Cortesão, it is demolished, with skillful use of the evidence, in the work of C. R. Boxer.[86] The misadventures of the Indian chief protected by the Portuguese authorities who was demoted in 1771 by the viceroy for "having fallen so low as to marry a Negress, soiling his blood by this alliance"[87] speaks volumes about the hierarchy of races in the Portuguese empire, as do the learned discussions about the origin of the Indians and the blacks: Were the former the descendants of the Jews deported by the Assyrians or were they the descendants of Cain? Was Cain black, in which case the blacks would be his offspring, damned like him? Debates such as these continued on into the eighteenth century.

There has been a tendency to see the *Lusiadas* as the first literary work which "in its grandeur and its universality speaks for the modern world" and constitutes "a true product of that Europe, Christian and classical, of which Camões was so faithful and so distinguished a son."[88] I find this interpretation unconvincing, for two reasons.

First of all, the ideology that motivated Camões and all the conquerors was still very deeply rooted in the world of medieval values: the work is a *chanson de geste* decked out in antique culture, which extolls the chivalric values, enlisting them in the service of religous designs through which the unrelenting spirit of the Portuguese against the "ignoble Moslem" perpetuates itself. The economic aspect of the discoveries did not attract the poet's attention; not surprisingly, for his idea was to create a heroic legend by singing of the intrepid mariners and not the money barons. But, above all, the concept of universality in the *Lusiadas* is already that of a world under the subjugation of a Europe that was "Christian, superior, and more enlightened" than the

other continents, as well as more civilized and more powerful, according
to the poet,[89] who, in my opinion, introduced to literature the Europocentric current of apologists for colonization. Camões is on the other
side of the barricades from Montaigne or Rabelais. Bowra implicitly
acknowledges this: to him, the classical Greco-Roman heritage with
which Camões is impregnated constitutes the *differentia specifica* of
Europe and, by its humanizing power, makes Europe a civilized world,
in contrast with the East, which, in spite of its wealth and its long history, "is in the last resort uncivilized." According to Bowra, Camões
was perfectly aware of this superiority which the culture of the ancient
world was assumed to confer on Europeans.[90]

All the same, the poet makes a clear distinction between Africa,
"divested of earthly goods, wild and full of brutality,"[91] largely inhabited by people who he considers guilty of every vice, and Asia,
"with vast lands rich in kingdoms."[92] The description of India, in particular, abounds in superlatives and epithets of wonder, while that of
China praises the Great Wall and, curiously enough, the advantages of a
constitutional monarchy based on merit.[93]

This discrepancy between ways of looking at the Africans, on the
one hand, and the Asians and the Indians, on the other, became more
pronounced as the slave trade developed. The same public who en-
thused about the noble savage of America saw the Africans in a completely different light. And yet Europe, at the end of the thirteenth
century and the beginning of the fourteenth, had shown a keen interest
in Ethiopia, and one of the Magi even changed color, becoming black—
which causes Henri Baudet to say that the black man, in our culture,
was canonized before the Indian was even discovered.[94]

This change can be explained only by the slave trade. Undoubtedly
there was no lack of generous sentiment or of impartial testimony to
the human qualities of the Africans in travel accounts. In the field of
literature, contrary to what some have said,[95] there are some black
heroes; the novel "Oroonoko," by Aphra Behn, is a good example, as
it dates from the end of the seventeenth century.[96] Toward the end

of the eighteenth century the writings of three emancipated African slaves living in London—Ottobah Cugoano, Alandah Equiano, and Ignatius Sancho—enjoyed great success.[97] In this connection, mention should be made of the amazing and little-known careers of three intellectuals of African origin, whose works, written in Latin, have just been reissued: Juan Latino (1516?-1606), who taught Latin at the university of Granada; Anthony William Amo (1703-?), born a slave, who became professor of philosophy at the universities of Wittenberg and Halle and returned to Africa after the death of his protectors, the dukes of Brunswick-Wolfenbüttel; and last, J. E. L. Capitem, raised in Holland by a rich merchant, who became the defender of the slave trade and published, in 1742, a work entitled *Dissertatio politico-theologica, de servitute, libertati christianae non contraria.*[98]

Certainly Montesquieu,[99] Diderot, Condorcet, Locke, Pope, Defoe, Adam Smith, Tom Paine, and many others spoke up against slavery. Toward the end of the eighteenth century the abolitionist movement acquired a great deal of importance. But one cannot help being surprised that thinkers as enlightened as Voltaire and scholars as scrupulous as Buffon[100] were convinced of the inferiority of Africans. Voltaire applied himself to finding arguments to justify the slave trade and was so inept at this that, in the Beaumarchais edition of 1785, the publishers (Condorcet?) traded polemics with him.[101]

It was common in the eighteenth century to consider blacks as devoid of intelligence, or, at the very least, as possessed of an intelligence vastly inferior to that of the Europeans. To the mind of Lord Chesterfield, a very popular figure in England in his time, they were so ignorant that they were "little better than the lions, tigers, and leopards and other wild beasts, which . . . [Africa] produces in great numbers."[102] Authors who were more closely involved in an economic system based on slave labor were even more virulent. Thus, a historian of the West Indies was able to write, in 1774, that an orangutan husband would be no dishonor to a Hottentot woman. The blacks were not, in his eyes, human beings, but animals susceptible of learning civilization in the same way as apes learn to eat, drink, and dress like men.[103]

It is curious that in America, even enlightened and open-minded persons endeavored to put together specious arguments for the reputed inferiority of the African. Jefferson's book *Notes on Virginia,* contains an entire proof on this subject which claims to be scientific. Jefferson would not grant that black slaves be emancipated except on the condition that they emigrate—or rather re-eimigrate—to Africa. For blacks are inferior to whites in various ways: first of all, they are ugly (like Caliban); then their existence is based more on feelings than it is on thought; their memory is comparable to that of white men, but their intellectual faculties are inferior and their imagination is "dull, tasteless, and anomalous" *[sic]* ;[104] their intellect and their external appearance improve by cross-breeding with white men, which "proves that their inferiority is not merely the effect of the conditions in which they live."[105] Deploring the fact that the Americans have not, since the beginnings of colonization, undertaken systematic studies of the blacks and the Indians, considered as "topics of natural history"—which would have made it possible to verify the hypothesis of African inferiority—Jefferson refuses to draw conclusions about blacks on the basis of the populations living in the heart of uncivilized Africa, because he wants to be fair-minded! He prefers to observe the black slaves of America, who have had the advantage of coming into close contact with the civilization of their masters. And yet these slaves, who live in better conditions than the slaves of ancient Rome, have produced nothing comparable in the field of the arts; the reason for this is that the slaves in Rome were white! The Africans' supposed incapacity for artistic creation constitutes the keystone of Jefferson's reasoning. At the very time when London was admiring the refined intellect of Ignatius Sancho, Jefferson was describing the Africans as fairly gifted in singing, but incapable of expressing themselves through rhetoric, painting, or sculpture.[106]

It is characteristic that Jefferson contrasts them in this respect with the Indians of America (whose defense he even takes up against Buffon).

Constance Rourke's quip comes to mind: "As the Indian perished or was driven farther and farther away from those fertile lands which the white invader wished to occupy, a noble and mournful fantasy was created in his place."[107] At the beginning of the nineteenth century, the popularity in America of plays and operas on Indian themes stemmed from the fact that the Indian could be easily cast in the role of an "improbable and phantasmagorical ancestor" for a people who wished to forge for itself a mythical genealogy. The noble savage was thus called on to play a quite different role than in Europe, a role which is comparable in certain respects to the one which he filled in the so-called Indianist movement in Latin-American romanticism— which, however, was rooted in the popular literature of the colonial period.[108]

After the French Revolution of 1789, the noble savage ceased to be indispensable to the development of European ideas and, furthermore, the race for colonies resulted in a hardening of attitude on the part of Europeans. As Charles Morazé has observed, "European man, in 1840, was no longer the man of 1780. In sixty years a profound transformation had taken place. As late as the eighteenth century, the Westerner did not dare to declare his superiority over the Indian or the Chinese. By the beginning of the nineteenth century, he no longer had any doubt of it."[109] The noble savage would still figure for some time in romantic literature, but the emphasis was increasingly to shift toward exoticism (at the metaphysical level as well), causing Goethe, for instance, to contrast Europe, caught in the whirlwind that toppled thrones, to the happy East where the Biblical wind blows; later, Baudelaire would speak of languorous Asia and blazing Africa—a vast and distant world which was to attract Gauguin, Rimbaud, and young soldiers and agents of commercial companies—the builders of colonial empires— in quest of fortune and also, to be fair, of adventure.

But where there is exoticism (and romanticism, unlike the century of the Enlightenment, would come to discover it also in European peasant culture and folklore), no real cultural confrontation can exist.

As Fanon has pointed out: "There is on one side a culture with recognized qualities of dynamism, of expansion, of depth. A culture in movement, in perpetual renewal. Opposing it, there are characteristics, curiosities, things, never a structure."[110] At the very most we see in the nineteenth century, and more and more rarely, a would-be cultural pluralism, cultivated somewhat awkwardly by orientalist academics and partisans of the *philosophia perennis* of the major Eastern religions.[111] In the realm of action, colonial conquest and imperialism were at their height; as Conrad put it, it was the joyful dance of trade and death. At the ideological level, the Europocentric and racist vision of the world prevailed. The great battle waged by the era of the Enlightenment was to result in philosophical victory but defeat in the realm of action.

It was only with the October Revolution and, even more, the end of the "Vasco da Gama era" that Europocentrism began to totter. Inevitably, ethnologists were among the first to become aware of its ascendancy and destructive effects, and to give their discipline an expiatory vocation, which was closely bound up with the phenomenon of colonialism—whether ethnographers admit it or not.[112] As Claude Lévi-Strauss has strikingly phrased it, anthropology aims to be "an undertaking which renews and atones for the Renaissance in order to extend humanism to the whole of humanity."[113] Will it succeed? At all events, the reflections of Bronislaw Malinowski, dating from more than fifty years ago, have not lost their timeliness as a program, not to mention a manifesto:

It is in the love of the final synthesis, achieved by the assimilation and comprehension of all the items of a culture and still more in the love of the variety and independence of the various cultures that lies the test of the real worker in the true Science of Man.

There is, however, one point of view deeper yet and more important than the love of tasting of the variety of human modes of life, and that is the desire to turn such knowledge into wisdom. Though it may be given to us for a moment to enter into the soul of a savage and through his eyes to look at the outer world and feel ourselves what it must feel to *him* to be himself—yet our final goal is to enrich and deepen our own world's vision, to understand our own nature and to make it finer, intellectually and artistically. In grasping the essential outlook of others, with the reverence and understanding due even to savages, we cannot but help widening our own. We cannot possibly reach the final Socratic wisdom of knowing ourselves if we never leave the narrow confinement of the customs, beliefs and prejudices into which every man is born. Nothing can teach us a better lesson in this matter of ultimate importance than the habit of mind which allows us to treat the beliefs and values of another man from his point of view. Nor has civilised humanity ever needed such tolerance more than now, when prejudice, ill will and vindictiveness are dividing each European nation from each other, when all the ideals, cherished and proclaimed as the highest achievements of civilisation, science and religion, have been thrown to the winds. The Science of Man, in its most refined and deepest version, should lead us to such knowledge and to tolerance and generosity, based on the understanding of other men's point of view.[114]

Notes to Chapter 2

1. J.-J. Rousseau, *Discours sur l'órigine et les fondements de l'inégalité parmi les hommes* (Paris: Editions Sociales), p. 179.

2. F. Rabelais, *Oeuvres* (Paris: Renaissance du Livre, 1935), vol. 1, p. 242. Cf. Erich Auerbach's fine essay on the world as related by Pantagruel (*Mimesis: The Representation of Reality in Western Literature,* tr. Willard Trask (New York, 1957), pp. 229-249.

3. This chapter is based in part on the article published in *Annales—Economies, Sociétés, Civilisations,* 21, 3 (May-June 1966), pp. 965-987.

4. R. Grousset, *Bilan de l'histoire* (Paris, 1962).

5. Federico Chabod, *Storia dell'idea d'Europa* (Bari, 1964).

6. Henri Baudet, *Paradise on Earth: Some Thoughts on European Images of Non-European Man* (London, 1965).

7. Thucydides, *The Peloponnesian War,* Book I.

8. Aristotle, *Politics,* Book III.

9. "As Europe is a construction of the human mind on the basis of an ill-defined geographical reality, ever since men have reflected on it there has been an immense variety of Europes." J. B. Duroselle, *L'idée d'Europe dans l'histoire* (Paris, 1965), p. 25.

10. Tacitus, *De Germania.*

11. Dante, *The Divine Comedy: The Inferno,* Canto 28, line 35.

12. See *Storici arabi delle Crociate,* ed. Francesco Gabrielli (Turin, 1966), pp. 73-84.

13. Baudet, *Paradise,* pp. 20-21.

14. W. Ullmann, *A History of Political Thought: The Middle Ages* (Harmondsworth, 1965).

15. Geoffrey Barraclough, *History in a Changing World* (Oxford, 1957), p. 62.

16. *The Alexiad of Anna Comnena* (Harmondsworth, 1969), p. 62.

17. C. M. Cipolla, *European Culture and Overseas Expansion* (Harmondsworth, 1970), p. 20.

18. C. Dawson, *The Making of Europe: An Introduction to the History of European Unity* (London, 1953).

19. Leopold Génicot, *Les Lignes de faîte du Moyen Age* (Paris, 1962).

20. Barraclough, *History,* p. 38.

21. J. Le Goff, *La Civilisation de l'Occident Médiéval* (Paris, 1964).

22. Cf. O. Beigbeder, *La symbolique* (Paris, 1961).

23. Cf. J. Baltrusaitis, *Le Moyen Age fantastique* (Paris, 1955), p. 183.

24. J. Ebersolt, *Orient et Occident* (Paris, 1954), pp. 34-95. Research on Byzantine and Oriental influences in France before and during the Crusades.

25. R. A. Jairazbnoy points out that in 1171 there were three thousand French merchants in Alexandria and that many Arab tradesmen regularly visited Montpellier and Arles (p. 31). The first chapter of his book provides a fine overall view of the contacts and relations between Europe and the East at the artistic and cultural levels. See *Oriental Influences in Western Art* (Bombay, 1965).

26. R. Grousset (*Bilan de l'histoire,* p. 111) stresses that Marco Polo's interest in the far-flung civilizations of Asia "could scarcely have gone beyond economic investigation."

27. See V. H. Debidour, *Le Bestiaire sculpté en France* (Paris, 1964), pp. 181-190.

28. Chantal Lemercier-Quelquejay, *La Paix mongole* (Paris, 1970), p. 75.

29. Etiemble observes that Lucifer trifrons wearing bat's wings is to be found in Dante's Hell. *Connaissons-nous la Chine?* (Paris, 1964), pp. 19-20.

30. This diplomatic cross-curent is briefly described in J.-P. Roux's small book, *Les Explorateurs au Moyen Age* (Paris, 1961).

31. Baltrusaitis, *Le Moyen Age fantastique*, p. 284.

32. Etiemble quotes as his authority the work of Pouzyna, Cecchi, Soulier, and Gennaro on Siennese and Tuscan painting, while putting forward the hypothesis that, these studies and, of course, those carried on by Baltrusaitis notwithstanding, "We can only conjecture on the role of Chinese art in Europe around the time of Marco Polo" (*Connaissons nous la Chine?*, p. 19).

33. The polemics on the interpretation of the famous *Garden of Delights* in the Prado Museum point to the difficulty of establishing the exact extent of Eastern influences on Bosch's imaginary world. See R. L. Delevoy, *Bosch* (Geneva, 1960), pp. 87-109.

34. It goes without saying that I have proved this only very sketchily. To be more thorough, I should also have to tackle the vast field of the development of literary themes and analyze the roles of the Byzantine, Islamic, and Jewish cultures as intermediaries between India and Europe. One example will serve to illustrate the complexity of the task: the *Historia septem sapientum*, known in Western Europe in two versions, one in Latin from the twelfth century and one in Spanish from the thirteenth *(Libro de los enganos)*, dates back to fifth-century India. In addition, there are an Arabic version (eighth century), a Syrian (eighth-eleventh), a Greek (eleventh), a Hebraic (thirteenth), and a Persian one (fourteenth). See J. Krzyzanowski, *Romans Polski wieku XVI* (Warsaw, 1962), pp. 88-89.

35. Extracts of which have been published under the title *Journal d'un bourgeois de Paris sous Francois Ier* (Paris, 1963).

36. *Journal d'un bourgeois de Paris sous Henri IV* (Paris, 1954).

37. See R. Mandrou, *De la culture populaire aux XVIIe et XVIIIe siècles, La Bibliothèque bleue de Troyes* (Paris, 1964), pp. 66-67.

38. A. Métraux, "Les Précurseurs de l'ethnologie en France du XVIe au XVIIIe siècle," in *Cahiers de l'histoire mondiale*, No. 3 (1963), pp. 723-724.

39. J. Tazbir, "O czarnych mieszkancach Ameryki" in *Mowia Wieki* (Warsaw), No. 1 (1968), pp. 14-18.

40. See B. Olszewicz, *Pierwsze wiadomosci o odkryciu Ameryki w literaturze polskiej*, vol. 1 (Warsaw, 1910); I. Chrzanowski, *Marcin Bielski—Studium historyczno-literackie* (Lwow, 1926); and last and most important, J. Tazbir's recent monograph, *Szlachta a konkwistadorzy* (Warsaw, 1969). This extremely well-documented work provides a complete description of Polish reactions to the discovery and the conquest of America.

41. See L. A. Chur, *Rossia i Latinskaia Amierika* (Moscow, 1964), pp. 6-7.

42. Robin Hallett, *Penetration of Africa to 1815* (London, 1965), p. 38.

43. G. Chinard, *L'exotisme américain dans la littérature française au XVIe siècle* (Paris, 1919), p. 242.

44. Lecture, department of history of the University of Paris VIII, 28 November 1970.

45. Chabod, *Storia dell'idea d'Europa,* p. 63.

46. "Where primitivism thought on the whole in terms of 'no longer,' utopism was mainly concerned with 'not yet'; if primitivism mourned the past, utopism looked toward the future. Despite their deep interaction, therefore, the two categories are still essentially different." (Henri Baudet, *Paradise,* p. 34).

47. See M. Zywczynski's introduction to the Polish translation of Las Casas, *Krotka relacja o wyniszczeniu Indian* (Warsaw, 1956), p. 63. This same Las Casas, however, accepted Negro slavery. R. Romano sees in the dispute between Las Casas and Sepulveda the opposition between the interests of the Spanish crown and those of the *encomenderos.*

48. Pero Vaz de Caminha, *Carta a el Rei D. Manuel* (São Paulo, 1963), p. 60.

49. Montaigne, *Essais,* book 3, chapter 6 (Paris: Bibliothèque de la Pléiade, 1943), pp. 1019-1020.

50. Jan Kott, *Szkice o Szekpirze* (Warsaw, 1961), pp. 182-226.

51. G. Atkinson, *Les nouveaux horizons de la Renaissance française* (Paris, 1935).

52. A. Métraux, "Precurseurs," p. 722.

53. Buffon, *Oeuvres completes,* vol. 9: *De l'homme* (Paris, 1833), p. 172.

54. A. Nikitin, *Wedrowka za trzy morza,* tr. from Russian into Polish by H. Willman-Grabowska (Warsaw, 1952), pp. 34-35.

55. G. Atkinson, *Les Relations de voyages au XVIIe siècle et l'évolution des idées: Contribution à l'étude de la formation de l'esprit du XVIIe siècle,* Paris, p. 3.

56. Montesquieu, *De l'esprit des lois,* XXI, 21 (Paris: Garnier, 1922), vol. 2, p. 37.

57. Voltaire, *Essai sur les moeurs et l'esprit des nations,* Supplément, XVIIIe (Paris: Garnier, 1963), vol. 2, p. 939. Around the year 380, Ammianus Marcellinus noted of Rome that "the use of silk hitherto limited to the nobility has now spread to all classes without distinction, even the lowest." Quoted by G. F. Hudson, in *Europe and China* (Boston, 1961), p. 77.

58. See Basil Davidson, *Black Mother,* Part 2 (London, 1961).

59. C. M. Cipolla, *European Culture,* p. 95.

60. "... Voltaire turned the history of China into a fable for Europeans." E. A. Kosminskij, "Wolter kak istorik," an essay published in *Wolter,* a collection edited by W. P. Wolgnine (Moscow, 1948), p. 174.

61. Already Montaigne (*Essais,* book 3, chapter 13) was writing: "In China, in whose kingdom civil administration and the arts, through commerce with and knowledge of ours, surpass our examples in several respects of excellence, and whose history teaches me how much more embracing and various the world is than either the ancients or ourselves do fathom. . . ." For the importance to the seventeenth century of the debate over Chinese ritual practices and the discussions of metaphysics and politics inspired by China, see Etiemble, *Connaissons-nous la Chine?,* pp. 42-67.

62. Etiemble has done a remarkable study of this in *Les Jésuites en Chine* (Paris, 1966).

63. See M. Luftalla, "La Chine, vue par quelques économistes du XVIIIe," *Population,* no. 2 (1962), pp. 289-296.

64. B. Baczko, *Rousseau: samotnosc i wspolnota* (Warsaw, 1964), p. 215.

65. See the recent work by J. Reychman, *Orient w kulturze polskiego Oswiecenia* (Wroclaw, 1964).

66. T. Mankowski, *Genealogia sarmatyzmu* (Warsaw, 1946), p. 81.

67. J. Tazbir, "O czarnych . . . Ameryki," and, by the same author, *Literatura antyjezuicka w Polsce 1578-1625* (Warsaw, 1963).

68. I follow here Baczko's interpretation (*Rousseau,* pp. 118-140), which is based on that of Lévi-Strauss and carries it further.

69. Published in the collection *Jean-Jacques Rousseau* (Neuchatel, 1962), pp. 239-248.

70. Claude Lévi-Strauss, *Tristes Tropiques* (ed. 10/18, Paris, 1963), p. 351.

71. J.-J. Rousseau, *L'Inégalité,* p. 166.

72. Diderot, *Ecrits philosophiques* (ed. Pauret, Paris, 1964), p. 277. In my opinion, Jean Giraudoux, in *Supplément au voyage de Cook* (1935), removes all its anthropological connotations and all its significance from Diderot's essay— which constitutes the most important result of the philosopher's collaboration in *l'Histoire des deux Indes,* by the Abbé de Raynal. Concerning the latter point, see M. Duchet's study, which appeared in *Cahiers de l'Association Internationale*

des Etudes Françaises, no. 13 (June 1961), pp. 173-187, and particularly the recent work by Yves Benot, *Diderot: De l'athéisme à l'anti-colonialisme* (Paris, 1970). The success enjoyed at the time by Giraudoux's superficial play is a clear indication that the public was not very sensitive as yet to the problems which appear to us today to be so important.

73. Kosminskij, "Woltor kak istorik," p. 160.

74. René Pomeau's introduction to Voltaire, *Essai sur les moeurs,* edition referred to, p. 1.

75. "One need only consider, from Petersburg all the way to Madrid, the prodigious number of superb towns, built in places which were deserts six hundred years ago. . . ." Voltaire, *Essai sur les moeurs,* CXCVII, vol. 2, p. 811.

76. Ibid., CXLIII, vol. 2, p. 325.

77. J. Ch. Adelung, *Pragmatische Staatsgeschichte Europens* (Gotha, 1762), quoted in Paul Hazard, *La Pensée Européenne au XVIIIe siècle: de Montesquieu à Lessing* (Paris, 1946).

78. Edward Gibbon, *Decline and Fall of the Roman Empire* (London, 1921), p. 163. In *Le Siècle de Louis XIV,* Voltaire also speaks of Christian Europe as a sort of large republic divided up into several states.

79. K. M. Panikkar, *Asia and Western Dominance* (London, 1959). Consulted in the French edition, *L'Asie et la domination occidentale* (Paris, 1955), p. 920.

80. Quoted by D. F. Lach, *Japan in the Eyes of Europe: The Sixteenth Century* (Chicago, 1968), p. 656.

81. See in particular Gilberto Freyre, *Interpretação do Brasil* (Rio de Janeiro, 1947), pp. 41-87.

82. Giberto Freyre, *New World in the Tropics: The Culture of Modern Brazil* (New York, 1963), p. 31.

83. K. L. Little, *Race and Society* (Paris, 1958), p. 12 and p. 52.

84. See *Arabskiye Istoshniki X-XII viekov po etnografii i istorii Afriki iugnee Sahary* (Moscow, 1965), and, in particular, the extract from Kitab Tabaquat al-Umam de Abou Quasim Sa'id (1029-1070), pp. 191-194.

85. A. N. Sherwin-White, *Racial Prejudice in Imperial Rome* (Cambridge, England, 1967).

86. C. R. Boxer, *Relações Raciais no Imperio Colonial Portugues, 1415-1825* (Rio de Janeiro, 1967).

87. Ibid., p. 153.

88. C. M. Bowra, *From Virgil to Milton* (London, 1945), p. 86 and p. 138.

89. Luis de Camões, *Os Lusiadas*, X, 92.

90. Bowra, *Virgil to Milton*, p. 103.

91. Camões, *Os Lusiados*.

92. Ibid., X, 98.

93. Ibid., X, 106 and X, 130.

94. Baudet, *Paradise*, p. 18.

95. "From the time of Montaigne's famous essay on the cannibals right up to Voltaire's *Ingénu*, no Negro played the role of the noble savage. . . . Negroes did not lend themselves at all to heroic roles; they worked hard on the sugar-cane plantations and were sold like beasts of burden to all the colonies. . . . They constituted too real an image of bourgeois society to be able to become its ideal image." J. Kott, *Szkola Klasykow* (Warsaw, 1955), p. 51.

96. Paul Hazard *(La Pensée européenne)* points out the immense success of this book, which was adapted many times for the stage and inspired painters, poets, and composers.

97. Hallett, *Penetration of Africa*, pp. 146-148.

98. *The Black Experience*, Klaus Reprint catalogue, annotated by J. Jahn (Neudeln, 1970), p. 15.

99. Chapter 5 of book XV of *Esprit des lois*, entitled "De l'esclavage des Nègres" remains in my opinion one of the finest texts bequeathed to us by the age of Louis XIV.

100. Buffon quotes the opinions of travelers who attributed little intelligence to the blacks but acknowledged that they had great sensibility (*Oeuvres*, vol. 9, p. 233). This was one of the most commonly held views of the period.

101. Here is the offending passage from Voltaire: "We purchase domestic slaves only from amongst the Negroes. We are criticized for such transactions: a people that trades in its children is even more blameworthy than the purchaser; this trade demonstrates our superiority; he who gives himself a master was born to have one." And the note to the 1785 edition: ". . . The Negores are but the accomplices and the instruments of the Europeans; the latter are truly the guilty ones" (*Essai sur les moeurs*, CXCVII, vol. 2, p. 805).

102. "The Africans are the most ignorant and unpolished people in the world, little better than the lions, tigers and leopards and other wild beasts, which that country produces in great numbers." (Quoted in Hallett, *Penetration of Africa*, p. 37.

103. "We cannot pronounce them unsusceptible of civilisation since even apes have been taught to eat, drink, repose and dress like men. But of all the human species hitherto discovered, their natural baseness of mind seems to afford the least hope of their being (except by miraculous interposition of Divine Providence) so refined as to think as well as act like men. I do not think that an Orang-Outang husband would be any dishonour to an Hottentot female" (Long, *History of Jamaica,* quoted in K. D. Little, *Race and Society,* p. 15).

104. Thomas Jefferson, "Notes on the State of Virginia," in *The Life and Selected Writings of Thomas Jefferson* (New York: Modern Library, 1944), p. 257.

105. Ibid., p. 250.

106. "But never yet could I find that a black had uttered a thought above the level of plain narration; never saw an elementary trait of painting or sculpture." (Ibid., p. 258.)

107. Constance Rourke, *American Humor: A Study of the National Character* (New York, 1971, p. 97).

108. Latin-American literary criticism puts a great deal of emphasis on this fact. To quote the great Brazilian poet Manuel Bandeira, "The idealization of the Indian was in perfect accord with national sentiment; it came before romanticism and did not disappear with it." (*Apresentação da poesia brasileira* (Rio de Janeiro, 1954), p. 58. This point of view is upheld for Hispano-American literature in A. Torres Rioseco, *Expressão Literaria do Novo Mundo* (Rio de Janeiro, 1945).

109. C. Morazé, *Les bourgeois conquérants* (Paris, 1953), p. 91. Etiemble (*Connaissons-nous la Chine?*, p. 67) points out that as early as the middle of the eighteenth century, there appeared as a backlash against Sinophilia, a Sinophobic current of thought which, around the middle of the nineteenth century, turned into an attitude of contempt for China.

110. Frantz Fanon, "Racisme et culture," in the anthology *Pour la révolution africaine* (Paris, 1964), p. 42.

111. Intellectuals from Third World countries are often very critical of the work of European orientalists. Thus an Indian writer has said, with some exaggeration, I think, that European Indology was "a purely literary creation, a self-sufficient presentation with its exclusive data, axioms, postulates, theorems and corollaries, a sort of Euclidian geometry of India, an abstraction in the literary dimension, with no necessary relation to anything that existed in fact though I cannot say that it did not at times touch hard ground" (N. C. Chaudhuri, "On Understanding the Hindus," *Encounter,* June, 1965, p. 22). But I do think that R. Grousset's observation is true: "Just as the West, at the end of the eighteenth

century and, it must be said, during the whole of the nineteenth, appreciated Chinese or Indian art only as a sometimes quite preposterous curiosity, so also with the Indian or Chinese religious and philosophical concepts which we have come to consider common knowledge, but which are only incomplete elements, artificially reassembled, even deliberately presented in such a way as to fit in more easily with our current intellectual attitudes" (*Bilan de l'histoire,* p. 112). Around the middle of the nineteenth century the previously keen interest in the Indian cultures of America exhausted itself (see Métraux, "Précurseurs de l'ethnologie").

112. See M. Leiris, *Cinq études d'éthnologie* (Paris, 1969), p. 84. The museum of Jewish culture in Prague owes its extensive collections to the efforts of Nazi ethnographers employed to create a museum of the exterminated race.

113. Lévi-Strauss, *Leçon inaugurale au Collège de France* (5 January 1960), p. 47.

114. B. Malinowski, *Argonauts of the Western Pacific* (London, 1922), pp. 517-518.

3

An Iconological Digression: The Image of the Black in European Art

A systematic study of the image of the "other" would require, as I have said, an interdisciplinary course in the history of ideas, the history of science, and the analysis of travel accounts, school textbooks and the stereotypes purveyed by the mass media; and, last, psychological research into the attitudes toward each other of men from different cultural areas and social environments. I think that a program such as this should be one of the priorities in "peace research," which has enjoyed a certain vogue during the last few years.[1] But the documents in the case of ethnocentrism include a particularly rich source of material which has so far been surprisingly little explored: the comparative iconological study[2] used in the plastic arts; thus, the study of the *image* of the other in the literal sense of the word, of the image created by artists who, whether they were following a program or not always aware of what they were doing, have provided us with expressive evidence of their and their societies' attitudes toward other peoples.

The following pages in no way claim to exhaust the subject. Their aim is twofold: to call the attention of researchers and readers to the problem that I have just posed and to try out a method of iconological analysis leading to a typology of attitudes toward the black man, thereby tracing the distinctive lines of the two opposing tendencies in European attitudes toward the other which were mentioned in the previous chapter.[3]

The first representations of blacks in European art date back to the second millennium B.C. As Przeworski has demonstrated, a few Cretan frescoes show men with clearly negroid features. Acquaintance with Africans, the result of commercial contacts between the Aegean islands and Libya especially, did not cause the artists of Crete to develop a stylized manner of depicting them, which would seem to prove that contacts were rare and knowledge of the African anthropological type was very imperfect.[4]

Some art historians have insisted on the fact that blacks were often represented in Greco-Roman antiquity in a somewhat caricatural and even grotesque and monstrous form.[5] And yet, in *The Iliad*, Zeus goes off to feast with the "perfect Ethiops."[6] This theme is taken up again in *The Odyssey:* "But he to the far-off Ethiops' country was gone— the Ethiops sundered apart, remotest of men, some towards the rising sun, some towards the westering sun."[7] Herodotus locates among the long-lived Ethiopians, the most beautiful and the most robust of men, the Table of the Sun; they live then in a land of plenty.[8] The Greeks were also familiar, by way of Egyptian sources, with the Pygmies, whom legend depicted as being attacked by cranes fleeing the European winter.[9] As for imperial Rome, the racial prejudice of the clean-shaven *togati* showed itself, as I have already remarked, against the barbarians of the North, *bracati* and *comati* (wearing trousers and covered with hair); the *Graeculi*; and the Jews, more than against the blacks.[10]

On this basis, an American scholar, Frank M. Snowden, in a recent and well-documented work, puts forward the thesis that "the Greco-Roman view of blacks was no romantic idealization of distant, unknown peoples but a fundamental rejection of color as a criterion for evaluating men."[11] According to Snowden, those who would see certain classic representations of blacks as caricatures underestimate the anatomical curiosity of the artists. As for literary texts, if they are wrongly interpreted this is sometimes the result of the intellectual approach that attributes to the ancients the racial prejudices of our own time. Snowden, on the contrary, seeks to draw from his study a lesson of humanism and tolerance which may serve as a model for his white compatriots in the United States. It must be admitted, however, that the impressive photographic documentation he has assembled and the facts he cites elicit some reservations about his generous, overidealized conclusion on race relations in antiquity. Although the problem was not as keenly felt as it is today, it would be exaggerating to say that it was totally absent, if only on account of the marginal position of the great majority of Africans in Greco-Roman society. But this in no way detracts from the interest of Snowden's work.

It was in the Middle Ages that the African became particularly important symbolically. Remote and scarcely known, he was to appear in two opposing forms.

First, as a black, he would be associated with night, the world of darkness, and the forces of evil, and would even, in popular tradition, personify the devil. While it is impossible to accept the exaggerated formulation of B. Baranowski, who claims that the black African was for Europeans the most common representation of the devil,[12] certain anecdotes and legends, related by, among others, the great Polish poet J. Tuwim, and dating back to the fifteenth and sixteenth centuries, clearly indicate that the devil was personified by the black Ethiopian.[13] Ethnographic evidence points in the same direction. Bystron relates that some peasants in Crakow referred to the nobles and the middle class as "blacks." One of the sayings now fallen into disuse in Polish rural areas is "black as a Swede."[14] Is this a recollection of the black-devil stereotype, linked with the memory of the Swedish invasion?

And, to stay within the Middle Ages, in the *Chanson de Roland* there is no equivalence at all between the way the white-bearded emir is presented—a real baron, were he a Christian—and the accursed tribe of blacks whose teeth are the only white thing about them.[15] Is the black striking Jesus in the *Mocking of Christ* in the Arena Chapel a harking back to this same interpretation? It is difficult to be absolutely sure;[16] nor, similarly, can one be fully satisfied with the interpretation often put forward for the blacks in Bosch's *Garden of Delights,* according to which they symbolize lust.[17]

Furthermore, living in a distant country alongside fantastic creatures of the animal and plant kingdoms, the black was to form part of the *Imago Mundi* of this marvelous world, recreated, invented upon the facades of cathedrals to the greater glory of God. In the fourteenth century he was even to know the extraordinary fate of becoming the Church's symbol of ecumenism, in the Adoration of the Magi.

This episode from the New Testament was usually illustrated, right up to the middle of the thirteenth century, at least, with three personages, white, "like everyone else," differing little in age. They had represented the three ages, or the three tribes of Shem, Ham, and Japheth, or, more rarely, the three continents. As for the black, he rarely appeared in Christian iconography. It is true that Saint Maurice was featured as a black knight in contrast to Saint George. The former was, according to legend, a Roman legionnaire of Egyptian origin, but it seems to have been the phonetic association of the Christian name with the generic term Moor—designating a dark-skinned man—that he became, according to Louis Réau, "one of the rare dark-skinned men in Christian iconography."[18] Apart from Saint Maurice, there are a few minor saints who are associated by tradition with Africa, without any definite indication, however, of their anthropological type. These include the patron saint of Verona, Saint Zeno, born in Morocco, whose effigy is a painted statue with a dark face, and the principals in edifying scenes, such as the Ethiopian eunuch baptized by Saint Philip. I am speaking, of course, of the Christian tradition in Europe. The Faras frescoes, recently exhibited at the National Museum of Warsaw, prove that in Christian Nubia, as was to be expected, Africans attained the highest ecclesiastical honors.

But then, at the beginning of the fourteenth century, a sudden change took place. In many paintings one of the Magi became a true black through a twofold intellectual development. First, in Cologne especially, where the cult of the Magi was very much alive, the legendary Prester John, the lord of a vast Christian kingdom situated at the far ends of the earth, came to be regarded as the descendant of one of the three Kings. Second, after coming into contact, in Jerusalem, with Ethiopian monks, some German pilgrims became convinced that Prester John was the Negus. As a result, Prester John's Empire shifted from Asia to Africa, and one of the three Magi had to change the color of his skin and become a black. Certain texts from the second half of the fourteenth century even have it that the Three Kings are the lords of three "Indies"—Black Africa, Persia, and Arabia.[19]

The career of the black in Christian iconography did not fail,

however, to produce resistance. The image of the black magus seems
to have been accepted above all in Northern Europe, where it aroused
no association with the realities of social life and served, as it were, as
a pure symbol, bordering on the marvelous and the fantastic.

I do not mean by this that Dutch, Flemish, and German painters
painted white men with black faces, although many paintings were
in fact conceived in this way. Stwosz's sculptures and above all the
magnificent anthropological study of the head of the black king in
Bosch's Adoration show that, during the second half of the fifteenth
century, at least, it was possible to observe here and there in Europe
a real flesh-and-blood black. These encounters were exceptional, however, and do not appear to have aroused any reflections on the social
condition of those who served as models for the portrayal of the
Magus.

Things were different in Italy, where there was a far greater number
of black slaves and servants possessing distinctly inferior social status.
The black servant who carries off the coffin after the resurrection of
Lazarus in the Giotto fresco at Assisi in no way participates in this great
event. He does not belong to the community of men and Christians.
Throughout the fifteenth century, in Venetian painting especially, it
was quite natural for black servants to appear in crowd scenes as, for
instance, in Carpaccio's canvases or in Bellini's painting of the Miracle
of the relic of the Holy Cross fallen into the Canal.

Can a servant or a slave be canonized? This was difficult for the
Italian painters to accept; and while some resigned themselves, as did
Andrea Mantegna, others, like Gentile da Fabriano or Leonardo da
Vinci, left the black king out of their compositions. Most preferred
halfway solutions. A painting by Lorenzo Monaco shows a black prince
closely following the procession of the Magi, all of whom are white. A
painting by Jacobello del Fiore shows a black page holding dogs on a
leash. In Gozzoli's great fresco in the Medici-Riccardi Palace in
Florence, and in other paintings, the impression of exoticism is created
chiefly by the backgrounds filled with strange animals, Oriental goods,

and dark-skinned servants. Veronese painted Moors who were not, strictly speaking, "blackamoors."

The typology I have just outlined is neither complete nor rigorous, but the two traditions and the intermediate variants certainly coexisted throughout Europe. Certain conclusions could be drawn in terms of the relative frequency of images of blacks in the different cultural areas, but to my knowledge no such study has been done. I might add that certain representations of the black in Italian or Spanish painting (such as the legend of Saint Cosmas and Saint Damian, in which, after a canon's leg is amputated, a transplant is made of a dead black man's leg) although very difficult to interpret,[20] seem to reinforce my impression of assymetrical social relations. On the other hand, in Hans Memling's *Last Judgment* (Gdansk Museum in Poland) a black man figures among the chosen ones going to heaven, and another among those who are about to be cast down into Hell. Here the chief concern is that of the equality of all men before God. In this sense Memling's painting belongs to one of the mainstreams of the development of humanist thought, which was to come into its own in the sixteenth century.

The great discoveries made it necessary for Europe to define itself in relation to the non-European cultures. Attitudes polarized and asserted themselves vigorously, even brutally.

Thus the attitude foreshadowed in Memling's *Last Judgment* would be enunciated in a series of studies of black men's heads. Those who painted them transcended the purely aesthetic interest aroused in painters by the observation of new anthropological types in order to find in these faces passions common to all human beings. I have in mind particularly the superb drawings of Dürer, still heedful to anatomical detail; the studies of Rubens, Van Dyck, and de Crayer which undoubtedly have served as inspiration for many generations of Othello and which deserve to be called psychological studies; or again, the boundless melancholy of Rembrandt's blacks and the serious and sad gaze of the black boy painted by Watteau.

In literature, humanist inspiration would produce the noble black savage, like the hero of the novel *Oroonoko,* of which I have spoken. It is doubtless present also in *Othello,* even if the interpretation suggested by Jan Kott seems one-sided: "Othello is black. Desdemona is white," writes Kott. "Although black, Othello is noble. *Othello* was written against this 'although'."[21] All the same Shakespeare made no bones about portraying the skin-deep racism of all the characters. And Othello, blinded by passion, it is true, exclaims: "Arise, *black* vengeance from the hollow hell" (Act 3, Scene 3). His transformation is sudden and total; he loses his reason, and it is this that Lawrence Olivier's interpretation perhaps overemphasizes, while remaining faithful to the text. For *Othello* fits into the tradition of the Elizabethan theater which, out of a taste for exoticism and in order to exploit novelty, made it a habit to put African characters on stage. The audience appreciated the character of the black and evil Moor—a tragic character—to whom they contrasted the white and pagan but nevertheless virtuous Moor. Shakespeare took these two stereotypes as his inspiration but transcended them in order to create a complex and superb character, fragile like all human beings, who nevertheless remains a Moor.[22]

But this trend of humanist thought was far from being dominant. Social reality prevailed. A brief and isolated episode—the conversion of the kings of the Congo to Catholicism at a time when the American Indians were being massacred, and the ensuing diplomatic contacts with the Vatican—has bequeathed to us the fine bust of Antoine Emmanuel Ne Vunda, the ambassador of King Alvaro II, who died in Rome in 1608. It was executed by Francesco Caporale and decorates one of the churches in Rome. Nevertheless, social reality for most blacks in Europe was servitude or slavery. They appear then in numerous mythological and Biblical scenes, as well as in genre painting, performing similar sinister tasks, like the servant with the earring in Andrea Mantegna's *Judith,* or trifling services, like the boy holding out the

letter to Bathsheba in Ruben's painting, or bearing the parasol of the
Marchesa Grimaldi posing for Van Dyck. Black servants suddenly began appearing in the North of Europe, and as far as Poland and Russia.
They were often well treated, as is shown by a Dutch family portrait
painted by Frans Hals, perhaps because the vogue for exoticism and the
scarcity of African servants made them much coveted by the neighbors.
Lozinski notes that the black who, in 1599, was in the service of a great
Polish lord, Andrzej Fredro, created a sensation throughout the province.[23] An exotic servant in motley, serving an exquisite drink—tea,
coffee, chocolate—such was the black's condition in Europe throughout
the sixteenth, seventeenth, and eighteenth centuries. Tiepolo's Moor,
sporting an earring, of course, thus becomes a social document.

The black also bore on his shoulders the colonial economy that was
making Europe rich. The monument to Doge Pesaro, in the Frari in
Venice, symbolizes this; and of course the theme of black atlantes and
caryatids was to be exploited both in architecture and cabinetmaking.

From this only one step was needed to make the black the symbol
of all the luxury wares which flowed in from distant countries. By the
sixteenth century, the palaces and houses of noblemen and rich merchants were decorated with thousands of exotic objects—carved goblets
made of coconuts or ostrich eggs, inevitably adorned with the figure of a
black, ivory sculptures, and so on. Maurice Rheims notes that, in the
eighteenth century, a portrait of a black boy in a turban was worth
three times as much as that of a Parisian child executed by the same
painter at the same period.[24]

So the black became a symbol again just as in the Middle Ages, but
at a lower level, devoid of spirituality. Exoticism is indeed, as Valéry
says, the evocation of the imaginary Orient, and in order for this evocation to produce its effect, it is necessary never to have been in the
vaguely determined place to which it refers. "One must know it solely
by way of pictures, hearsay, reading, and a few topics of the least
learned, the most inexact, and even the most confused variety. This is
how we collect good dream material. It requires a mixture of space and

time, of pseudo-truth and false certainty, of minute details and vast, inexact perspectives."[25] With the help of the legends handed down from antiquity and the Middle Ages, as well as of the lack of information, accounts, and drawings modeled on reality,[26] the public of the Renaissance and the Age of Enlightenment had no difficulties in creating for itself an Orient of the mind, which happened in this case to be an imaginary Africa. But as colonization and the slave trade developed, the image of the black man became debased and became charged with racial prejudice. The persistent tradition of the black as the symbol of darkness was revived and certain stereotypes of the emotionality and the sexuality of blacks, in contrast with the intellectuality of Europeans, began their long and tenacious career.

On the iconographic plane, racial prejudice was to be expressed by a shift from the exotic toward the grotesque, which was characteristic of the rococo style. Certainly, the individual black, even if he was a servant, continued to be endowed with human and even sympathetic features; however, allegories of Africa, and therefore collective portrayals of the blacks, became distinctly caricatural.[27] Dinglinger's Moor with emeralds and, even more, the porcelain statue of the African king in the Metropolitan Museum collection present a stereotype which has been perpetuated right up to the present, as is to be seen in numerous illustrations in children's books.

In the nineteenth century, generally speaking, portrayals of blacks were devoid of any significance other than the search for exoticism in combination with an aesthetic interest in the interplay of colors. The same was true for the United States. The intellectual climate was scarcely favorable to the portrayal of blacks. The few paintings which do exist convey a false and idyllic image of the slaves on the plantations. It was only after the Civil War that the black became a serious subject of study for painters and attracted attention because of his folk tradition and his human qualities. Winslow Homer and Thomas Eakins are commonly considered to be the first artists of talent to have seriously attempted to paint black persons from 1875 onward. Was this guilt, in Homer's case, since he had often depicted blacks in a caricatural manner in his paintings and sketches of the Civil War? At all events, his new attitude caused him to be reviled by the righteous-minded.[28] It was not until American intellectual life became more radical, during the Great Depression, that painters and novelists discovered the human dimension of the Southern black farmer's wretchedness.

One might have thought that the "discovery" in 1905 of African sculpture by Vlaminck and Matisse would bring about a radical change in attitude toward the African peoples. But while for European art this was of an importance comparable, in some respects, with that of the discovery of America for anthropological thought, it was not accompanied by the awakening of a pluralistic consciousness at the cultural level, although it finally contributed to it. The discovery of Africa took place in the plastic arts and then in music, both of which are supremely asemantic areas. The Europeans discovered Africa art at a time when they needed it to deliver the death-blow to the classical tradition and the ascendancy of Greece, which had been renewed by the Renaissance, a tradition which doubtless had fastened onto the Greco-Roman heritage in order to give greater credibility to the central position of Europe in the world.[29]

It was only Picasso, according to John Berger's brilliant interpretation, who, through his simple, emotional, and direct borrowings from African masks, pursued a goal whose implications were more than aesthetic. It appears that, in painting the Demoiselles d'Avignon, he was in no way concerned with problems of form. What he wanted was to offer a challenge to civilization. "The dislocations in this painting"—writes Berger—"are the result of aggression, not aesthetics; it is the nearest you can get in a painting to an outrage."[30] What was involved, however, was not a reevaluation of African culture and, consequently, of African man. It was not, with a few commendable exceptions, until almost half a century had passed that Europe gave its full attention to the idea of African emancipation.

Such was not the case in Brazil and in the Antilles. It was here—and especially in Brazil—that, for the first time, in an art belonging to European culture, and even before the rebirth of African cultures, that the black was to become a hero. The Brazilian artists, led by Portinari, have paid homage to the true builders of the Brazilian economy, be they black, half-caste, or caboclos. Their feet are enormous and flat because they never wear shoes, Portinari once told me; their hands are horny and their arms muscular from work. When they cry, their tears are very big, for their lives are full of suffering. But they also know how to enjoy themselves like no one else; they have built Brazil with their sweat. A large part of Portinari's work constitutes a collective portrait of the Brazilian nation and, quite naturally, the blacks have found a place in it.

Such, in its essential features, is the tormented history of representations of the black man in European art.

Notes to Chapter 3

1. I made this proposal in an article entitled "Ethnocentrism—Source and Aggravating Factor of Conflicts," published by the UNESCO review, *Impact,* 18.2 (April-June 1968).

2. There is a perfect analogy with iconology, defined by G. Michaud as the branch of comparative literature which studies through written documents the ways in which peoples portray each other (see his preface to L. Fanoudh-Siefer's study, *Le mythe du nègre et de l'Afrique Noire dans la littérature française (de 1800 à la 2e Guerre mondiale)* (Paris, 1968), p. 3.

3. A first version of this chapter, accompanied by illustrations, appeared in *Annales—Economies, Sociétés, Civilisations,* 24.4 (July-August 1969), pp. 883-892. Hans-Joachim Kunst's recent monograph, *Der Afrikaner in der Europäischen Kunst* (Bad Godesberg, 1967), is an inventory rather than an iconological study.

4. Stefan Przeworski, "Typy afrykanskie na zabytkach kretenskich," in *Opera Selecta* (Wroclaw, 1967), pp. 17-35.

5. Paribeni, *Saggi di storia antica e di archeologia offerti a Guilio Beloch,* 1910, quoted by S. Przeworski, ibid., p. 30.

6. Homer, *Iliad,* Lord Derby's translation (Everyman's Library).

7. Homer, *Odyssey,* S. O. Andrew's translation (Everyman's Libary), p. 1.

8. Herodotus, *History,* book III.

9. Homer, *Iliad.*

10. A. N. Sherwin-White, *Racial Prejudice in Imperial Rome* (Cambridge, England, 1967).

11. F. M. Snowden Jr., *Blacks in Antiquity; Ethiopian in the Greco-Roman Experience* (Cambridge, Mass., 1970), p. 217.

12. B. Baranowski, *Pozegnanie z diablem i czarownica* (Lodz, 1965), p. 33.

13. J. Tuwim, *Czary i czarty polskie* (Warsaw, 1960), pp. 16-17 and 154-155.

14. J. Bystron, *Megalomania narodowa* (Warsaw, 1935), pp. 66-69.

15. See *Chanson de Roland,* stanzas LXXII and CCXXIX, for the description of the emir; CXLIII and CXLIV for vituperations against blacks.

16. I should like to thank Professor Enrico Cerulli, who was good enough to communicate to me his interpretation of this painting. Professor Cerulli, in pointing out that it is clearly the improperium that is depicted and not, as is commonly believed, the flagellation, disagrees with art historians who stress the formal importance of the black area in the composition of the painting, or else mention Byzantine influences. He considers the problem insoluble. For his part, Professor Jacques Le Goff inclines to an interpretation which admits of the existence of black slaves in medieval Italy.

17. See, for instance, Mario Bussagli, *Bosch* (Florence, 1966), p. 26. On the other hand, W. Fraengler, in *Le Royaume millénaire de Jérôme Bosch* (Paris, 1966) sees in this painting paradise regained by the Adamites.

18. Louis Réau, *Iconographie de l'art Chrétien* (Paris, 1955), vol. 3-2, p. 937.

19. See Jean Doresse, *L'Empire du Prêtre-Jean, L'Ethiopie médiévale,* vol. 2 (Paris, 1957), pp. 211-231. Interpretations of details vary from author to author.

20. Once again, I express my thanks to Professor Cerulli for having shared with me numerous details of the legend of Saint Cosmas and Saint Damian. The legend originated in medieval Rome, and the transplanted leg came from the corpse of a recently deceased black, whose remains were of course restored to their original state by transplanting the canon's amputated leg (gangrenous and consequently black). But in Spanish art, the legend has a more tragic interpretation: a living black, screaming with pain, is severed from a leg which is to be used to cure the patient. The theme was used by the Italians Beato Angelico, Lorenzo di Bieci, and Saco di Pietro; the Spaniards Pedro Burruguete and Fernando Callego; and

the Fleming Ambroise Franken, among others. In Valladolid, at the College of Santa Cruz, it is the subject of a relief in gilded and polychromed wood.

21. Jan Kott, *Szkice o Szekspirze* (Warsaw, 1961), p. 233.

22. See Eldred Jones's excellent study, *Othello's Countrymen: The African in English Renaissance Drama* (London, 1965).

23. Wladyslaw Lozinski, *Zycie polskie w dawnych wiekach* (Cracow, 1964), p. 94. Already at this time King Stefan Batory had a black boy among his servants, according to B. Baranowski, *Znajomosc wschodu w dawnej Polsce do XVIII w.* (Lodz, 1950), p. 203.

24. M. Rheims, *La vie étrange des objets* (Paris, 1959), p. 163.

25. Paul Valéry, *Regards sur le monde actuel* (Paris, 1945), pp. 200-201.

26. See in particular the collection *Monumenta Ethnographica Africae.*

27. P. D. Curtin, in *The Image of Africa; British Ideas and Action, 1780-1850* (Madison, Wis., 1964), p. 36, observes that toward the end of the eighteenth century several authors began to present a dual image of the African, fairly favorable to individuals but hostile to the community.

28. Sidney Kaplan, "The Negro in the Art of Homer and Eakins," in *Black and White in American Culture,* ed. J. Chametsky and S. Kaplan (Amherst, Mass., 1969), pp. 273-279.

29. On this last point see A. Jakimowicz, *Zachod a Sztuka Wschodu* (Warsaw, 1967), p. 73.

30. J. Berger, *Success and Failure of Picasso* (London, 1965), p. 73.

In Swift's antitravelog, the King of Brobdingnag, after he has listened to Gulliver's account of moral standards in his homeland, makes the following judgment about Europeans: "I can only conclude the bulk of your natives to be the most pernicious vermin that nature ever allowed to crawl upon the surface of the earth."[1]

Here then, once again, we have a settling of accounts between Europeans by characters brought in specially for the occasion. A rhetorical device? Doubtless so, but also the foreshadowing of a virulently Europophobic image which colonization could not fail to produce in the minds of those colonized.

The Spaniards, the very image of the horsemen of the Aztec Apocalypse, arrived in Mexico preceded by omens of doom. People believed that they were witnessing the return of gods with faces and bodies white like limestone, accompanied by a few "dirty gods"— Cortez having brought a few blacks with him, including Francisco Eguia, who is reputed to have transmitted smallpox to the Mexicans.[2] The Spaniards were offered gifts and human blood to drink. They recoiled before the blood but accepted the gifts, then immediately put the country to fire and the sword and pillaged the treasures of Montezuma. The presumed sons of the sun hurled themselves on the gold "like starving pigs," "snatched it up like monkeys." The sight of all the wealth accumulated by the Aztec sovereign took their breath away: they bared their teeth like wild animals and hugged each other for joy. The Indian chronicles to which we are indebted for these details are damning evidence against the conquerors because they make no attempt to judge. They record the chain of events produced by supernatural intervention; they describe the ineluctable tragedy of their people. World literature contains few texts as poignant as these.[3]

This scene was to go through many encores and variations. Pigafetta, in 1519, tells of his arrival in the bay of Rio de Janeiro: "It should be taken into account that, by chance, there had been no rain for two months prior to our coming there, and the day of our arrival it began to rain; from this, the people of the forementioned place

concluded that we came from the sky and that we had brought the rain
with us, which showed a great simple-mindedness." Then he adds:
"This people would easily be converted to the Christian faith."[4] More
than four centuries later, toward the end of the Second World War, the
strange "cargo cult" made its appearance in the New Hebrides. The
founder of one of these millenarian and eschatological movements an-
nounced the imminent arrival of "America"; all the adepts of the cult
would receive vast quantities of goods and would live eternally without
having to work; but, in the meantime, all goods, beginning with objects
purchased from the whites, had to be destroyed. The "Americans" were
the Ancestors, the dead who would return in triumph laden with gifts,
the whites being generally considered as spirits of the dead, as ghosts
and phantoms. This did not, however, keep the cargo cults from having
a strong anti-European element. The natives were in fact convinced
that the cargo boats sent to them by their dead and rightfully belonging
to them had been intercepted by the whites.[5]

At the other extreme of attitudes toward Europeans are numerous
instances of rejection, hand in hand with, at the very most, a certain
curiosity about the exotic, like the desire to see a real flesh-and-blood
Latin which caused Marco Polo to be invited to the court of the Great
Khan. The universe of Ibn-Batutah, as vast as it was, was a world without
Europe because medieval Europe had little to offer him, but above all
because it was situated completely outside Islam, and therefore outside
what he regarded as the inhabited world. In contrast, in all the territories Ibn-Batutah visited, from China to the heart of Africa, he found—
no matter how small—Moslem communities.[6]

Babur, the prince of Fergana, who ruled over India as the Great
Mogul at the beginning of the sixteenth century, left behind him a brilliant autobiography, written in his mother tongue—Turkish. Where,
then, were his boundaries? On one side they took in China, on the
other the Ottoman Turks; but Babur does not mention Christian
Europe even once, and not because he was unaware of its existence.
The circumnavigation of Africa and the landing of Vasco da Gama on

the Indian coast, twenty-one years before Babur invaded India, are not referred to in his writings. Was he ignorant of these facts, or did he consider them to be unimportant?

In the sixteenth century the Jesuits complained that the Japanese nobles had no wish to visit distant countries. Only with a great deal of effort did they manage finally to organize a Japanese mission, which visited Europe from 1584 to 1586 and which was, moreover, given a triumphal reception. Instructions were compiled, detailing the best way of presenting the wonders of Europe to the Japanese, in order to charm and instruct them, while preventing them "from seeing or learning other things which may create the opposite impression."[7] One of the major concerns of the organizers of this "guided tour" which anticipated by some centuries the practices of modern diplomacy, was to keep them away from the baneful influences of Protestantism. This is why they did not have permission to visit Germany and Saxony.

Without any doubt, the Japanese embassy produced a great deal of stir in the cultural life of Europe. We do not know what its effects were in Japan, but we can assume that they were very great, since 1589 saw the beginning of the massacres of Christians, which were to last for almost half a century and cost the lives of tens of thousands of people.

As for China, missions were tolerated there for a longer time and enjoyed a certain prestige at the court: the religious brethren excelled in mathematics and in the art of casting guns.[8] But the impact of Catholicism was superficial there, in spite of the flexibility of the Jesuits and their effort to adapt to the local culture. Indeed, in Japan Saint Francis Xavier found a stumbling block in the form of the following question, which was very difficult to answer: "If yours is the true faith, why have not the Chinese, from whom comes all wisdom, heard of it?"[9]

The respect accorded to the European mathematicians and bombardiers did not extend to other areas of science and technology. The Chinese emperors assembled a vast collection of European clocks, the skill and variety of which they greatly appreciated, but they considered

them as toys and nothing more. In his fine essay on clocks, Carlo
Cipolla quotes the following opinion of Western science at the end of
the eighteenth century: "In regard to the learning of the West, the art
of surveying the land is the most important, followed by the art of
making strange machines. Among these strange machines, those per-
taining to irrigation are most useful to the common people. All the
other machines are simply intricate oddities, designed for the pleasure
of the senses. They fulfill no basic needs."[10] Finally, at the commercial
and diplomatic level, the ethocentrism of the Middle Kingdom caused it
to reject British proposals for an exchange of ambassadors. The English
envoys who arrived in Peking were treated there as the representatives
of a country paying tribute to the Celestial Empire, to demonstrate
thereby its loyal submission, which was the only form of relationship
with the barbarians which was recognized.

The two letters which the Emperor Ch'ien-lung sent to George III of
England in 1787 admirably sum up the attitude of the Chinese toward
the barbarians of the western peninsula of the Asian continent. These
are the main points: The British request is without precedent and cannot be granted, for Europeans residing in Peking do not have the right
to return to their country or to communicate with it; furthermore,
they are obliged to dress in the Chinese manner and to live according
to the customs of the country, which would present some difficulties
for a foreign ambassador. Likewise, major difficulties would arise if
China were to decide to send an ambassador to England, not to mention the fact that Europe is divided up into many countries and that it
would be impossible to receive so many ambassadors. In a word, the
Celestial Dynasty is not going to change its customs and established
etiquette just to suit England. European merchants are accorded the
right to settle in Canton, but there is no reason for an embassy to be
established at the Court of Peking. Assuming that the English are
moved by the desire to acquire Chinese civilization, Chinese laws and
ceremonies are so different that, even if the English ambassador were
to manage to master the rudiments, it would be impossible to transplant

them to England. As for English merchandise, the Emperor attaches no importance to it.

The second text is even more explicit. China is not interested in importing manufactured articles from barbaric countries. But as Europe cannot do without the tea, silk, and porcelain produced by the Celestial Empire *[sic!]*, the Emperor has consented that trade be carried on in Canton. England is dealt with on an equal footing with other nations and its proposals could create an awkward precedent. It is only out of concern for the isolation of the British Isles, separated from the world by the oceans, and its misapprehension of Chinese laws, that the Emperor has decided to close this incident by sending back the English envoys laden with munificent gifts, but also with a detailed memorandum in which the English requests are rejected one by one and which over and over again stresses the doctrine of the most strict separation between the subjects of the Empire and the barbarians.[11]

Europocentrism was opposed, then, by a traditionalist Sinocentrism, which was not even Europophobic because it did not yet deign to admit the irreversible interference of the Fo-lang-ki in the destiny of Asia. It was not until the middle of the nineteenth century and the brutal military and economic expansion of colonialist Europe that this haughty isolationism began to crumble.

Then began the age of modernization, incomplete and rarely effective, sometimes imposed by the colonial administrations, sometimes passionately espoused by embryonic national movements. I can give only a brief outline here of the typology of attitudes which began to emerge, from the moment when those on the periphery of the capitalist world began to realize that they had been reduced to impotence and often to wretchedness by the technical and military superiority of the Europeans and that, in order to liberate themselves, they had to master Western science, the Western art of warfare, and Western technology.

We may distinguish five principal types of reaction to the European challenge.

The first attempted to separate technological knowledge from

cultural, religious, and ideological values as completely as possible and
counted simultaneously on the transfer of European techniques and
the reinforcement of local values. This is what the Japanese leaders
practiced from the time of the Meiji restoration in 1868 right up to
1945, when the system of traditional, political, and cultural values collapsed.[12] This undoubtedly proved to be an effective procedure tech-
nologically and economically, since Japan very rapidly rose to the rank
of a great industrial and military power. But the social price of this exploit was exorbitant: a particularly rapacious form of capitalism was
thereby introduced, based on a hierarchical social structure and relations of production directly inherited from feudalism; Japan set out on
the path of imperialism, as we know with disasterous consequences,
first, for the peoples colonized by Japan, and, second, for the Japanese
themselves, laid low by the defeat of 1945.

Thus, by the end of the nineteenth century, the Japanese were, to
the other peoples of Asia, the "satraps of the white world,"[13] bearing
the superior technology adapted from Europe and pressed into the service of their own colonialism. The Korean writer Younghill Kang has
devoted a few fascinating passages of his autobiography to his discovery of the West, at the beginning of this century, through the agency
of Japanese invaders, who, in Korea, with its pride in its Confucian tradition, were nevertheless considered to be culturally very inferior. "It
may seem strange to the reader who is not familiar with the politics of
the Far East that Korea, an independent nation for more than forty-two
centuries, should have been so helpless during those first ten years of
the twentieth century before the clandestine but persistent intrusion of
Japan. The reason, however, for the latter's power in the East was that
it had been rapidly Europeanized, especially from the point of view of
its weapons. This is the sole subject which it has learned thoroughly,
since Perry's arrival; so much so that it is capable of instructing its
neighbors. The vigor it possesses as a young nation, its gift for imitation, the total transformation already accomplished, have enabled it
easily to shed a borrowed culture in order to assimilate another. But

what was relatively easy for Japan was not so for the older countries, China and Korea."[14]

In short, in Japan the most modern techniques of war and of production were placed in the service of a conservative and traditionalistic ideology, containing a strong element of hostility toward the European cultural area. The scroll depicting the arrival of Commodore Perry[15] takes on a symbolic dimension. The fascination exercised by the steamboat can be seen, but some of the Americans are portrayed as veritable devils. The contrast with the well-known lacquer screens representing the arrival of the Portuguese in the seventeenth century is striking. What one immediately notices in the screens is the incapacity of the Japanese painters to distinguish the physical features of the European from those of the African sailors (except for the color of the skin); both are painted in a stereotyped way, the ironic curiosity of the artists dwelling on a few generic features—their large size, their long noses, their small, elongated heads—but above all on the details of their dress; the baggy trousers must have caused great delight to their audience, together with the monkeylike agility of the sailors perched high up on the masts. On the other hand, Perry and his companions are portrayed with a particular malevolence. As these portraits were not done from life but were products of the artist's imagination, these terrifying faces tell us a great deal about underlying feelings. The same is true of the famous toy, made at the end of the eighteenth century for Sultan Tipu, the maharajah of Mysore, featuring a tiger in the process of devouring a European, the whole of which was life-size and equipped with sound devices, the roaring of the tiger mingling with the screams of his victim.[16]

In Latin America, throughout the nineteenth century and at the beginning of the twentieth, the attitude of the local élites was almost completely contradictory. They remained aloof from modern techniques of production which were being introduced everywhere through the investment of foreign capital; on the other hand, they attempted to vie with Europe on the cultural level by accepting its values, its tastes, and its fashions. They learned to consume rather than to produce, as Gustave Beyhaut justly has observed,[17] and they willingly accepted intellectually a situation in which they were the colonized ones, as well as all the racial, climatic, and cultural prejudices promoted by the colonizers to justify colonial expansion. The very pessimistic psychological portrait of the Brazilian which is sketched in Paulo Prado's famous book is a striking example of this.[18] This excessive Europophilia of the élites was to go hand in hand with the Europophobia of the common people in marginal situations, who were attracted either by repressed native cultures or by religious and cultural syncretism, halfway between Christianity and animism. The difficulty Latin American nations experience today in reducing their dependence on the outside world actually stems from having imported this dependence along with the model of culture which I have just described.

We are therefore faced with a situation similar to that of colonies where the colonizers succeeded, willy-nilly, in creating groups which were assimilated to such an extent that they became more Europeanized than the Europeans. They did this according to the well-known guidelines laid down by Lord Macaulay in 1834: "We must at present do our best to form a class who may be interpreters between us and the millions whom we govern; a class of persons Indian in blood and colour, but English in tastes, in opinions, in morals, and in intellect."[19] In fact, the colonial enterprise resulted in a deculturation and a denaturalization of the native,[20] in the production of "white niggers."[21] Kwame N'Krumach has clearly described the ridiculous aspects of an education which was supposed to turn Africans into poor copies of the English: "We were neither fish nor fowl. We were denied the knowledge of our African past and informed that we had no present. What future could there be for us? We were taught to regard our culture and traditions as barbarous and primitive. Our textbooks were English textbooks, telling us about English history, English geography, English ways of living, English customs, English ideas, English weather."[22]

Such a way of molding minds could only corrupt the weak and revolt the strong. The reaction of those who revolted took three forms
which I shall examine in turn.

Some sought to find a solution in the glorification of traditional
values, to some extent following the Japanese model in the cultural
sphere but without necessarily doing so in the technical sphere. In
India, in particular, there are still signs today of attempts to legitimize
this or that contribution of Western culture by endeavoring to find a
local genealogy for it, aimed at proving both *nihil novi sub soli* and
that the Indians were first in the field. Thus, an Indian historian recently applied himself to proving that the philosophical schools of
Kant and Hegel would have been unthinkable without the impact of
Indian philosophy and, since Hegel influenced Marx, "It can be said
that Marxism also contained, at least in its dialectics, the essential attributes of Indian thinking."[23] Undoubtedly this is more valuable
than the traditional opposition between the spiritualism of the East
and the crude materialism of the West, preached by Vivekananda[24]
and all the traditionalists who reject any possibility of interchange,
on opposition which is nevertheless far removed from cultural
pluralism as we understand it. K. T. Shah, who is rightly considered
to be the father of Indian planning, did not hesitate, in 1951, to interpret the Artha Shastras and other classical Indian writings as an example of global planning that no nation today is in any position to
introduce.[25]

This attitude is merely a step away from negritude,[26] which, for the
most part, is the same intellectual maneuver, nostalgia for the traditional past more than revolt, and the invention of an Africocentrist historical myth, contrasting with the Europocentric myth and constructed
as its opposite, sometimes resulting in a veritable racism against racism,
as Sartre has strikingly phrased it.[27] In her fine essay, *Négritude et
situation coloniale,* Lilyan Kesteloot reassures us: black writers, although sometimes possessed by their hatred, are aware of the dangers
of a neo-racism such as this,[28] and I am glad to concur. This is true, in

particular, I believe, of those who, like Mphahlele, reject negritude,
either as an artificial intellectual movement of a Europeanized elite,[29]
or as an unfortunate confusion between the creation of an *engagé* national culture on the one hand and folklore or an abstract populism on
the other, like Fanon.[30] Moreover, Africans and American blacks have
many motivations for seeking a set of common cultural values to hold
up against the cultural nationalism of the groups that dominate the
world's economy and politics—a nationalism which has no place for
them.[31] After all, the process of nation building, which Africa is presently experiencing, has, as the Polish sociologist Nina Assorodobraj has
observed, caused it to go through a period of romanticism, in which history plays the same role as it did in Eastern Europe, in the nineteenth
century, in the writings of the Slavophiles.

The basic conflict is the same. "When a group of people define
themselves historically as a nation and as a part of a much larger ethnic
group, because they feel that they are lagging behind (be it in relation
to democratic Europe of the nineteenth century or to industrial civilization), they must take a stand on the question of whether they are pur-
suing an original path of development or Westernization. History
becomes equally necessary to both sides, but they interpret it by applying different standards of values."[32] In other words, it would be naive
not to expect history to be manipulated according to ideological needs.

But these considerations should not prevent us from seeing where
Africocentrist mythology leads and from stigmatizing its excesses in
the same way as those of all ethnocentric history, sustained as they are
by falsifications and serving this or that ideology. In the United States
especially, black historians and ideologists have increasingly been advocating a revision of African history which, instead of correcting the
image which has been falsified by European historiography, would be
satisfied with glorifying real or mythical facts that can prove, whatever
Lilyan Kesteloot may say, the superiority of the black race and can
propagate antiwhite racial stereotypes.

Let us take, by way of example, Malcolm X's lectures on Afro-

American history.[33] They contain very relevant statements on the affiliation of the American blacks with the great dark majority of mankind and the rejection of the status of Negro: "Whenever you see
somebody who calls himself a Negro, he's a product of Western civilization—not only of Western civilization, but of Western crime."[34] But
immediately afterwards, he criticizes anthropologists for having deliberately falsified the classification of races, and says that the Sumeri-
ans, the Dravidians, and Egyptians are black people. The description of
the exploits of black people results in a stereotype of the black man:
". . . The black man by nature is a builder, he is scientific by nature,
he's mathematical by nature. Rhythm is mathematics, harmony is
mathematics. It's balance. And the black man is balanced. Before you
and I came over here, we were so well balanced we could toss something on our head and run with it. You can't even run with your hat
now—you can't keep it on. Because you lost your balance. You've
gotten away from yourself. But when you are in tune with yourself,
your very nature has harmony, has rhythm, has mathematics. You can
build. You don't even need anybody to teach you to build. . . ."[35]

In opposition to this image of the black, Malcolm X sets the stereotype of the European. At the period when the blacks of Egypt had already created a sophisticated civilization, Europeans walked around
naked or dressed in animal skins, lived in caves, ate raw meat. Their
preference for underdone beefsteak stems from the fact that they have
only recently acquired the habit of cooking their food. A characteristic feature of the European is his taste for killing. The Chinese were
the first to invent gunpowder, but for peaceful ends. The Europeans
immediately transformed it into a deadly weapon. "In Asia and in
Africa we kill for food. In Europe, they kill for sport. Have you not
noticed that? Yes, they're bloodthirsty, they love blood; they love to
see the flow of other people's blood, not their own."[36] Gunpowder
and lies made it possible for the Europeans to dominate the world, in
spite of their technical and cultural inferiority right up to the period
of the Crusades: "And it was during the Crusades that many of the

people in Europe realized what a high culture existed in Asia and in Africa. Why, these people were living in huts in Europe, and in holes in the hills, still in that day—they were savages almost, didn't know what learning was, couldn't read and write. Their king couldn't even read and write, and he was over all of them. They got their reading and writing and arithmetic from you and me. And you see what they did with it? They turned around and used it on us."[37]

Before setting aside this text, which it would be wrong to treat as a simple curiosity or as an example of ignorance—falsifiers of history usually know their history—it should be noted that Malcolm X takes up and turns against the Europeans the stereotype of black sexuality, so frequently called on by white racists. Since Hannibal—a black at the head of an army of 90,000 black Africans—conquered Italy, it is not surprising that so many Italians have dark skins even today. This, for Malcolm X, is an object of pride, as is the fact that American soldiers briefly passed through Europe during the Second World War, as is borne out by the large number of mulatto babies. "You've spread your blood everywhere. If you start to talk to one of them, I don't care where he is, you can put him right in his place. In fact, he'll stay in his place, if he knows that you know your history."[38]

Malcolm X seems to have founded a school among certain American history teachers. Even the massacres of Africans perpetrated by European colonizers are sometimes described in such a way as to allow mention, on the side of the victims, of the fabulous exploits of mythical warriors who proved to be better commanders than some of the best military minds of Europe. This brings back to me a childhood memory. At the Lycée Pasteur in São Paulo, the person who taught us Brazilian history, who was, moreover, known for his Fascist sympathies, took great pains to explain to the group of Europeans who attended his courses that the anonymous heroism of the pioneers of the northeast of Brazil, in the sixteenth century, had no equivalent in European history. Not even Joan of Arc, he would say, and in order to make his point more effectively, he would make foreigners stand up when he

delivered his account of the cowboys who created the "leather civilization" in Pernambouc. Which just goes to show that the loathsome face
of chauvinism is the same everywhere.

What Malcolm X wishes is not only the glorification of the past of
the black peoples, but also the categorical rejection of European civilization. This, in my typology, is the second form of revolt against
European domination, and it is undoubtedly destined to have wider
and wider repercussions among the peoples of the Third World unless
there is a fundamental change in the interplay of world politics and
world economics.

This brutal rejection is based on direct experience. It stems first of
all from colonization, which turns the colonized into objects and cor-
rupts the colonizer. Consider Aimé Césaire's famous speech: "Between
the colonizer and the colonized, there is room only for forced labor,
intimidation, pressure, police, taxes, theft, rape, serfdom, scorn, mistrust, arrogance, complacency, rottenness, brain-washed élites, and debased masses. No human contact, only relationships of domination and
submission which transform the colonizer into a warder, a sergeant-
major, an overseer of convicts, and the native into an instrument of
production."[39]

But the rejection stems also from the genocide and the "white civil
wars," to use Keith Irvine's expression,[40] which to some are the end
product of the pseudohumanistic European culture. For Europe, from
the point of view of the Third World, is indeed the universe where the
Mediterranean myth of man made in God's likeness has been trampled
on and delivered to the crematorium. As the Polish poet and writer
M. Jastrun has recognized, "Europe, which has created, or at the very
least absorbed and adopted, almost all the humanist faiths is, at the
same time, the mother of almost all the antihumanist myths, which it
has shown far greater skill in putting into practice than it has positive
values."[41] At the sight of a concentration camp, the hero of the novel
Los pasos perdidos by the Cuban writer Alejo Carpentier exclaims: "I
could never imagine the failure of Western man to be so absolute as

that which here is revealed to my eyes, amongst the débris of terror."[42]
Fanon is even more virulent: "That Europe which never stopped talking about man, never stopped proclaiming that it was concerned only
about man, we know today by what sufferings mankind has paid for
each of the victories of its spirit."[43] Can we then be astonished, although we may deplore it, that he decides to defy the European heritage: "Let us make up our minds not to imitate Europe and let us turn
our muscles and our brains to a new end. Let us endeavor to invent
the total man that Europe has been incapable of setting in the lead."[44]

This directive, applied literally, leads to the rejection of all that
Europe produces, right up to its most radical thought, which is also incapable of grasping with its Europocentric conceptual framework the
realities of the periphery. "The revolutionary utopias of the intellectuals of industrial cultures are absolutely inadequate when it comes to
furthering the liberation of our countries," writes an Argentinian philosopher attacking Sartre, Nizan, and Gorz.[45]

In these circumstances, which lead to extremism and fanaticism, a
great deal of intellectual courage and a very broad outlook are necessary to take up a third form of revolt—the last in my typology—which
is a dialectic striving between rejection and assimilation, leading beyond one's frame of reference to a more finely shaded position than
that which consists in purely and simply anathematizing the European
heritage.

Initially, what is required is an awareness of the ambiguity in the
Third World's attitude toward Europe, which is described by the well-
known specialist in Arab history, Bernard Lewis, in these terms:

Even after liberation, the intelligent and sensitive Arab cannot but be
aware of the continual subordination of his culture to that of the West.
His richest resource is oil—but it is found and extracted by Western
processes and machines, to serve the needs of Western inventions. His
greatest pride is his new army—but it uses Western arms, wears Western-
style uniforms, and marches to Western tunes. His ideas and ideologies,
even of anti-Western revolt, derive ultimately from Western thought.

His knowledge even of his own history and culture owes much to Western scholarship. His writers, his architects, his technicians, even his tailors, testify by their work to the continued supremacy of Western civilization—the ancient rival, the conqueror and now the model, of the Muslim. Even the gadgets and garments, the tools and amenities of his everyday life are symbols of bondage to an alien and dominant culture, which he hates and admires, imitates but cannot share. It is a deeply wounding, deeply humiliating experience.[46]

I differ from Lewis on many points. The situation in Saudi Arabia is not the same as in Algeria, to take two extreme cases; the political context alters the main premises of the problem. Modern industrial technology no longer has to be borrowed solely from the European area (in the broad sense that we give to this term) constituted by the ancient metropolises and the great capitalist powers. The ideological trends of the Third World cannot be explained simply in terms of external influences (which would be to fall back into Europocentrism). It is appropriate, on the contrary, to focus on the effective and potential, positive and negative, contribution of local tradition and to explain its impact on politics. R. Garaudy has rightly insisted on the possibility that in the elaboration of socialism the great and lofty traditions of Islamic culture, the philosophy and the sociology of Ibn Khaldun, the utopian socialism of Carnathes, and the rationalism of Averroes may come to play a role similar to that played by Hegel, Ricardo, or Saint-Simon,[47] provided that they are shown to be compatible with the European school of socialist thought.

But as to the crux of the problem, Lewis is undoubtedly right. The Third World must take a stand in relation to Europe in three areas—intellectual equipment, technologies, and ideologies.

Abdel-Malek rightly insists on giving a central place conceptually to the dialectic of specificity and universality. He supports his case by showing up, through historical analysis, the incompleteness of the conceptual instruments of the social sciences (developed at a time when three quarters of humanity was in no way involved in the dialogue and was at the very most treated as a topic of discussion). But he also emphasizes that it is impossible to go beyond the present stage merely by rejecting this Europocentric apparatus, since the critical approach cannot be reduced to a simplistic Manichaeism.[48]

With regard to Western technologies, both production-oriented and military, the assumption that they will inevitably be assimilated by the Third World underlies, as we have seen, the ambiguous relationship between the Third World and Europe, but it also delivers up that relationship to the domination of the industrial countries. People have recently begun to realize that there is a need in this area, as in all others, for a critical examination of the initial hypotheses and in particular of the idea that there exists a scale of technological values of universal significance. I shall return to this problem later; here I shall observe merely that the heroic resistance of Vietnam, in the face of aggression by the most powerful army in the world, challenges even the universal value of military technologies, except, of course, for the total destructive power of nuclear and biological weapons, since the military aid provided to the Vietnamese by the U.S.S.R. and China cannot explain by itself the failure of the American operations.

There remains the most controversial aspect: that of ideological exports from Europe, of the ideology of the Enlightenment,[49] of Marxism, of socialism, and also of Christianity, the impact of which should not be judged by the failure of missionary enterprises, but by the influence that it had on Gandhi, by the role that Martin Luther King might have played, by the vitality of millenarian movements of vaguely Christian inspiration,[50] and finally by the appearance of a church of protest in Latin America.

The ideological history of the Third World is largely a series of definitions relating to this heritage. That is the picture which emerges from an anthology of contemporary Arab political thought[51] and especially from an important work by Abdallah Laroui, whose overriding concern is the problem of critical assimilation of positivism and Marxism, defined as the "system of systems," the "methodical summary of

Western history," and the "epitome of the West."[52] Naturally rejecting Europocentrism, Laroui also rejects pluralism, which he considers
to be a pseudosolution, and generously postulates a dialogue leading
to a truly universal anthropology.

The same concern with the universal, as against pluralism, is to be
seen in the debate on socialism. Should one speak of socialisms in the
plural and assign national adjectives to them, as many leaders in the
Third World tried to do? Or, on the contrary, should one admit the
existence of only one socialism and, by extension, of only one universal method of building it?

European socialists are congratulating themselves on having taken
an important step toward making Marxism more flexible, by simultaneous recognition of the specificity of situations in the Third World[53]
and of the right of peoples to seek their own path toward socialism—a
principle solemnly set forth at the Twentieth Congress of the C.P.S.U.
and brutally violated subsequently with the invasion of Czechoslovakia.
By a curious paradox, their counterparts in the Third World think it
necessary to insist on the universality of socialism.

This may be because they fear another Europocentric trap in the refusal to apply the same all-encompassing categories to the European
nations and to the Third World, as is the case of the Chinese. Did not
Guo-mo-ro, taking a stand against traditional Sinocentrism, but also
against the nondogmatic interpretation of Marxism, state, in 1929:
"The Chinese have an old saying: 'The conditions of our country are
specific.' Almost all nationalities have national prejudices of this kind;
however, the Chinese are neither gods nor monkeys, and the society
organized by the Chinese should have no special features."[54]

Or perhaps it is because they have seen the fall of regimes which
have eagerly and hastily proclaimed national socialisms and have not,
so to speak, gone beyond the stage of verbal incantation, serving extremely various aims and interests in each case.[55] We are indebted to
Kwame N'Krumach for one of the most penetrating texts on African
socialism, a soul-searching reexamination since it was composed by

the former president of Ghana when he was in exile, in 1966, with all
the free time necessary to analyze the reasons for his own lack of success. N'Krumach[56] considers that the very term African socialism is
devoid of meaning, appropriate to anthropology rather than to economics. To assume that there can be tribal, racial, or national socialism is to get bogged down in chauvinism. African tribal society should
not be idealized, and the task of African socialists is to identify themselves with the spirit of communal societies more than with their structure. It would be futile to seek solutions to the complex problems of
modern society in a return to the mythical past. For, according to
N'Krumach, Islamic civilization and the colonial experience are both
historical experiences of traditional society in Africa, profound experiences which have brought lasting changes to the configuration of that
society. They have introduced new values and a social, cultural, and
economic organization of African life. Modern African societies, although backward, are not traditional, and they are clearly in a state of
socioeconomic imbalance, because they are not anchored in a firm
ideology. The solution is certainly not to reject all Islamic and Euro-
colonial influences, in a vain attempt to recreate a past which cannot
be revived. The solution is in a flight forward, toward a higher and
more harmonious form of society, in which the quintessence of the
human scheme of traditional African society will be expressed in a
modern context; in a word, toward socialism by means of policies
scientifically developed and correctly applied."

In other words, there must be an effort to learn from and to progress beyond the old models, not wholesale rejection of them. Nehru
was guided by the same intention—whatever may be said about his indecisiveness at moments of major decision for the Indian nation. This
is admirably summed up in his testament. As a nonbeliever, Nehru re-
fused all religious ceremony after his death, but he asked that a handful
of his ashes be committed to the Ganges and that the rest be scattered
across the fields of India from a plane. The text is a love poem to the
people of India and to the Ganges, the symbol of the past and of

tradition but also of the course toward the ocean of the future. After recalling that he himself dreamed of liberating his people from oppressive traditions, Nehru adds, however, that he never wanted to cut himself completely off from the past: "I am proud of this great heritage which has been and which remains ours. I am also aware that I, like all of us, am a link in the endless chain which goes right back to the dawn of history, in the unfathomable past of India."[57]

I shall now sum up. Beginning with popular culture, which is stimulated by the mass media, governed by school instruction, disseminated by what have come to be called the applied arts—and they form the public taste and sensibility far more than do masterpieces—average Europeans continue to see the inhabitants of the Third World and, more generally, colored people (this term has not yet disappeared from our vocabulary) through two contradictory stereotypes which are, however, frequently linked together in very different combinations. This "other" appears now as the cannibal, the Anti-Christ, the destructive demon preparing to overwhelm the developed countries in his demographic tidal wave, and now as the being on the right side of the angels, the child of nature, the creator of exquisite cultures, worthy of our greatest respect: kindly do not touch the objects on display in the planetary museum of ethnology! This is a convenient way of atoning, in thought and in words, for colonialism, and of confirming for ourselves the generous power of our intellect, capable of going beyond the limits of ethnocentrism. Is not the theory of cultural pluralism founded on the absolute value of the principle of tolerance, that most precious jewel of our humanist heritage?

But still, in spite of the intentions of those who recognize the past connection of ethnography with colonialism,[58] despite the enormous importance, to European intellectual development, of having left behind the pseudoscientific justifications of European superiority, cultural pluralism lacks effectiveness in the eyes of the Third World. It is inoperative, and since at the same time it unintentionally makes the

European public susceptible to the most banal form of exoticism, it even becomes a nuisance. The reason for this is that it is certainly no longer sufficient to give protection to and to understand a few marginal cultures nor even to discover the harmony of their social systems, the virtues of their ethics, and the beauties of their art (an end which is, moreover, a long way off, since the "white peace" is sometimes based on ethnocide).[59] The redemption of the Third World, be it accomplished solely through the efforts of those concerned or through action on the world scale, will be carried out by the peasant populations, already affected by industrial civilization and, in one way or another, partially integrated in the market economy, and therefore holding little attraction for anthropologists always on the lookout for cultures in the pure state or for preliterate populations.

Moreover, there are many anthropologists who, in the name of cultural pluralism, reject in principle any action intended to change economic and social structures, because they fear, not without reason, that the irremediable destruction perpetrated in the name of an ill-defined material progress is an excessive price for the advantages obtained. In other words, they challenge the soundness of the development options that planners currently espouse and emphasize the complexity of value systems which the arrogant reductionism of economists translates into a few dubious indexes. This criticism is completely to the point and goes to the very heart of the problem. Economists, wherever they work, should learn a lesson from it, the lesson being relativism: at a time when the progress of econometrics and the availability of computers create extremely dangerous technocratic illusions, it is important more than ever before to insist on the specificity of the social sciences, on the need to acquire, with a view to action, a sense of continuity, which only familiarity with history can give, and a sense of the global social phenomenon, which comes from the patient study of anthropology.

But the imperatives of continuity demand immediate action. The radical intellectuals of the Third World, impatient, rebellious, distrustful—as they have every reason to be—see in the theory of cultural pluralism a new ideological mystification to justify inaction, the perpetuation of the status quo, that is to say, the exploitation of the Third World by the advanced countries. Doubting the intellectual honesty of this theory, they reject it. All dialogue becomes impossible, and Europe is subsumed in the stereotype of the white colonialist. From this vantage point, European culture has only one aim: to conceal real social relationships. The crematorium becomes the emblem of Europe and genocide the end product of twenty-five centuries of history. The Auschwitz executioners, the jailers of the prisons described by Solzhenitsyn, the American expeditionary forces in Vietnam, all the colonials from Cortès to Massu are the inheritors of Greek civilization, the most barbaric which has ever existed.

The reader will object that I have oversimplified matters by completely disregarding in this first conclusion the diversity of the trends of thought on either side, in Europe and the Third World, and that in particular I have not paid enough attention to the commendable attitude of thinkers who attempt to synthesize and to free themselves from the present framework instead of seeking confrontation. But the effectiveness of ethnocentric stereotypes stems precisely from their terrifying primitivism, from their capacity to simplify history and social relationships and to draw from these the power to mystify and to alienate. To my knowledge, no form of fanaticism has ever truly been sustained by complex thought constructs, although they have often served as ornament and disguise. On the other hand, our way of thinking—even in its scientific and philosophical manifestations—encounters a great deal of difficulty in liberating itself from the prejudices underlying our education and the culture which envelops us. It is for this reason that stereotypes of the other must be exposed to the light of day, as painful as this operation may be to us. How humiliating it is, indeed, to discover the distance between creative thought and the real motives for certain attitudes and actions, those of individuals and those of societies! When it cannot destroy illusions, reason finally delivers itself into their service; and the more persuasive it is technically, the more devastating the possible effects of its enslavement.

In brief, the social sciences, founded on what Jacques Berque has termed the dialectic of the Same and the Other, the alternating or cumulative process of identification and "distancing," acquire, in this world fascinated by technological prowess, a responsibility for which they are not always given credit. They can pave the way for a civilization which is at once industrial and worldwide, "a civilization in which the plurality of cultures, the right to be different and the individual's right to be liberated would hold sway."[60]

Notes to Chapter 4

1. Jonathan Swift, *Gulliver's Travels* (Harmondsworth, England, 1970), p. 173.

2. Aztek Anonim, *Zdobycie Meksyku,* edited and annotated by T. Milewski (Wroclaw, 1959), p. 103.

3. See in particular M. L. Portilla's anthology, *Vision de los Vencidos, Relaciones Indigenas de la Conquista,* Mexico, 1961.

4. Antonio Pigafetta, *Premier voyage autour du monde par Magellan* (Paris, 1964), p. 98.

5. Mircea Eliade, *Méphistophélès et l'Androgyne* (Paris, 1962), pp. 155-161.

6. Quoted by Arnold Toynbee, *Civilization on Trial* (London, 1948), pp. 64-67.

7. Instructions of Father Valignano, S.J., quoted by D. F. Lach, *China in the Eyes of Europe* (Chicago, 1968), p. 691.

8. Etiemble, *Les Jésuites en Chine* (Paris, 1966), pp. 41-43.

9. Quoted by Lach, *China in the Eyes of Europe,* p. 764.

10. C. M. Cipolla, *European Culture and Overseas Expansion* (Harmondsworth, 1970), p. 159.

11. Text reproduced in V. Simone, *China in Revolution; History, Documents and Analyses* (New York, 1968), pp. 70-77.

12. Compare R. A. Scalapino, *Ideology and Modernization: The Japanese Case,* Institute of International Studies, University of California, Berkeley, reprint 162.

13. See R. Segal, *The Race War* (new York, 1967), p. 6. "For the colored peoples, by and large, Japan is part of the very same status quo against which they are rebelling, and Japan herself, though of course in theory recognized as colored, is viewed in practice as no more than a satrap of the white world." This passage by an Indian author suggests the relativism of the concept of color. Did not Francis Xavier write in 1552 that the Chinese are white just like the Japanese? (Quoted in Lach, *China in the Eyes of Europe,* p. 795.)

14. Younghill Kang, *Au pays du matin calme* (Paris, 1967), p. 193.

15. O. Statler, *The Black Ship Scroll* (Tokyo, 1963).

16. Tipu's tiger is on display at the Victoria and Albert Museum, London. For a detailed description see M. Archer, *Tipu's Tiger* (London, 1959).

17. G. Beyhaut, *Raices contemporaneas de America Latina* (Buenos Aires, 1964), p. 72.

18. Paulo Prado, *Retrato do Brasil, Ensaio sobre a Tristeza Brasileira* (São Paulo, 1944). See also the chapter on cultural transplantation in Nelson Werneck Sodré, *Historia da Literatura Brasileira* (Rio de Janeiro, 1964), pp. 471-488.

19. Quoted by K. Damodaran, *Indian Thought: A Critical Survey* (Bombay, 1967).

20. J. Berque, *Dépossession du monde* (Paris, 1965).

21. The Yorubas call them *"oyinbo dudu,"* the Ibos *"beke oju,"* which is the equivalent of "black white man" (see B. Obichere, "African History and Western Civilization," in *Black Studies in the University: A Symposium* (New Haven, 1969), p. 87).

22. K. N'Krumach, *Africa Must Unite* (London, 1963), p. 49.

23. G. K. Mookerjee, *The Indian Image of Nineteenth Century Europe* (Bombay, 1967), pp. 12-13.

24. See the interesting essay by Raghavan Iyer, "The Glass Curtain between Asia and Europe," deploring the superficial images that the Europeans form of Asia and the Asians of Europe. The essay is the introduction to a book published under the same title (London, 1965), pp. 3-27.

25. K. T. Shah, *Ancient Foundations of Economics in India* (Bombay, 1954), pp. 41-42.

26. In her interesting essay *Négritude et situation coloniale* (Yaoundé, 1968) Lilyan Kesteloot makes a survey of the most important themes dealt with by writers on negritude.

27. Jean-Paul Sartre, preface to the *Anthologie de la Nouvelle poésie nègre et malgache de langue française,* edited by L. S. Senghor (Paris, 1948).

28. Kesteloot, *Négritude et situation coloniale,* p. 84.

29. E. Mphahlele, "What Price Negritude," in *The African Image* (New York, 1962), pp. 25-40, and, by the same author, "Littérature Africaine," communication presented to the first International Congress of Africanists at Accra, December 1962, the collection *Problemy Afrykanistyki* (Warsaw, 1963), pp. 181-195).

30. Frantz Fanon, *Les damnés de la terre* (Paris, 1961), pp. 174-175.

31. See H. Cruse, "The Integrationist Ethic as a Basis for Scholarly Endeavours," in *Black Studies in the University,* p. 3.

32. Nina Assorodobraj, "Rôle de l'histoire dans la naissance de la conscience nationale en Afrique Occidentale," communication to the World Congress of Sociology, Evian, 1966.

33. Malcolm X, *Malcolm X on Afro-American History* (New York, 1967).

34. Ibid., p. 15.

35. Ibid., p. 22.

36. Ibid., p. 28.

37. Ibid., p. 29.

38. Ibid., p. 25.

39. A. Césaire, *Discours sur le colonialisme* (Paris, 1955), pp. 21-22.

40. Keith Irvine, *The Rise of the Colored Races* (New York, 1970). As early as the First World War, the Korean novelist Younghill Kang noted: "The great war contradicted all that the missionaries had been preaching since they came to the East. They said that all were brothers in Christ, and all these brothers were killing each other" (*Au pays du matin calme,* pp. 293-294).

41. M. Jastrun, *Mit Srodziemnomorski* (Warsaw, 1962), p. 185.

42. A. Carpentier, *Los pasos perdidos,* quoted from the Polish translation *Podroz do zrodel czasu* (Warsaw, 1961), p. 139.

43. Fanon, *Les damnés de la terre,* p. 239.

44. Ibid., p. 240.

45. C. P. Mastrozilli, with F. Alvarez, *Marcuse, Sartre, Nizan y el Tercer Mundo* (Buenos Aires, 1969).

46. Bernard Lewis, *The Middle East and the West* (London, 1964), p. 135.

47. R. Garaudy, "Traits spécifiques de l'option socialiste en Algérie," in *Economie et Politique* (May 1965), p. 13.

48. See A. Abdel-Malek, *L'avenir de la théorie sociale,* communication presented to the Seventh International Congress of Sociology, Varna, September 1970. I should mention once again the difficulties which confronted European sociology when it attempted to deal with two quite distinct cultures, equipped with a vocabulary which sometimes acted as a screen. See in this connection F. Balandier, *La vie quotidienne au royaume du Kongo du XVIe siècle* (Paris, 1965), pp. 7-8, and Bernard Lewis, *The Arabs in History* (London, 1966), p. 20: dichotomies of church and state, spiritual and temporal, ecclesiastical and secular were unknown to medieval Arab society; the terms which designate them were introduced into the language only recently.

49. In 1790, the Portuguese colonial authorities took severe measures in Brazil against the readers of the Encyclopaedia and, in 1794, they arrested people on the charge of "encyclopaedism," according to J. Cruz Costa, *A filosofia no Brasil* (Porto Alegre, 1945), p. 43. More than a century later, the French colonial authorities prevented Vietnamese youth from reading the reputedly subversive works of Rousseau and Montesquieu. Phan-chu-Truh, a Confucian scholar and an enthusiastic follower of these two philosophers, became acquainted with their works through Chinese translations. See J. Chesneaux, *Le Vietnam* (Paris, 1968), p. 30.

50. The famous "confession" of Nat Turner is just one example of the way in which Christian doctrine functioned as a source of inspiration for social protest movements and, it so happened, for an American slave uprising; see Herbert Aptheker, *Nat Turner's Slave Rebellion* (New York, 1966). The mural painting in the youth center of a Guinean town, showing the president Sekou Touré as Saint George killing the hydra of colonialism (see *The New York Times,* International Edition, January 7-9, 1967) expresses a highly meaningful syncretism.

51. A. Abdel-Malek, *La pensée politique arabe contemporaine* (Paris, 1970).

52. A. Laroui, *L'idéologie arabe contemporaine* (Paris, 1967), pp. 117-169.

53. I must cite once again the proceedings of the recent conference on the Asian mode of production and in particular the volume published by the *Le* Centre d'Etude et de Recherches Marxistes, *Le mode de production asiatique* (Paris, 1969).

54. Guo-mo-ro, *Zhongguo gudai shehui yenjiu* (Peking, 1960), p. 1.

55. For a serious attempt at a critical analysis of African socialisms, see Y. Benot, *Ideologies des independances africaines* (Paris, 1969). With regard to Asian socialisms, consider the harsh words of Govind Sahay, former minister

of the State of Uttar Pradesh in India: "Those who speak of Indian socialism ignore history. Indian socialism is going to degenerate into Hindu socialism, then into caste socialism and then be transformed into Fascism, as happened in Germany." (*Link,* New Dehli, December 22, 1963).

56. K. N'Krumach, "African Socialism Revisited," communication sent to a seminar on the national and social revolution in Africa, organized by the review *Al Talia* in Cairo, October 24 to 29, 1966.

57. "Le Testament de J. Nehru," *Le Monde,* June 5, 1964, p. 2.

58. See M. Leiris, *Cinq études d'ethnologie* (Paris, 1969), pp. 83-112.

59. See in this connection R. Jaulin, *La Paix Blanche—Introduction a l'ethnocide* (Paris, 1970), a book which, however, I consider to be too full of bluster, for it often substitutes invective for proof.

60. J. Berque, "L'Orient et l'avènement de la valeur monde," *Esprit* (September 1970), pp. 323-335.

II

The Europocentric Limitations of Science

There will always be Eskimoes to instruct
the inhabitants of the Belgian Congo on
the best way to withstand hot weather.
—J. J. Lec

The Responsibilities of Science

Science, progress, humanity, harmony. Does the association of these concepts define our hopes or our illusions? Are they a program for action or an ideological hocus-pocus intended to make us wait patiently and to disarm our anger at the inconsistences of industrial civilization? This is the question I asked myself when I visited the World's Fair at Osaka. Undoubtedly it was also asked by the tens of millions of Japanese who passed through the exhibits, fascinated, perhaps, by the advance of technological and industrial power in their country, satisfied that it should take the lead over the United States in areas which had enabled the Americans a quarter of a century earlier to win their victory over Japan. The visitors to the Fair would then be transported by the supermodern subway back to the asphyxiating realities of their daily lives; pollution, wretched housing conditions, frugality decked out with industrial gadgets and the automobile, alienating labor relationships. It is the question that must be asked and, moreover, will be asked, by the several billion inhabitants of the Third World not belonging to the local elites who alone benefit personally from the amenities of industrial civilization.

For, to the Third World, the science and the technology of the industrialized nations, our pride and what we claim to be our part in redeeming the wretched everywhere, assume a monstrous appearance and seem to conceal an evil intention. This is primarily because of the destructive bias of our science and technology and the importance which they accord to research on more and more sophisticated weapons, but also because of their role in the perfecting and the functioning of the world economic order. Nigel Calder is therefore right in saying: "No caricature is involved in describing modern science as a European invention which enabled the white nations to achieve military, economic and cultural domination over the rest of the world, and to make themselves prosperous while leaving the natives of the poor countries to progress very much more slowly. No injustice is done to say that most research workers and technologists have unthinkingly connived in these uses of science which are, at bottom, racist. Declarations about using science to feed the world's hungry have not stopped the prosperity gap growing wider; nor can they alter the fact that the intellectual interests of the great majority of research workers are far removed from any such program and that the preoccupation of technologists is with machines that enrich the rich."[1]

This is a clear statement of the problem of scientists' moral responsibility. It cannot be eluded by pointing out supposedly objective trends of development in scientific thought—Marxism is not a convenient fatalism—nor by projecting the false image of a neutral science and of the career scientist as a sort of British civil servant. Scholars and technologists are better placed than anyone else to evaluate both the positive and the negative fallout from their inventions, from the choice of research topics and from the methods employed, and therefore from the political decisions which are not perhaps their province, but on which they are morally obliged to express an opinion, as citizens and as professionals. It is only too convenient to plead the part of the sorcerer's apprentice.

Researchers are required to play an increasingly active role in politics, and their profession can bring to bear a certain pressure because there are more and more of them; because, as educators, they live on campuses where a student population, which likewise is becoming larger and larger, is challenging the soundness of industrial civilization. And because the awakening of political awareness, the radicalization of thought, and a militant approach are a more and more frequent answer to the questions raised by the extraordinary development of science and technology and the absurdity of the uses to which they are put.

Insofar as an international scientific community is beginning to take shape, one of its most urgent tasks should be to prevent science from being used against the nations of the Third World on the pretext that it is for their advancement; or, at the very least, to see that the most negative effects of scientific and technological progress in industrial countries are controlled, and at all events compensated for by organized assistance. Its task should also be to make sure that researchers from underdeveloped countries have free access to the knowledge acquired by world science and that substantial foreign aid, endowed by independent sources, enable them to establish a research potential geared to their own problems. Exclusive reliance on the imitative transfer of knowledge in the form of finished intellectual products and technological processes, is in fact a fallacious shortcut to modernity.[2]

In the meantime, we must become aware of the Europocentric character of contemporary science and technology. This idea is making headway in the social sciences and, in particular, economics, with which I shall deal at greater length in the following chapters; and this awareness is in itself a step forward. But does the same hold good for the natural sciences and technology?

The reply, whatever certain scholars infatuated with the universality of their knowledge may say, can only be affirmative. In an excellent report prepared for the United Nations, a team of British researchers has recently described the main features of the situation.[3] It may be summed up as follows.

The present international division of scientific work serves the needs of the Third World countries badly since, when it comes to practical application, they have no indigenous science. Research and development funds constitute only 0.2 percent of their gross national product. This represents approximately 2 percent of the nonsocialist world's R&D expenditure, or, on a per capita basis, a ratio of 100 to 1. This last figure slightly undervalues research in the Third World, because wages paid to researchers are considerably lower than those in Western countries; but an adjustment for this factor would not alter the initial impression of a huge disparity. Since, moreover, scarcely 1 percent of the funds devoted to research in industrialized member countries of the O.E.C.D. is allocated to problems specific to the Third World (that is, less than a fiftieth of the funds earmarked for nuclear, military, and space research), the transfers of science and technology on which the Third World must rely—encountering, in addition, enormous difficulties in obtaining access to knowledge and especially to technologies protected by private patents—such transfers are based on findings and processes established essentially to meet the requirements of the developed countries. But the urgent problems, the natural, social, and economic conditions, are quite different there. In particular, Western technology aims to replace human labor by capital, whereas the Third World, on the contrary, needs technologies which are sparing in their use of capital and call for as large a supply of manpower as possible. Furthermore, Western technologies are designed for a scale of production which is too vast for the narrow market outlets of the Third World countries.[4] Finally, models for consumer goods and equipment are conceived for markets in the developed countries; the pattern of supply therefore presents very serious gaps in relation to the Third World's requirements; on the other hand, scientific effort is concentrated within areas which are sometimes of no benefit to it. What is more, about one billion dollars—or the equivalent of all the research expenditure of the Third World—is committed each year to the development of synthetic goods which are in direct competition with the raw materials produced by underdeveloped countries.

The scant efforts of the Third World to establish its own scientific base are undermined by the brain drain on researchers, attracted by the better material conditions in the laboratories of industralized countries, and also by the appeal for the scientists who remain where they are, of research topics which cater to foreign fashions and to the activities of the international scientific community. But the major obstacle to the development of science resides in the very structure of underdeveloped economies, which create no demand for autonomous science or technology and make do with imported technologies, valid only for modern industry, which remains a foreign enclave.

This gloomy tableau rehearses in its main themes the criticism of the negative impact of modern science and technology which, for some years now, has occupied many intellectuals in the Third World and, in particular, in Latin America. Essentially, what is being challenged is the Europocentric limitations of that science, conceived for other ends and working in such a way as to put the Third World increasingly at the mercy of the industrial powers. The following points should be stressed.

In its present form, the international scientific community exercises a baneful influence on researchers in Third World countries: it molds them to its needs and fashions, the latter being dictated by the specific situations of industrialized countries; it imposes on them goals which often isolate them from the realities of their countries, along with a scale of values and prestige which makes them exiles, even when they stay at home. I am not, of course, attempting to deny the universality of scientific results, wherever they may be achieved, but to explain that the importance of a scientific result cannot be evaluated outside a frame of reference which reflects the concrete realities of a country and, more generally, the requirements of society. Recent advances in science and technology have as yet in no way contributed to the elimination of social injustice on a world scale, and this remark is true a fortiori of the Third World. On the other hand, the danger of collective suicide has increased. If we want to make science play a positive role, we must make a radical change in the distribution of the human and financial resources placed at its disposal and, at the same time, revise the hierarchy by which importance is assigned today to the different disciplines[5]—without, however, expecting immediate and spectacular results.

From this perspective we must rank research priorities according to the needs of Third World countries and reintegrate alienated and alienating science into efforts toward development. Generally speaking, there is agreement on the necessity of according far more importance to biology and to the social sciences, but on condition that biology tackle the long-neglected problems of tropical agriculture and of finding possible new food resources[6] and that the social sciences concentrate on the interdisciplinary study of change in societies, thus rejecting the all too convenient simplication of "ceteris paribus."[7]

This of course implies that universities be radically transformed. Rather than turning out batches of "functional technocrats," they would be required to carry on an action-oriented critique of society, to educate public opinion, and to develop self-contained blueprints for society, thereby transcending the alienating and alienated concept of underdevelopment, which implies a mere quantitative lag in relation to developed societies and an imitative concept of modernization.[8] According to Darcy Ribeiro,[9] modernization that is a mere mirror image, experienced passively and accomplished by importing computers and ideas, would play into the hands of conservatives, whereas the autonomous development of the Third World culture can be accomplished only within a radical framework, which would transform the university into a focus of the struggle against underdevelopment, for formulating goals as well as mobilizing resources.

This resistance extends, in principle, to a large part of Western technology. As O. Varsavsky has written, "Accepting the technology of the North [North America] means producing the same thing as they, competing with them in a field which they are more familiar with and, consequently, in the end losing the battle against their great corporations—assuming that there is even the desire to wage such a battle. If we accept their science and their technology, that is to say, if we accept their teaching us to think, we shall do the same things they do, we shall be like them, and then the struggle for economic and even political independence loses its meaning. The logical solution in this case is the one which Puerto Rico has chosen."[10] These statements should not be taken literally; all the authors I have referred to in fact recognize the necessity and the benefit of properly managed international scientific cooperation, and they reject all exaggerated forms of autarky. They merely protest against the present state of affairs: they no longer want to be towed along by the industrialized countries.

I shall have occasion to return to the choice of appropriate technologies for industry and agriculture and to the negative effects of imitation in a more detailed discussion of development theory.[11] For the time being, I will stress the possible importance, for the Third World, of introducing, in the field of social services—more particularly, health, sanitation and education, technologies and forms of organization

which differ from European models. As paradoxical as it might appear
at first sight, the poor countries could quickly set up welfare states (in
the literal and technical sense of the term) if they wanted to and if
they managed to develop original formulas based on extensive employment of manpower and only the bare essentials in equipment. There is
no reason for the welfare state to require, at the outset, a high per
capita income; the historical experience of Western Europe could be
challenged, as that of the U.S.S.R. already is by Cuban educational and
health policy.[12]

There is no doubt, in fact, that action on a large scale in this field
would bring about a considerable improvement in the standard of living, although I am not in a good position to evaluate it quantitatively.
Indeed, orthodox Marxists exclude social services from the calculation
of national income, on the pretext that they represent redistribution of
income and not its creation. As for Western accounting of this type, it
falls prey to two errors of a different kind: first, it acknowledges no
difference between the services of a doctor or teacher and those of a
policeman or a pen-pusher in some overstaffed administration, bloated
by political patronage; furthermore, for lack of a more satisfactory way
of quantifying the value of these services, they are measured in terms of
cost, that is to say, essentially as wages. This amounts then, to considering the value added by those in social service jobs to be equal to their
wages; and to vary as do the scales used to determine their remuneration, which is absurd. A Pakistani doctor working in a provincial hospital in England does not become five times more productive than he
was in his home country by the mere fact that he gets five times as
much salary; nor is a French primary-school teacher ten times more
productive than his Indian counterpart, if their wages are in a ratio of
10 to 1. It would, on the contrary, be more plausible to assume that
the two teachers perform more or less equivalent tasks and that, consequently, the cost of eduction in India, in absolute terms, is far lower
than in France and, in relative terms, not nearly as high as any expenditure on equipment and facilities, the prices of which are generally

higher in the Third World than in the industrialized countries. This provides an excellent opportunity for the poor countries, provided that they are able to take advantage of it.

It will be objected that this calculation does not take into account the difference in per capita income, which makes the relative share of expenditure on education higher in India than in France. But, in my opinion, this argument is based on a misunderstanding. It assumes a given income whose allocation is to be determined, whereas, in my opinion, expanding social services, which are not capital-demanding, might make it possible at the same time to increase national income by going beyond the goals previously fixed by conventional methods. As has been demonstrated on many occasions by M. Kalecki,[13] the problem of financing such an increase in employment amounts, in the last analysis, to having an adequate supply of foodstuffs—the main counterpart of wages paid. Now, in some of the Third World countries at least, agricultural production seems recently to have taken a sufficient stride forward for it to meet an increased demand for food products. From this angle, then, there are no obstacles to the creation of a large number of jobs in the social services, which would present two immediate advantages: (1) an increase in the well-being of the populations served; (2) a reduction in unemployment and underemployment, particularly among holders of certificates or diplomas.

In the long run, improving health standards and raising the level of education would also have positive effects on the economy. But I do not think that this assumption, although it is the mainstay of theoreticians' argument for investing in human resources, is very important. One should insist on the welfare state as an end in itself, not a means. Moreover, I share the skepticism of Myrdal and many English authors about the soundness and usefulness of quantitative exercises which seek to demonstrate the high return on investments in human resources.[14] I prefer to stress the complementary character of profit-making and educational investments at the level on which theoreticians of human resources work. It is, however, possible to envisage some marginal substitutions between investments for profit (and the educational investments which complement them) and social expenditure. A slight reduction in investments could, in certain conditions, have fairly spectacular effects on mass consumption, if one were to decide, on the one hand, to sacrifice an investment with a high capital/output ratio and, on the other, to use the funds thus released to finance inexpensive social services that did not demand much capital. In other words, there would, at the most, be a choice between two patterns of development: one ensuring a higher conventional growth rate, the other resulting in a lower rate but making it possible for mass consumption to reach a higher level than is suggested by standard GNP accounting, which is a prisoner of its own imperfect categories. Let me stress this again: many countries could see the way to expanding their social services without at the same time sacrificing their accustomed rate of economic growth, provided that they find adequate technologies and forms of organization. This would mean breaking away from their present systems, based on European models.

The absurdity of an elitist and alienating educational system thus becomes glaring. While, however, critics are unanimous in denouncing it and in proposing a new system, better adapted to local realities, less wasteful of effort, and open to educational experimentation,[15] concrete proposals or experimental attempts are, in my knowledge, very rare—except in China, where very large-scale reforms, praised by some, attacked by others, have been launched, so it is said, to shatter the cultural foundations of mandarinism, to bring education in closer contact with work, and to replace booklearning by the communication of experience.

Ivan Illich criticizes, not without justification, the too frequent confusion between schooling and education and, on a more general level, between the institutions whose function it is to administer social services and the services themselves; between the acquisition of knowledge and learning of a social role.[16] According to Illich, in Latin America the school has inculcated the myth of the school to such an extent that the inhabitants of the countries where the school attendance rate is the lowest are those who believe most firmly in the need for universal schooling. In fact, in view of the economic conditions in underdeveloped countries, only a small minority can benefit from prolonged school attendance, in an educational system defined by American or European standards, whose alienating function is teaching its pupils to think rich and to live poor. But the widespread cult of the school makes it possible to assign large sums for the education of a minority with the acceptance of the majority. Even worse, by its very existence, the school discourages the poor who consider taking their own education in hand.

This devastating, impassioned criticism from the pen of an eminent educationist, a social thinker whose commitment demands respect and admiration, ends, in fact, by proposing inadequate solutions which aim at making education more flexible through an "educational loan" system and seek the deprofessionalization of education, the active participation of the community, and the opening up of education to the problems of life; in a word, the dissemination of knowledge by networks other than those of the traditional school. From which it emerges that, all in all, criticism is easy in comparison with the thankless task of proposing alternative solutions.

Illich has also denounced the elitist system of hospital and medical services in the Third World, and made a vigorous and passionate appeal— in my opinion perfectly justified—to replace private consumption with mass consumption as soon as possible.[17] In particular he advocates the setting up of a paramedical system in Latin America, staffed by medical aides and midwives working at the village level, unequipped, it is true, to perform complicated surgery, but in a position to save thousands of human lives by the teaching of simple hygiene and by vaccination campaigns. This paramedical service is not an alternative solution to more costly medical services, as Illich seems to think, but a valid priority in a social services program until the hospital network has grown and it is possible to ensure more complete medical care for the whole population.

Moreover, this type of service calls for resources different from those required to set up modern medical services and therefore does not prevent a parallel effort toward the latter.

What must be stressed, on the other hand, is the need to adapt the modern medical system to the specific conditions of the Third World and, in particular, to the very different ratio of equipment and personnel costs.[18] We could profit from our negative experience and develop preventive medicine on a large scale, thereby reducing hospitalizations and thus diminishing the "room and board" component of the cost of medical services. At all events, the rate of advancement of modern medical services is determined by the possibility of installing the necessary equipment and is consequently affected by bottlenecks in industrial production or by a shortage of foreign exchange.

Doctors who are trained to use modern equipment cannot work without it: their function is therefore reduced to that of health officers of the paramedical service. The expenses of training them constitutes under some circumstances an intolerable waste of resources, not to mention the frustrations engendered and the strong probability that unemployed doctors will emigrate. In the last case, a mechanism is set in motion whereby technical aid from the underdeveloped countries is provided for the rich countries, financed to the last penny by taxpayers in the poor countries.

The main features of a health service conceived to meet the needs of an African country are defined in an excellent article by Oscar Gish.[19] He emphasizes the setting up of dispensaries and of rural health centers, preventive medicine, and, in particular, medical care for children, whose numbers, as we know, are large and who die at an alarming rate of diarrhea, pneumonia, malnutrition, and even common infantile diseases such as measles (in underdeveloped countries, the death rate for babies less than a year old is four times higher than in industrial countries; for infants between one and four years, it is forty times higher). A rural dispensary serving a population of 20,000 can be set up for 20,000 pounds sterling, or the cost of four beds in a hospital equipped to train doctors, of ten beds in a district hospital, and of fifteen to twenty beds in a rural hospital. In Zambia, 250 health centers—enough to take care of the entire Zambian population—could have been set up with the money allocated for the construction of the university hospital in Lusaka alone. Health services provided chiefly by hospitals cannot, in a poor country, serve more than a fraction of the population. (In Ghana—where, in fact, economic standards are relatively high—this fraction is estimated at a third of the population.) The ordinary expenses of a health center are estimated at 10,000 pounds per year, that is 10 shillings yearly for each inhabitant. According to Gish, these centers can effectively treat, and above all prevent, many illnesses, one case out of a hundred, on an average, having to be sent to a district hospital. In their turn, the district hospitals have to transfer one case out of a hundred, on an average, to the regional or national hospitals, which offer highly specialized services. An effective and adequate hospital network would therefore require no more than 10 shillings per head. Consequently, for one pound sterling per person per year it would be possible to operate a health service that would supply the needs of the whole population—on the condition, however, that there is a radical change in methods of training doctors who will for the main part become both foremen and paramedical instructors. Many medical schools in the Third World presently turn out doctors who are very competent but ill-prepared to serve the needs of their countries. This extremely costly education serves only to increase the brain drain: 25,000 doctors trained in the Third World are presently in practice in the United States and approximately 10,000 in Great Britain.

I shall now turn to the example of India.[20] In 1961, in this country, there were 75,000 "allopathic" doctors, that is to say, trained along Western lines (including 20,000 in rural areas) and about 170,000 traditional doctors and healers (ayurvedic, homeopathic, and so on). In rural areas, a modern doctor cared, on an average, for 17,912 patients; in the towns, 1,438. Figures for the traditional doctors and healers were, respectively, 3,164 and 1,107 patients per doctor. It was estimated, moreover, that 43.5 percent of the urban population and scarcely 16.8 percent of the rural population had access to the services of modern doctors. The government of independent India made an immense effort to develop the network of medical schools. Numbering 30 in 1950-1951, with 2,675 first-year students, they increased to 91 in 1967-1968, with 11,106 first-year students and 7,407 graduates. A reasonable projection allows one to assume that in 1976 the country will possess 179,200 doctors and in 1986, 293,650. Supply will be greater than demand—which is limited principally by the growth rate of public medical services—at least 20 percent in 1976 and 30 percent in 1986. A considerable proportion of these unemployed doctors will undoubtedly emigrate. Already, between 1961 and 1966, the number of Indian doctors working abroad increased from 3,000 to 7,500, that is to say, about 8 percent of the total profession. It is pointless to dwell on the cost of this unfortunate circumstance, which was undoubtedly brought about by the desire to rival developed countries in saturation indexes for doctors. It might have been thought that, in India's situation, special attention would have been given to creating a paramedical service and rationalizing the network of traditional doctors and healers. But the Indian Medical Board decided against relaunching a training program for medical aides, which had been abandoned in 1954, on the grounds that it would represent a step backward.

This attitude is typical of an inferiority complex which colonialism instilled in part of the intellectual élite of the Third World. Certain dark-skinned Europeans admit of no universities other than Oxford and Cambridge, and they enjoy reiterating that (as the author has been told on many occasions) "only the best is good enough for Africa." Of all forms of dependence, that which confuses independence and sovereignty with the passive acceptance of the developed world's scale of cultural values is the most dishonest and undoubtedly the most dangerous, because it alienates the person who subscribes to it. This, moreover, is the only plausible explanation why there has been so little progress in the direction I have just suggested—forgetting even what was valid in the Gandhian village social worker, the *sewak*,[21] who at best was transformed into a bureaucrat in charge of rural community development.

This brings us face to face with the second major obstacle to setting up the welfare state of our dreams in a poor country. Illich is undoubtedly right to denounce the bureaucratic welfare state, as we see it operating in the Third World, meting out costly privileges to small minorities and baiting the unprivileged with the promise that they too will gain access, sooner or later, to the circle of the chosen. This model of the welfare state leads to a dead end—as, moreover, the welfare states set up in industrialized countries to evade a change in the capitalist structures of production. But whatever verdict we reach with regard to this or that model of organization, it is technically possible, in my opinion, to define all public social services as constituting the welfare state in the strict sense of the word, and to examine the problems raised by its introduction in different social systems. In this sense, it is also the duty of the socialist state to be a welfare state, because it has a greater opportunity to choose a truly democratic model for its social services and the potential of making great strides in this field. The experiences of Vietnam, China, and Cuba are proof.

In short, I believe that effective action is not impossible within the framework of a mixed economy, in countries whose governments make a minimum of political promises and are moved by a sincere desire to seek original solutions to the problems of underdevelopment.

I have just stressed education and health as representing two pillars of the welfare state. The same argument applies to other social and cultural services, ranging from a special food program proposed by Pirie,[22] birth control, and the promotion of social and cultural activities, all the way to services more directly linked to production, such as rural development and public housing schemes using local building materials. The importance that this last activity could assume may be measured by the fact that, according to United Nations estimates, a billion people live in slums, and new building meets less than one fifth

of current needs.[23]   In other words, it is necessary to free from bureaucratic fetters and to develop all activities which, in principle, should
serve village community development. In most cases, it is true, such
programs have been resounding failures, but in my opinion this is owing
to the sociological and technological unimaginativeness of the solutions
proposed and to a bureaucratic style of operation. The welfare state in
poor countries must be decentralized and democratic; initiative and
participation at the local level are essential for success. What has characterized all activity of this kind up to now is the assumption that it
should rely on vast amounts of manpower, employed either full time or
part time or mobilized in different forms of paramilitary service or voluntary labor. For many reasons I do not believe in the long-term effectiveness of voluntary labor, which, moreover, does not completely
side-step the problem of financing, since increased work implies additional consumption of foodstuffs. Furthermore, as I have already said,
provided that there is a sufficiently flexible supply of basic goods,
there is no reason why workers in the social services should not be paid
at a normal rate, if this involves within reasonable limits deficit spending, and after exhausting the usually considerable possibilities for using
taxation to make the privileged classes bear the burden. This operation
should act as a spur to the economy without causing serious inflationary pressures provided it is kept within the limits imposed by the capacity of the economy to meet increased demand for industrial and
imported goods. Which means that it must be carried out on a relatively modest scale in relation to overall activity, but nevertheless very
considerable comparison with the volume of social services provided by
conventional methods.

Apart from this limitation imposed by the structural rigidities of
underdeveloped economies, the operation of the welfare state in poor
countries would, especially at the outset, come up against two other
obstacles. First, the personnel recruited for different social services
must have appropriate qualifications. This entails setting up a system
of specialized education or of retraining for unemployed professionals,

which would become, for a while, the privileged sector in this operation and at the same time a veritable laboratory for experimentation with unconventional teaching methods. Second, throughout my discussion I have assumed, for the sake of clarity, that social services would not, for all practical purposes, require an investment in equipment. Judging from the evidence, this is an unrealistic assumption and, insofar as equipment is necessary, a new economic constraint is introduced. Research on inexpensive technologies in the field of social service should be counted among the most pressing problems to confront contemporary science. What is needed, to quote Illich once again, is "counter-research," aimed at finding, within reasonable limits, substitutes for the hospital, for the traditional school, for the house built by the mason, and for numerous other accessories of modern life. More generally, it is necessary to rethink all the elements of our civilization, of the social organization which underlies it, and of the technologies which serve it, while fully aware of the difficult choices that this implies for the scale of values and the social costs that each solution must necessarily entail. Counterresearch would be a war cry against Europocentric science, a banner for all scientists of the Third World aware of their responsibility, and a challenge to us. For may one not hope that we will want and will know how to go beyond the limitations of our science, that we shall become aware of the devastating effects of extending our mode of technological civilization to the entire globe, and that we shall consequently agree to participate in counterresearch instead of ridiculing it?

Notes to Chapter 5

1. Nigel Calder, *Technopolis: Social Control of the Uses of Science* (London, 1970), p. 252.

2. See chapter 14.

3. United Nations, "World Plan of Action for the Application of Science and Technology to Development," draft of introductory statement prepared for Advisory Committee on the Application of Science and Technology to Development,

98
Europocentric Limitations of Science

Document E/AC.52/L.68, October 19, 1969. The authors of the document belong to the Science Policy Research Unit at the Institute of Development Studies of the University of Sussex.

4. Whence the trend, in the Third World countries, toward monopolistic or oligopolistic structures (see, in this connection, M. Merhav, *Technological Dependence, Monopoly and Growth* (Oxford, 1969).

5. See O. Varsavsky, *Ciencia Politica y Cientificismo* (Buenos Aires, 1969).

6. See, in particular, N. W. Pirie's excellent little book, *Food Resources Conventional and Novel* (Harmondsworth, 1968).

7. D. F. Maza Zavala, "Ideas sobre la investigacion y la enseñanza de la economia en America Latina," in *Revista de la Facultad de Ciencias Economicas y Sociales* (Caracas, 1969), p. 20; see also P. Streeten's excellent study, "Economic Models and Their Usefulness for Planning in South Asia," published as an appendix to Gunnar Myrdal, *Asian Drama* (New York, 1968), vol. 3, pp. 1941-2004.

8. O. Sunkel, *Reforma Universitaria, Subdesarrolle y Dependencia* (Santiago, 1969).

9. D. Ribeiro, "Politica de Desarrollo Autonomo de la Universidad Latino-americano," in *Gaceta de la universidad* (Montevideo), 9.43 (April 1968), pp. 27-39.

10. Varsavsky, *Ciencia Politica*, p. 44.

11. See part 3 of this book.

12. Students of Cuba are unanimous in praising the social accomplishments of the revolutionary regime which made these a priority without consideration of the cost (see L. Hubermann and P. M. Sweezy, *Socialism in Cuba;* New York, 1970) whereas my conception of the welfare state in poor countries stresses technologies requiring small capital investment.

13. See, in particular, M. Kalecki, "Problems of Financing Economic Development in a Mixed Economy," in *Essays on Planning and Economic Development,* vol. 2 (Warsaw, 1965), pp. 37-50.

14. See Myrdal, *Asian Drama,* vol. 3, pp. 1533-1551, and also T. Balogh, "Comments on the Paper by Messrs. Tinbergen and Bes," in *The Residual Factor and Economic Growth* (Paris, 1964), pp. 383-395.

15. R. Dumont, *L'Afrique Noire est mal partie* (Paris, 1962); R. Dumont, "Le Développement Agricole et l'Education," in *Readings in the Economics of Education* (Paris, 1968), pp. 654-664; T. Balogh and P. Streeten, "The Planning of Education in Poor Countries," in *Economics of Education* (Harmondsworth, 1968), vol. 1, pp. 385-395.

16. Ivan Illich, "Déscolariser la société," in *Les Temps modernes,* No. 289-290, August-September 1970, pp. 483-484.

17. Ivan Illich, "Le Tiers Monde peut faire autrement," in *Analyse et Prévision,* June 1970.

18. To realize the difference in this proportional cost, it is enough to observe that wages in the Third World usually constitute only a fraction of the wages paid in the industrial countries, while the cost of equipment—especially when it is imported—is considerably higher than the prices paid in the industrial countries.

19. O. Gish, "Health Planning in Developing Countries," in *The Journal of Development Studies* (London), 4. (July, 1970), pp. 67-76.

20. All the statistical data on India are quoted from the unpublished thesis by P. N. Mathur, "Supply and Demand for Critical Human Skills in India's Developing Economy: A Case Study for Doctors," University of Delhi, 1969.

21. When questioned in 1946 on his conception of the village social worker, Gandhi gave a definition which, in my opinion, underlies all the efforts toward subsequent conceptualization of the community development of villagers "reinvented" by social researchers in the West and adopted by the United Nations. See in particular M. K. Gandhi, *Economic and Industrial Life and Relations,* ed. V. B. Kher, (Ahmedabad, 1957), vol. 2, pp. 206-207.

22. See Pirie, *Food Resources.*

23. United Nations, Center for Economic and Social Information, *Crisis in Housing and Urban Development,* Background Note No. 180, March 30, 1970.

6   Politics in the Third World: Similarities and Differences

The finest exports from Europe to the Third World were the ideals of liberty, equality, fraternity, democracy, and socialism. It was the contradiction among these ideals, also received from the West, and the oppressive practices of colonial regimes, which caused the dawn of awareness: under their banner revolts against imperialist domination sprang up (the attempt to find local genealogies for them was not made until later), and the revolutionaries themselves made use of European weapons and techniques of war.

Incorrigible racists would see this as a confirmation of their prejudices. I prefer to see it positively as the unification of the cultural microcosms which dotted our planet before world trade. This is the chief stake in the crisis of the Third World's emancipation, for I persist in believing, in spite of everything, that the European cultural heritage has aspects which are worthy of dissemination to the whole of humanity, that it is not made up simply of crematoria and genocide, of racism and of secular or religious ideologies used to justify the conquest of the victors and the submission of the vanquished.

Is there a universality to the progressive political ideas of Enlightenment and the French Revolution that allows the extension of European political science to other latitudes and other situations? Is there a common nucleus of political science that is serviceable to the partisans of present regimes and to the revolutionaries who are struggling for their abolition, to the dominated countries and to the great world powers? Or, on the contrary, should we resign ourselves to having two political cultures, as long as there are oppressors and oppressed, and to accepting a few ethnocentric interpretations of the vast world scene? In the field which I am about to enter now, scientific knowledge and ideology are closely intermingled. The reflections which follow will therefore inevitably be marked by my personal preferences, despite my efforts to cast them aside.

National Phenomena[1]

If there is a field in which Europocentrism has produced useful results, it is the study of national movements. Curiously, the Marxists used this line by extending to continents dominated by imperialism the analysis of the national question as it was stated by Marx for Central and Eastern Europe and Ireland and then by Lenin for the Tsarist Empire. The awakening of the colonial peoples became one of the two key points of the strategy which was to ensure the success of the world revolution, and the only one after the hope of a speedy revolution in the industrialized countries had faded. Through all the policy changes in the Communist International and the U.S.S.R., in spite of the profound differences which on several occasions set the partisans of very wide-ranging tactical alliances (whether with Chiang Kai-shek or with the Emir of Afghanistan, as long as those parties pursued an anti-British policy, Stalin explained)[2] against those who advocated the autonomy of the Communist movement, and despite errors of judgment and decisions on detail which were sometimes disastrous in their consequences, the basic analysis has proved to be correct. The victory of the Chinese, Vietnamese, and Cuban revolutions justifies those who placed their trust in the revolutionary potential of the peripheral countries at a time when their analysis of the situation was treated as fanciful and completely unreal by the mandarins of Western political science.

It will be objected that the political emancipation of former colonies did not bring about the collapse of the world capitalist system. In most Third World countries, nonsocialist, often capitalist, and sometimes frankly neocolonial regimes have been firmly established; but national emancipation has not resulted in social revolution, at least yet. The very inception of the Third World would therefore be a setback for world revolution, for it would present the Communists with a painful choice between precipitating armed social revolution in the Third World here and now, and developing a waiting strategy.

The rift between Peking and Moscow closely follows, at least in this one aspect of the dispute, the line of cleavage which, half a century ago, separated the supporters and the opponents of continuing revolution. The Chinese think that the country should immediately launch a global assault on the city, whereas the Soviets endeavor to show that adventurism can only push the Third World countries into the arms of imperialism and that, furthermore, that time is on the side of the growing revolutionary forces. And this is not to mention the neutralist tendencies of the foreign policy of many Third World countries which will continue to undermine imperialism and therefore contribute in the course of history to world revolution, even if this entails temporarily reinforcing certain localized forms of capitalism.[3]

While theorists of national liberation movements have managed to grasp chief trends in the development of the periphery of the capitalist system, their effectiveness stops there, as is shown by this controversy. Even if we make allowance for the distortions to which it has been subjected to make it fit in with the evolving interests of Soviet foreign policy, and, recently, those of China, it provides no answer to many disturbing questions. Where is the boundary to be drawn between retrogressive nationalism and progressive nationalism? What limits should be set for concessions to national unity, balanced against the hope of swinging the country into the anti-imperialist coalition? How to reconcile the interests of national liberation and the requirements of internationalism, which are equated with Soviet defense? What is one to think of a country with a reactionary government, which imprisons or murders Communists but pursues a neutralist foreign policy?

This list of questions, while incomplete, calls to mind dramatic events for which the Communists of China, India, the Arab countries, and then Indonesia in turn paid the price. It also calls to mind embarassing alliances with retrogressive monarchies and the toleration of the chauvinist and even racist excesses to which certain overzealous "nationalist" movements finally sank. In general, all these episodes may be explained by the exaggerated importance accorded to the interplay of international forces and the underestimation of internal factors in the dynamics of each country. Armed with the all-encompassing theory of national liberation movements, some Marxists set Marxism on its head, forgetting that the analysis should, on the contrary, begin with class structures, relationships of power, specific social problems, and established ideologies in each country in order to understand their specificity and, where possible, to deduce foreign policy trends from them.[4] In short, a country did not become progressive simply by having a neutralist policy; rather, the question to be asked was: Why were the conservative governing classes of certain Third World countries interested in taking a neutralist tack? But above all, what should have received attention were the pivot points of local policy, its broad outlines, its particular problems. For this kind of analysis, however, Marxists were no better prepared than other researchers, insofar as they persisted in employing a Europocentric conceptual framework and apparatus.

A Digression on India

The tradition of Europocentric description of the Third World's social and political systems goes back to the first accounts of European travelers. It could not have been otherwise. Confronted with a different and sometimes more complex reality, as in India, brought up in a culture in which relativism had an extremely small part at the time, Europeans were naturally led to see around them institutions similar to those they already knew, or to make more or less felicitous deductions. It is understandable that someone like Anastas Nikitin, a Russian merchant who visited India shortly before Vasco da Gama set sail, was baffled by the caste system.[5] But it should be borne in mind that most contemporary descriptions of India continue to use the concepts of caste and of subcaste as though the subcastes were divisions of the caste whereas on the contrary the caste is a globalizing concept, sanctioned by religion and roughly corresponding to the order of feudal society, and it is the subcaste which forms the main unit of the social structure. Moreover, in Sanskrit there are two quite different terms to designate these concepts: *varna* and *jati*.

This is not the place to go into the merits of the various theories on the origin of the *jati* system; but insofar as it was, in the beginning, a hierarchy of tribes governed by a despotic power and obliged to pay tribute in products or specialized services, we may find certain analogies with the villages of artisan-serfs of the high Middle Ages in Europe; the caste system would appear to be less exceptional, at least with regard to its origins, than is commonly thought.

In political science Europocentrism usually takes two extreme forms. Either the phenomena observed are reduced to European models, or, on the contrary, their specificity is exaggerated whenever this reduction seems to be too extreme. To stick to the example of India, this is what usually happens to analyses of the social and economic doctrine of Gandhi. He, however, had deep roots in European solidarism and in his rejection of industrial capitalism merely followed the trend of all agrarian doctrines, or, more accurately those of the retrogressive variety which look to a golden age in a mythical past. Now these doctrines made their appearance more or less everywhere, with astonishing regularity, at a rudimentary stage of capitalist development, in the United States, in Russia, and in China. In America, agrarianism was soon to fade away in the face of industrial expansion; in Russia, it succumbed to the Bolshevik Revolution; in China, it was assimilated by Maoism; in India it became for a while, at the prompting of Gandhi, the dominant ideology of the nationalist movement.

At all events, the three fundamental premises of Gandhi's economic and social doctrine make him an unrecognized precursor (unrecognized on account, perhaps, of his oft-proclaimed distrust of economics) of modern theories of underdevelopment. Indeed, at a time when the reification of economic relations is the rule, Gandhi treats them, as, moreover, does Marx, as interpersonal relations; was this because his thinking was turned to the golden age of premercantile collectivist economies?[6] At a period when the fate of the peasant masses did not figure prominently in economic discussions, Gandhi made it the focal point of his thought, both economic and social. He proposed, in particular, that caste relations be humanized and that the untouchables be accorded a little dignity. He did not, however, challenge the caste system, which was sanctioned by religion and by a philosophy of the individual's progress toward perfection which, taken out of context, is a source of delight to a few European humanists and religious thinkers who are incapable of seeing its true social implications.[7] Finally, he glimpsed the importance of relying on traditional techniques. These promises were to be adopted by the Chinese Communists. And yet, Gandhi's program of action is diametrically opposed to that which the Chinese implemented. The *ambar charka*—the already perfected spinning wheel—is economically disastrous, the value added by the spinner being vastly below a starvation wage.[8] The rejection of industrialization and the idealization of the self-sufficient village economy could in the long run only aggravate the wretched plight of the Indian masses.

Then why this program? The answer must be sought in two places.

First, one must go back to Gandhi's moral philosophy. Imbued with Christian and solidaristic ideals—in his autobiography he admits to having read the *Baghavat Gita* for the first time while a student in England[9] —he transposed them into the context of Hindu religious philosophy, which accounts for his appeal to the Indian masses; and he ended by giving an absolute character to the ethical aspect of economic relations, to such an extent that he saw only the intentions of people providing each other with services. The concepts of value and, consequently, of productivity, such as we use them in economics, have no meaning in his system. Orthodox Gandhian economists strained to invent curious theories on the origin of value in order to justify the master's thought after the fact: one of them places the source of all value in solar energy, immediately adding that man is a more effective converter of this energy than machines.[10]

Above all, it should not be forgotten that the chief aim of Gandhi's economic and social program was to forge solidarity through the united action of a people profoundly torn by social divisions but joined by a common cultural background and by the desire to shake off colonial

oppression. It lost all meaning in independent India, as the few orthodox Gandhians were to discover. Vinoba Bhave, one of Gandhi's
spiritual disciples, attempted to promote an original type of agrarian
reform by convincing landowners to make a voluntary gift of a part of
their lands. This has had only marginal effects, but, to a European,
the very fact that such a campaign could be conceived is fairly significant.

I have dwelt at some length on the example of Gandhi's thought to
show the intellectual approach which seems necessary for studying
Third World politics. We must give their due to solutions for problems
which have no exact parallel (either in the Europe of today or in that of
the nineteenth century), to the advance of imported ideas, and finally to
the cultural tradition and the extremely heavy burden of a living past.
But distrust of Europocentrism should not lead us to reject comparisons
and to exaggerate specificity.

Social Stratification

The study of social stratification in the Third World seems to me to be
the most urgent task, and also the most neglected one. We certainly
have data, in increasingly large quantities, on the distribution of income
for each income bracket, particularly for Latin America (table 1).
These data show a heavy concentration of wealth and allow us to speak
of dualistic or pluralistic societies in the Third World, a pyramid of
groups with such disparate incomes and life styles that they belong to
different worlds. But this criterion, a convenient one for statisticians,
is unsatisfactory since it groups members of very different social classes
in the same brackets just because they happen to have the same income;
consequently, it obscures the social structure underlying income distribution. If the picture conveyed by the statistics is to be accurate, different categories should be used, those set up by sociologists based on
the controversial concepts of class and social stratum.

Moreover, two obstacles should be removed at the outset: First is
the aversion of governments in the Third World, which control the
statistical services of their countries (and indirectly those of the United

Table 1. Income Distribution in Latin America

Population by Category of Income	Percentage of Total Income	Income Compared with the Regional Average (100)	Per Capita Income in U.S. Dollars (Data for 1965 in 1960 Dollars)
Poorest 20 percent	3.1	15.5	60
Next 30 percent	10.3	34.0	130
Next 30 percent	24.1	80.0	310
Next 15 percent	29.2	194.0	750
Richest 5 percent	33.4	680.0	2,600

Source: United Nations, Economic Commission for Latin America, *La distribución de ingreso en America Latina,* working paper (Santiago, Chile, 1969).

Nations) to exposing social injustice in their countries. But the imperfect data of which table 1 affords a good sample are enough to indict most of these governments, since they make it easy to identify the richest and the poorest groups.

The second obstacle is the still very unsatisfactory state of pilot studies necessary to develop categories of classification, in spite of ongoing work,[11] as non-Marxian sociologists do not accept the conceptual framework of social classes, while Marxists have for a long time neglected empirical research. Dogmatic Marxism in fact contented itself, for the analysis of social structures, with a standardized framework, anchored in the realities of urban nineteenth-century Europe and in the Russian model of peasant stratification, as it was when Lenin studied it. The analogies, probably far more striking, with the social structures of the period of transition from feudalism to capitalism[12] have never been systematically explored. However they should not be exaggerated either: the demographic and economic conditions of the Third World are in no way a replica of those of Europe in the

sixteenth to the eighteenth centuries, and, above all, the international
environment is quite different. The somewhat belated discovery of
Mao Tse-tung's studies on the social stratification of China has not
made things much easier, since his precise and minutely detailed cate-
gorizations of classes and strata do not necessarily correspond to the
realities of societies very different from the Chinese; thus a new dogmatism takes the place of the old.

As far as I know, the most ambitious attempt to present income
distribution in terms of social classes in a Third World country is that
of Hassan Riad, for Egypt. The accuracy of his data, summarized in
table 2, is somewhat suspect; what counts, however, is not the detail
but the overall picture, which is quite different from what we are accustomed to seeing in Europe.

Variations from one country to another are certainly very pronounced, and there is no question of extending the model of Egyptian
society to the entire Third World, or even to countries characterized
by a very high population density in terms of square kilometers of
arable land. On the basis of this table, however, it is possible to make
certain general observations and to formulate hypotheses for comparative studies yet to be undertaken.

Rural Areas

The analysis is most difficult for rural areas, on account of the complexity of agrarian structures. As always, the easiest thing to detect
is the opposition between landowners and landless agricultural workers
(that is to say, farmhands, seasonal workers, small sharecroppers, and
sharecroppers whom the landowners pass off as workers in order to
get around the agrarian reform laws).

It should be pointed out that the concept of landowner covers both
noblemen possessing vast domains and the owners of a few acres which
are worked by hired laborers or sharecroppers. Small landowners, who
are characteristic of overpopulated countries, are often the most heart-
less exploiters: from their small pieces of land they have to obtain a
sufficient income to live a little better than their employees, and they

Table 2. Social Structure and Incomes of the Population of Egypt

	Thousands	Percent of Total Population	Total Income (Millions of Egyptian Pounds)	Average Per Capita Income (Egyptian Pounds)
Urban Categories				
Not counted	2,983	37		
Servants	934	12	20	21.4
Subproletariat	186	2	5	26.8
Wage earners in the traditional sector	400	5	16	40.0
Proletariat	790	10	48	60.8
Lower-level employees	1,117	14	118	105.6
Traditional entrepreneurs	736	9	94	127.7
Intermediate-level employees, civil servants, etc.	614 614	8 8	83 83	133.5 133.5
Bourgeoisie and aristocracy	240	3	203	845.8
Totals	8,000	100	587	73.4
Rural Categories				
The common people				
without land	14,000	73	50	3.5
poor peasants (< 1 *feddan*)	1,075	6	7	6.1
Intermediate strata (1-5 *feddans*)	2,850	15	76	26.8
Privileged strata				
rich peasants (5 *feddans*)	875	5	76	87.4
agrarian capitalists	150	1	116	773.1
Totals	19,000	100	325	17.1

Source: Hassan Riad, *L'Egypte Nassérienne* (Paris, 1964), p. 41.

put their hearts and souls into the task, having nothing else to do. Between these two classes there are the peasants who cultivate their own land without using hired labor; the sharecroppers who own plots of land; the wealthy sharecroppers, who are real capitalist entrepreneurs; the agricultural workers who rent out their tiny plots of land to rich peasants; nonagricultural workers who nevertheless possess a tiny family farm; traders and moneylenders who also possess land; civil servants who are also farmers or merchants. The relations among all these people are complicated by the persistence of tribal, clan, and family ties, if not by castes. This criss-cross of relations reflects centuries of history, the interweaving of traditional and European legal and fiscal systems (the European systems having usually been imported without the least consideration for the social realities of the country), the coexistence of the most diverse forms of bondage (such as the *pongaje* and the *peonaje*) with incipient capitalist structures and increasing demographic pressure—real where there is no fallow land left, or artificial where such land is kept in reserve by large landowners. The more agonizing the cry for land, the more complicated these relations become. The system of "shared poverty"[13] is the logical outcome; the fantastic criss-cross of mutual obligations, of leasing and subleasing land, of snowballing indebtedness, stands in the way of all technological progress; the result is involution in the true sense of the word, a tangled web of obstacles tied up together.

   This sketchy description does not apply to regions where a tribal economy prevails or where village communities have survived. But there too the social reality is often different from the idyllic image of primitive communism for at least two reasons. First, there exist, even in tribal societies, forms of social inequality which are regarded as unjust by a part of the population; it is therefore illusory, as Meillassoux has shown,[14] to dwell on all forms of collective activity without taking the analysis any further. Then, mention should also be made of the subjugation and the exploitation of entire tribes, within the framework of more evolved societies. Such is the case with many tribes in India, treated as untouchables, and with the Indians in Latin America, driven away from their traditional homes.

The sociologist can deal with such complicated forms in two ways: either by plunging into the labyrinth of description, stressing the peculiarities of this or that local institution, or by using reduction to bring out essential relations without being distracted by the multiplicity of details. There is a risk that the first approach will divert sociology toward empiricism and toward the accumulation of detailed knowledge which ends up being a burden more than anything else. As for the second, it is vulnerable to dogmatism.[15] If one is concerned with finding an operational approach, it is necessary to apply oneself to discovering the real fronts of the class struggle or, more accurately, the objective divisions and the misconceptions, for it would be naive to think that the disinherited classes can easily achieve self-awareness in the conditions described above. In many countries, the landowners, the money-lenders, and the merchants belong to minorities which have been established for centuries but which are still alien. In these circumstances, racism can easily be stirred up, to the benefit of those in power (Indonesia, Burma, East Africa). And to this may be added the pressure of the administrative and policy apparatus, the dispersion of the rural population in certain countries (either because there are no villages or because they are cut off from each other) and, lastly, a fact which is too often overlooked, that, for better or for worse, the system of "shared poverty" makes it possible at least to survive. The astonishing stability of the caste system in India is to be explained not only by the fact that it has religious sanction but also by the division of labor which it underlies; similarly, hatred of the moneylender is tempered by the knowledge that he is the sole insurance against distress.[16]

In these circumstances, the aspirations of the peasant masses do not easily find expression in taking over land or in the uprisings that precede an agrarian revolution. On the other hand, millenarian movements[17] and the practice of robbing the rich to feed the poor[18] sometimes assume considerable proportions. While Mao Tse-tung's analysis of the revolutionary potential of rural areas in the Third World is probably basically correct, one should not conclude from it that it will be easy to mobilize the peasantry and to achieve armed conquest of land and power. The failure of the rural guerillas in Latin America who had followed the Cuban example is highly significant in this context, as is the passivity of the poor peasants in Egypt and Algeria toward governments which have promised radical agrarian reform and have not kept their promises. The argument is valid a fortiori for India. It is small wonder that recent movements to take over land came so late and have remained so moderate in the face of vacillation about agrarian reforms named as priorities when independence was proclaimed, in 1947. The only country in the Third World where a serious armed struggle has taken place between poor peasants and landowners backed by the army is Indonesia. It was brought on by the landowners, who felt that their privileges were being threatened; and we know the outcome of the struggle: the massacre of several hundred thousand men and women, Communist Party activists or members of their families.[19]

The attitude of the peasant masses is the same with respect to the anti-imperialist struggle, except when the land belongs to foreigners, as was the case in Cuba, in Algeria, and in Guatemala, and as is the case today in Peru. The antifeudal and anti-imperialist alliance of workers, peasants, and the national bourgeoisie, proclaimed the Communist International as the equivalent of the popular front in industrialized countries, has proved impossible to achieve. It was merely a theoretical construct, removed from the social realities of both the countryside and the cities.

The Cities
Of the 250 cities in the world with a population of 500,000 or more, nearly half are in the Third World. Unlike the large European cities created by the Industrial Revolution, they have sprung up in advance of such a revolution.[20] Most of the time they are a conglomerate of three cities: the traditional city, the former administrative, religious and commercial center; the new city which has risen up as a

consequence of European colonization; and the shantytowns where those who have foresaken the rural areas collect, driven by poverty rather than attracted by the prospect of steady jobs.[21] The yearly rate of urban expansion of the Third World, between 1940 and 1960, has been estimated at 4-5 percent, more than twice the rate calculated for nine industrialized countries of Europe, at the period when the growth of their cities was at its most dynamic. Some demographers expect this high growth rate to become even more pronounced. According to Kingsley Davis, the countries of the Third World are confronted with the following dilemma: "If they do not substantially step up the exodus from the rural areas, these areas will be swamped with under-employed farmers. If they do step up the exodus, the cities will grow at a disastrous rate."[22] Davis is undoubtedly right, so long as one agrees to see the duplication of the European model of development as the only path of salvation for the Third World. But we know that the Chinese, for instance, claim that there can be development without urbanization; they are making their greatest effort to find agricultural and industrial employment for populations that have remained rural.

The stratification of urban populations results from the phenomena that I have just mentioned. What is striking is the large size of the subproletariat of recent origin, whose members find it difficult to get steady jobs outside domestic service, traditional retail selling, and occasional work as dockers or unskilled construction workers. The personal services and small business sectors, both overgrown, are symptomatic of a pathological situation which has nothing to do with the rise of the modern "tertiary" stratum in industrial societies. The shantytowns function, as it were, as waiting rooms for the city proper and serve as catchbasins for the overpopulated villages. The millenarian hopes aroused by independence have contributed enormously to the expansion of the shantytowns. Each time industrialization takes a step forward the same effect is produced, the number of people fleeing to the towns being very much higher than the number of jobs created in the modern sector.

Compared to the subproletarians, whose standard of living is scarcely higher than that of the most abject of the rural population, the industrial workers employed in the modern sector are privileged: there is a considerable gap between the wages paid to unskilled and those paid to skilled workers. Although we should beware of oversimplified explanations and remember that these workers are the classic proletariat to the industrial bourgeoisie, we must stress the importance of this cleavage in the working class for analyzing the political balance of power. Although access to this privileged world is not completely closed off to the subproletarians (the building up of new factories ensures a certain social mobility despite the reduced number of new jobs created by industrialization), certain political parties and governments work to widen the gap, by establishing, for instance, fairly advanced social security systems which are limited in practice to a minority of urban workers.

Above the working-class aristocracy are the cohorts of civil servants and office workers. Overstaffed administrations are the rule. Their object is the creation of political appointees loyal to the distributors of patronage or ready to support the politicians who promise to play the game once they are in power.

Obviously, the military is a universe apart, politically very influential because it is organized more efficiently than the civil administration, able to resort to force and familiar with modern technology through the use of weapons. Although, in many Third World countries, the higher ranks of the army are traditionally recruited from the aristocratic élites, the regular officers who, more and more frequently, attain the higher ranks are of more humble origins and, by the very nature of their profession, they are inclined toward nationalism in all its gradations, from the most chauvinistic and reactionary to the most progressive. As a result, it is very dangerous to judge in one body the political tendencies and the role of the military in the Third World. The events of the last fifteen years are there to prove it.

Potential candidates for public employment are diploma holders (ranging from the primary-school-leaving certificate to the master's degree) who have not been able to find jobs in private enterprise equal to their ambitions. For several countries in Asia and Latin America, unemployed white-collar workers represent a not inconsiderable proportion of the urban population; the same is true of primary-school diplomaholders in Africa who have no way of entry into the modern sector and who are kept out of the traditional sector by the education they have received.

At the top of the pyramid are the high-ranking public officials, numerous and influential, who have often obtained their wealth illegally by dividing their time between public affairs and private business. Alongside them are the liberal professions, the industrial and commercial bourgeoisie, and absentee landowners living in the cities. Following the Chinese scheme, many authors attempt to subdivide the bourgeoisie into the local bourgeoisie and the "compradors," the former exploited by imperialism and the latter serving as the agents of foreign capital. But this division is often ambiguous, as is the line drawn between the industrial bourgeoisie and landowners. It overlooks the genealogy of the great fortunes of the Third World, all those family alliances between landowners, industrialists, agents of foreign capital, and high-ranking public officials. Take a Brazilian coffee planter who has invested his capital in domestic industries; he speculates at the same time in real estate and he is connected with foreign capital as a minority partner in industrial and business firms: so, to which of the three categories does he belong? It would perhaps be better to limit ourselves to distinctions between big- and small-capitalists, and then to the petty ones who are drawn to moneylending and trade or who rent out a few hovels at exorbitant rates, in order to have an income which is scarcely higher than that of the subproletariat whom they exploit, and exploit all the more fiercely in that they are poor themselves.

As was to be expected, the social stratification of the cities leads to political configurations which are different from those we know in

Europe. Misconceptions about this subject are all the more dangerous because, for a while now, the cities have been playing a dominant role in Third World politics, out of proportion to their demographic importance. This is particularly true in countries where illiterates do not have the right to vote.

The most serious error probably concerns the phenomena of urban populism in Latin America—peronism in Argentina and getulism in Brazil—equated in some cases with fascist movements, in other cases presented as social democracy in domestic affairs and anti-imperialism in foreign affairs. The error stems from juding everything by a European yardstick. Populism was an original attempt to create a middle-of-the-road majority between the traditional oligarchies and the extreme left, which, at the time, was possible provided that a balance was achieved between the more or less demagogic concessions made to the working-class aristocracy and the middle classes (concessions offset, in the eyes of the bourgeoisie, by the control acquired over the trade union movement) and a policy of support for industrialists and nonhostility toward the landowners. At no moment did either Vargas or Goulart think seriously of allowing the masses of the poor Brazilian peasantry to participate in the political life of the country. A nationalism more verbal than active and economic growth raised to the status of a national ideology were the two ideological components of these regimes which, in an eclectic manner, took their inspiration from fascism and the welfare state, from *Rerum Novarum* and the New Deal. In foreign affairs, neutralism would have been the natural extension of this policy; Peron and Vargas, each at different times, made a few vague attempts in this direction. But, before Bandoeng, the situation was scarcely favorable, especially since Latin America was being closely watched by the United States. Goulart, who had become suspect in the eyes of the bourgeoisie and the workers on account of his reformist demagogy with no action to back it, did not dare to appear neutral in foreign affairs. His indecisiveness brought him nothing except for the increasingly open hostility of the United States. The coup d'état of 1964 made Brazil a police state.

Intermediate Regimes

In classical Marxist analysis, situations of class equilibrium were considered to be exceptional and transitory. But in view of the particular special stratification of the Third World countries, as well as of an international situation characterized by competition between two world systems, I have been led to formulate, along with M. Kalecki, the hypothesis of the appearance of relatively stable regimes of a new type, which we call "intermediate regimes."[23] These regimes would be essentially formed of a coalition of all the *middle* classes in town and country areas, around a nationalist state, highly interventionist in the economic and social fields and willingly using a socialist vocabulary to capture the popular imagination. Our analysis was based on the Egyptian example, where the nucleus of the new government apparatus and of the economic bureaucracy (the managers of the public sector) was provided by the army; this condition is not necessary, although it is likely to recur.

Furthermore, the case of Egypt is instructive on two other levels:

1. The regime, forced to become more radical by the turn of events, covered a lot of ground from the time of the 1952 revolution right up to the nationalization decree of 1961. It finally put out of the picture, or at least neutralized, the large landowners and capitalists, even going so far as to dispossess all capitalists belonging to ethnic minorities. But it put an end to agrarian reform at a stage which keeps the rural proletariat on the fringe of the economic, social, and political life of the country and leaves intact the system for exploiting hired farm workers. The lot of the urban subproletariat has not substantially changed, except for the opportunities afforded by military careers. The apex of the social pyramid has thus been lopped off, but there has been no shift of power toward the base.

It is possible to demonstrate that all the intermediate strata of the

urban and rural population have, in one way or another, shared all the
benefits of this policy implemented under the banner of a militant and
highly popular nationalism: small and large capitalists have benefited
from buying at low prices the properties of the expelled minorities; a
vast bureaucracy enjoying a relatively high standard of living has been
created around the government capitalist sector formed by the nation-
alized industries,[24] industrial workers have been able to expect advantageous social legislation, and agrarian reform and all the measures aimed
at the development of agriculture have worked to the special benefit of
the average and small landowners, who still seem to hold local political
power to the detriment of the landless peasants. Repressive measures
against the extreme left are a logical part of this framework. Since the
extreme left represented the disinherited members of society and,
moreover, could aspire to the support of the working-class aristocracy
brought back by the regime, it represented a real threat.

2. Right up to the Six-Day war, Egypt managed to play the neutralist game with rare success, ensuring itself of substantial aid from
both sides at the same time and a privileged position among the Afro-
Asian nations. Siding in with the U.S.S.R. in order to counterbalance
Western influences is part of the logic of the "intermediate regime," as
is virulent anti-Communism at home.

As we see them, "intermediate regimes," which in our view are in no
way to be confused with socialism, comprise radical variants, as in Syria
or Algeria, and very moderate variants as in India. There, a *modus
vivendi* was established from the outset with the upper middle class,
which renounced for a good twenty years all desire to assume the direct
responsibility of power, thus increasing its economic force (and therefore its influence).

Of course, the stability of these regions is only relative, and the history of the last few years provides proof of this. But while the possibility is not to be discounted that intermediate regimes may here and
there sink into state-bureaucratic capitalism or into some crippled form
of capitalism promoted by neocolonialism, or that they may open the

way to genuinely socialist revolutions, one should not underestimate their capacity for survival, even in the face of violent coups d'état leading to substantial changes in the composition of the bureaucratic élites in power.

"Intermediate regimes," on which I have dwelt because of their novelty, enrich the typology of paths of development in the Third World. It is an extremely broad typology, since it includes, in my opinion, not only socialisms (I insist on the plural) and intermediate regimes, but also state-bureaucratic capitalism (which appears as a possible degeneration of both socialism and intermediate regimes), peripheral capitalism, and neocolonialism.

Key Ideas

Nationalism and economic and social development are the two key ideas which are stressed by all Third World politicians who seek to ensure themselves of popular support and to maintain for as long as possible the unity which was solidified either in the demand for independence or in the struggle for liberation. Immediately after independence, when euphoria was at its height and millenarianism was in full swing, inordinate promises were made to the masses, either because the leaders were demagogues or because they themselves believed in miracles—in the benevolence of the industrial powers repentant of colonialism; in the commitment of the United States and the U.S.S.R. to a massive program for redeeming the Third World; in the capacity of the Afro-Asian countries, united by a common intent set forth at Bandoeng, despite deep-seated differences in regimes, to influence the international system; in fantastic rates of growth without sacrifice or suffering and without any reform of structures; and above all in the possibility of attaining full employment in a few years, even in a country as afflicted by unemployment as India. There was a great abundance of unrealistic plans, intended to convince the various strata of the population that they all had something to gain from rapid economic development, which indeed was true:

the expansion of the forces of production and the setting up of a modern infrastructure answered everyone's purposes and could serve as the basis of a temporary political compromise even between opposing social classes.[25] The acceleration of history which the world had just experienced in promises of decolonization was transposed into economic and social affairs, projected into the future.

The fever spread to Latin America. The building of Brasilia (in my opinion economically ill-advised) became the symbol of this faith in growth raised to the status of an ideology—an ideology capable, so it was thought, of making Brazil advance with giant strides and of making up in a few years a lag of a century or hardly less in relation to the most developed powers. Ideological syncretism was in fashion, and there were wild attempts to reconcile a few scraps of Marxism and socialist ideology with the most disparate ingredients. Nehru attempted to accommodate his convictions as a Fabian socialist to a purely formal Gandhianism; in Burma, U Nu proclaimed himself Marxist at the base and Buddhist in superstructure;[26] N'Krumach forced his cadres to learn consciencism—one of the most absurd concoctions ever produced by political philosophy.[27] Nyerere glorified the values of the indigenous socialism of tribal economics;[28] Nasser and the leaders of the Arab revolution hastily attempted a progressive reinterpretation of Islam.[29]

This was to forget the harsh social and economic realities inherited from the colonial past, the accumulation of nationalistic, religious, tribal, and linguistic conflicts, the different loyalties that divided peoples, the cultural gap between urban and rural areas, the unwieldiness of administrative machines ill-adapted to the new tasks and often used for personal gain, regional parochialism sustained by economic inequalities, cultural differences and nationalistic or tribal antagonisms, and finally the skill of the major powers in stirring up antagonisms and in exploiting every situation to suit their own ends.

The solidarity of the Third World collapsed as a result of armed conflicts, economic rivalries, and civil wars; almost everywhere the economic and social programs ended in failure, at least when measured by the divergence between ambitions and reality, between promises and results. A wave of coups d'état, most of them regressive, swept across the three continents, reflecting the disillusionment of the masses, who remained passive as the gangs in power changed.

It is natural, when they are faced with the bankruptcy of overambitious programs, for the men in power, whether they belong to the old shift or the new, to attempt to make good their losses by a new bid for nationalism or even racism. Since the opposition does the same and public opinion is receptive to this persuasion, we are witnessing today a veritable proliferation of nationalist movements and parties, ranging from the revolutionary left to the extreme right, reactionary and obscurantist, gladly exploiting all forms of ethnocentrism.

I thus return to my subject, to questions which have remained unanswered: Where is the boundary to be drawn between retrogressive nationalism and progressive nationalism? How can we prevent nationalism, the motivating concept of revolutions for national liberation, from shifting toward chauvinism and racism? How can we keep it from degenerating into wrongheadedness legitimizing a *Weltanschauung* of opposition between colored and white, and keep skin color from being merely symbolic of affiliation with the poor or the rich?

Notes to Chapter 6

1. The Egyptian sociologist A. Abdel-Malek dwells at length on what he calls the "nationalitarian" process, which he compares unfavorably with "nationalism." I am not as sure as he is that we can or know how to draw the line between them (see his introduction to *La pensée politique arabe contemporaine*; Paris, 1970).

2. See Joseph Stalin, *Leninism* (Polish translation; Warsaw, 1947), p. 51.

3. This interpretation of the philosophy of history, currently subscribed to in official circles in the U.S.S.R., emerges in particular from reading the documents of the C.P.S.U. and scientific works which appeared during the Krushchev era.

4. In this chapter I again take up several ideas which I developed in my brief introduction to Third World politics, which appeared in Polish in Warsaw in

1966 under the title *Ksztalt Niepodleglosci* (The shape of independence). I wrote then that one of the major sins of Marxist analysis of international politics is "presentism," which is judging the domestic policy and the ideology of the Third World by its foreign policy: "In practice, we sometimes invert the correct assertion that foreign policy is an extension of domestic policy, and whenever, on the international scene, a country practices neutralism or seeks cooperation from us, we endeavour to find leftist trends in its domestic policy" (p. 64).

5. A. Nikitin, *Hozenie za tri morja* (Voyage beyond the three seas), referred to in the Polish translation *Wedrowka za trzy morza* (Wroclaw, 1952). It should be pointed out in passing that this vivid account abounds in prejudiced statements about the "black" inhabitants of the country and, in particular, against the women, who scandalized Nikitin with their uncovered heads and breasts.

6. This interpretation was suggested to me by O. Lange.

7. To my knowledge, the best anthology of Gandhi's economic and social writings is the three-volume *Economic and Industrial Life and Relations,* ed. V. B. Kher (Ahmedabad, 1957). For Gandhi's relationship to Christian thought and, in particular, to Ruskin and Tolstoy, see Gandhi, *An Autobiography: The Story of My Experiments with Truth,* consulted in the French edition, *Expériences de vérité ou autobiographie* (Paris, 1950); K. Nag, *Tolstoy and Gandhi* (Patna, 1950); and K. Rivett, *Economic Thought of Mahatma Gandhi* (New Delhi, 1959); The last essay shows up the European influences on the thought of Gandhi, but embarks on a highly dubious psychoanalytical interpretation. Gandhi's economic ideas have been the subject of a very large number of studies. For an apologetic but modernized interpretation, see S. Narayan, *Principles of Gandhian Planning* (Alahabad, 1960). For a nonsectarian Marxist monograph on Gandhi's personality, see H. Mukerjee, *Gandhiji. A Study* (Calcutta, 1958).

8. C. Bettelheim, *Problèmes théoriques et pratiques de la planification* (Paris, 1966). See also A. K. Sen, *Choice of Techniques* (Oxford, 1960).

9. Gandhi, *An Autobiography,* p. 87.

10. R. B. Gregg, *A Philosophy of Indian Economic Development* (Ahmedabad, 1958).

11. I must mention once again the efforts of Latin-American sociologists, in particular the work of F. H. Cardose (published in French as *Sociologie du développement en Amérique Latine;* Paris, 1969, particularly pp. 97-150), R. Stavenhagen (published in French as *Les classes sociales dans les sociétés agraires;* Paris, 1969), F. Fernandes (*Sociedade de classes e subdesenvolvimento;* Rio de Janeiro, 1968) and O. Ianni (*Industrização e desenvolvimento social no Brazil;* Rio de Janeiro, 1963).

12. See Fernand Braudel, "Dans le Brésil Bahianais: Le présent explique le passé," in *Ecrits sur l'histoire* (Paris, 1969), pp. 239-254.

13. See Clifford Geertz, *Agricultural Involution* (Berkeley, Calif., 1963).

14. C. Meillassoux, *Anthropologie économique des Goure de Côte-Ivoire: De l'économie de subsistance à l'agriculture commerciale* (Paris, 1964).

15. D. Thorner's small book, *The Agrarian Prospect in India* (New Dehli, 1956), remains in my opinion a valid model of "reductionism."

16. This is observed, for instance, in a study on Madagascar by E. Chapuis, "Conditionnement socio-culturel de l'économie dans la région de Tuléar (Madagascar)," in *Cahiers de l'I.S.E.A.,* "Economies et Sociétés," Série Economie, Ethnologie, Sociologie, No. 7, January 1964, pp. 199-225. See also C. T. Nistet, "Moneylending in Rural Areas: Some Examples from Colombia," *The American Journal of Economics and Sociology,* 30, 1 (January 1971).

17. See M. I. Pereira de Queiroz, *Réforme et révolution dans les sociétés traditionnelles* (Paris, 1968).

18. E. J. Hobsbawm, *Primitive Rebels* (New York, 1965).

19. See the interpretation of these events given by the Dutch sociologist W. E. Wertheim, in "Indonesia Before and After the Untung Coup," *Pacific Affairs,* 39. 1-2 (1966), pp. 115-127.

20. N. K. Bose, "Calcutta: A Premature Metropolis," in *Cities* (A Scientific American Book, Harmondsworth, 1967), p. 67.

21. Y. Lacoste, *Géographie du sous-développement* (Paris, 1965).

22. K. Davis, "The Urbanization of Human Populations," in *Cities,* p. 28.

23. Our articles were published in Polish in *Ekonomista,* no. 3/1965. A more recent version of Kalecki's article appeared in English, in *Co-existence,* no. 1/1967.

24. Some Egyptian analysts speak of "the new class" in Egypt: see in particular Adel'Abd Al-Rahim Ghoneim's very interesting study in Abdel- Malek, *La pensée politique arabe contemporaine,* pp. 192-200.

25. I develop this idea in my work *Patterns of Public Sector in Underdeveloped Economies* (Bombay, 1964).

26. U Nu, *Towards a Socialist State* (Rangoon, 1958).

27. K. N'Krumah, *Consciencism: Philosophy and Ideology for Decolonization and Development with Particular Reference to the African Revolution* (London, 1964).

28. J. K. Nyerere, *Freedom and Socialism (Uhuru na Ujamaa)* (Oxford, 1969). A selection from writings and speeches, 1965-1967.

29. See, for instance, *République Arabe Unie. La Charte,* and Nasser's speech of June 30, 1962 (Cairo, 1962).

7   The Emancipation of Development Economics

It is possible to trace the origins of development economics to classical economics and profitably to reread, from this point of view, Adam Smith and Ricardo, leading up to Marx.[1] This means, so to speak, following the path Marx took and then skipping over the unfortunate interlude of neoclassical analyses of market equilibrium, which separates these writers from the revival of interest in growth that was inspired by the threefold impact of the great crash of 1929, the consolidation and the material progress of the socialist economy in the U.S.S.R., and finally of the discovery of the Third World.[2] Going back to the sources in this way, however, presents two dangers: it inclines one to consider as absolute the laws of capitalist development and to universalize the historical experience of Britain and of Western Europe. We know, however, that this experience was, in many respects, very particular, simply because, to begin with, the birth of capitalism in Western Europe created the world market and the colonial empires and thereby affected conditions of development on a world scale. Moreover, Marx was very sensitive to this problem: although in the preface to the German edition of *Das Kapital,* he did not hesitate to say that England corresponded exactly to what Germany was going to become,[3] he was conscious of the features which made Russian development distinctive, as is proved by his correspondence with Vera Zasoulich.[4] The reason for this was that, in the latter half of the nineteenth century, Russia was, in comparison with the countries of Western Europe, quite clearly an underdeveloped country, if this neologism may be used in such a historical context. And this was particularly so in that the Tsarist empire was a prison of nations and practiced colonialism within a unified territory. This underdevelopment was a serious obstacle to the expansion of Russian capitalism and predetermined its characteristics of development.

The special problems of development economics in the Third World may be defined as (1) the "coexistence of asynchronisms"[5] within the systems studied and (2) the anachronism of each of these systems, taken as a whole, in relation to the economies and societies of industrialized countries, both capitalist and socialist. The industrialized countries are characterized not only by a higher development of the means of production but, above all, by the greater homogeneity of the relations of production. This asynchronism imposes on the underdeveloped countries an international position which is marked by asymmetrical economic, political, scientific, and cultural relations. It is a serious obstacle to their development, but it also—perhaps—affords them the hope of finding short cuts through critical analysis of the course taken by the more developed countries and intelligent use of acquired knowledge of world science and technology.

The necessity of operating with these two criteria—degree of development of the means of production and character of the relations of production—is bound to give rise to certain difficulties, considering that the correlation between the two is imperfect when one tries to apply it to individual countries. Probably the most convenient method is to distinguish between developed countries and underdeveloped countries, within both capitalist or socialist systems, while keeping in mind potential of the socialist underdeveloped countries to move ahead very fast; for the social emancipation of the masses, when it is effective, completely changes the behavior of the system from bottom to top and, consequently, the basic premises of development strategy.

At all events, looking at development in diachronic terms in no way implies reducing the multiplicity of paths of development to a single model. It merely emphasizes the historicity of development theory by isolating a scale of material progress, both synchronic and diachronic, and a logical order of succession of the relations of production and economic mechanisms. However, these relations may be shaped in terms of quite a variety of sequences and combinations. This all comes down to emphasizing the importance of the context in which the development of each country is achieved, or, if one prefers, of the interaction of the world economy considered as a system and of the subsystems which make it up.

What is important is to realize that development economics, when applied to the problems of the Third World, does not simply merge into general economics; and that, despite certain parallels, overlaps, and common features, it differs from both the theory of capitalist dynamics and that of the dynamics of socialist economies. These differences stem from the fact that underdeveloped economies and societies are, as I have already said, structurally heterogeneous. For each of them, development therefore entails the transformation (and usually the homogenization) of structures, whereas it is possible to consider that the dynamics of evolved capitalism and of established socialism act within the given structures. Furthermore, since the rate of growth of a developed capitalist economy is, roughly speaking, dependent on the evolution of effective demand and that of a well-managed socialist economy on increased supply, two approaches must be combined—starting with the limitations of both supply and demand—to analyze underdeveloped mixed economies, as we shall see in the third part of this essay.[6]

Four Cases of Mimetic Transfer: Keynes, Schumpeter, Harrod-Domar, and Dogmatic Marxism

Immediately after the Second World War, when the problem of economic development in the Third World arose, the tendency of economists was at first to disregard its specificity and to apply themselves to extrapolating, for the Third World, the theories then in vogue in developed countries. This outbreak of Europocentrism had a positive result: it rendered obsolete many colonialist theories, highly colored by racism, which undertook to justify European protectionism on the pretext that the colonial peoples were incapable of using the economic opportunities presented to them, since their primitive mentalities prevented them from understanding market rationality, considered, of course, as the only possible expression of economic rationality.[7] But the mimetic transplantation to underdeveloped countries of the theories of Keynes, Schumpeter, and Harrod-Domar resulted, as was bound to happen, merely in resounding failures at the practical level.

For indeed, to build a long-term development policy for an

underdeveloped economy on the basis of Keynesian precepts for short-
and medium-term policy (conceived for a developed economy) was to
close one's eyes to the fundamental difference between underutilization
of existing productive capacities and the absence of such capacities; between the capacity of the developed economy to meet the growth of
world demand and the paralyzing effect of bottlenecks specific to underdeveloped economies. In the former case, a flow of public expenditure and the stimulation of private investment and consumption by way
of credit policy has a multiplier effect, whereas in the latter case,
nothing like this can occur; if the bottlenecks are not eliminated, a violent jump in inflation is inevitable, while in the meantime unemployment continues unabated.[8]

It should be pointed out, all the same, that the infatuation with
Keynes helped to modernize the teaching of economics and the intellectual apparatus of economic and financial administration and that it also
cleared the way for the idea that a government policy of action was indispensable at the macroeconomic level. This undoubtedly cut two
ways, as the same modernization could have been achieved with the
help of a theory better adapted to the needs of Third World countries
and supported by a highly selective development policy, a plan with
firmly established priorities, which would have avoided the disastrous
consequences of an increase in overall demand. I am willing to admit
this. But for the time being I am merely noting the facts, trying not to
oversimplify the realities.

The fate of Schumpeter's theory was quite different. While it was
simplified to such an extent that only the skeleton was left, it was made
into an ideological hobby-horse. What was lacking in the Third World
were truly enterprising entrepreneurs, capable of innovating, that is to
say, of working with new combinations of the factors of production
(which in no way imply invention). This lack was due, among other
reasons, to the lack of infrastructure necessary for setting up modern
industries. Consequently, development policy had to pursue three goals
at the same time: build up the economic infrastructure, through

government action, by establishing poles of development capable of attracting private enterprise; create, by financial, fiscal, and educational policy, a class of small, medium, and large-scale entrepreneurs; last, do all that was necessary to attract foreign investment (a particularly curious conclusion in that Schumpeter was the first to understand that development was essentially bound up with the capacity to make autonomous decisions).[9] At all events, this interpretation of Schumpeter becomes, roughly speaking, the doctrine of the World Bank, of the governments of the United States and of the other industrialized countries, and of many governments of Third World countries.

There was a great rush, backed by funds from the World Bank, to construct dams and to implement regional development schemes for the river basins, modeled on the Tennessee Valley Authority in the United States. But these projects proved more costly than planned; they took an inordinately long time to realize; and their economic effects were often disappointing, especially since serious errors were committed, causing the negative impacts to surpass on occasion the results of irrigation of new land. It is, at all events, certain that the concentration of resources and the timing of these spectacular projects within the development strategies were, more than once, ill-advised. They prevented other, more urgent, projects with more immediate goals (for instance, irrigation with artesian wells) from being carried out.

Furthermore, the new poles of development did not prove to have the magnetic properties which had been attributed to them: local capitalists preferred to invest in these areas where external economics were the most powerful, that is to say, in a few cities which shot ahead of the rest of the country in industrialization; foreign capitalists were not generally inclined to venture into the Third World so long as business was satisfactory in the developed countries. The failure of the open-door policy toward foreign capital was, in a sense, a stroke of luck for the underdeveloped countries; the foreign stranglehold on the economy of certain countries indeed enables us to imagine the results had this policy been successful. With regard to these centers of development which enjoyed some success, it is important to note that this result was obtained through sustained government action, which implied abandoning the economic philosophy underlying their creation: the initial push is not in fact enough to arouse the dormant initiative of private entrepreneurs; they can be had only on the assurance of permanent hothouse facilities.[10]

What then is the value of entrepreneurs, still in Schumpeter's sense of the word?

The same question arises with regard to many government corporations and development banks created under the impetus of development policy inspired by Schumpeter. These institutions often take on the functions of entrepreneurs at the most delicate moment for setting up new industries and then abandon them to private entrepreneurs who prove incapable of discharging the very function which, it is claimed, justifies their existence and the privileges which they are lavishly accorded. Thus the practice challenges the soundness of the theory on which it is based. In reality, this is a misguided attempt to justify the policy of introducing capitalism; the imported commodity is not Schumpeter and his explanation of the development of European capitalism, but capitalism conceived as a universal model of development, as though it could take the place of development theory and policy.[11] Certain literal applications of the Schumpeterian model, moreover, have had results which are more comical than anything else. Thus, some American psychologists have decided that what Indian entrepreneurs are lacking is ambition, the motivation for success, and courses have been organized to inculcate it in them. This, they contend, is the way to create Schumpeterian entrepreneurs![12]

The same thing happens with growth models of the Harrod-Domar type, but for quite different reasons. They disregard institutions, and are therefore reduced, in their practical applications, to the banal discovery that there is a causal connection between investment and an increase in national income. Undoubtedly the advantage of this was to attract the attention of Third World governments to the possible importance of increasing savings and turning them into investment. But the macroecenomic argument on the allocation of income between savings and consumption may be wrongly employed to justify restrictions on mass consumption on the pretext of increasing savings, which happened very soon. Furthermore, stressing the role of investments almost exclusively makes it possible to relegate to the background the thorny problem of structural change and of the policies which pave the way for it; this is to confine oneself to the economic sphere, cutting it off from the political and the social.[13] This was exploited, and, as paradoxical as it may appear, the governments of the Third World were able for a while to use models of growth to justify their immobility.

The reader may reproach me for underestimating the theoretical contribution of models of growth. This is in no way my intention. But I am concerned here with grasping the practical significance for the Third World of the mimetic transfer of models of the Harrod-Domar type and the ideological uses to which they were put. I may add that, as intellectual apparatus, these models contributed to the popularity of the concept of capital-output ratio, which is certainly useful when applied with precaution and carefully defined for each case, but very dangerous when it is improperly used and even more so when it is made to serve as the very basis for planning.[14]

At bottom, it is fairly understandable that economists, educated to believe that they were cultivating a discipline at once suprahistorical and universal; convinced, moreover, of the need to transfer to underdeveloped countries the superior technology of the West; and ignoring the true history of development theory (which will be discussed subsequently), should have been so profoundly influenced by Europocentrism and should have persisted for so long in this outlook before turning to the study of underdevelopment in its real contexts. But curiously enough, the same error was made by most economists with Marxist backgrounds, who should have been the first to recognize the specificity of the Third World. Their minds fogged by dogmatic Marxism and Stalinist orthodoxy, they contented themselves with a twofold reduction. The path of development, they said, is through socialist revolution; while waiting for it to occur, the condition of peoples subjected to the twofold exploitation of imperialism and local capitalist and landowning oligarchies can only get worse. Once the revolution has been achieved, it will be enough to follow the example of the building of socialism in the U.S.S.R., a model of universal scope, applicable to all latitudes, to all countries, large or small, rich or poor.

The increasing political weight of the Asian, Latin-American, and then the African countries and the obvious lack of success in hastily transplanting theories and policies caused a real boom in specialized studies, both in the countries concerned and elsewhere. As a result of the Cold War the great powers found themselves having to perform increasingly complex manoeuvers on the chessboard of the Third World. Gunnar Myrdal, undoubtedly the Western scholar most committed to a veritable crusade against the misdeeds of Europocentrism, has recently drawn up a very sobering balance sheet for twenty years of economic research on the Third World. His main grievances may be listed as follows.

This research continues to use concepts and analytical methods ill-adapted to the realities it seeks to grasp. Moreover, it is not capable of freeing itself from a somewhat naive opportunism which resorts to euphemisms in order to be agreeable to the élites in power in the Third World and to boost their morale. Myrdal is right in seeing here a condescending paternalism, which the intellectuals of the Third World should be the first to reject. The overoptimistic vision of the underdeveloped economy is too well served by an obstinate tendency to isolate the economic sphere, to construct models which completely exclude the institutional and social framework, or which pay lip-service to the importance of noneconomic factors without taking them into practical consideration. Although Myrdal has been rightly criticized for exaggerating the paralyzing effect of institutions in his too static analysis of the Indian economy and society, his methodological caution retains its validity. The approach which starts off by building simplified economic models and then adding on to them a few non-economic considerations is not valid. "The very act of clarifying what should be meant by 'economic' problems or 'economic' factors must, in fact, imply an analysis that includes all the 'noneconomic' determinants. From a scientific point of view, the only permissible demarcation—the only one that is fully tenable logically—is between relevant and less relevant factors. And that demarcation will vary with the characteristics of the society under study."[15]

Furthermore, a large number of writings on the Third World are imprisoned by that major vice of nineteenth-century liberal theories which consists in separating the problem of the distribution of income and wealth from that of the spheres of production and exchange. Egalitarian principles apply at the very most to distribution, but production and exchange are subject to almost natural laws; Myrdal calls this theoretical escapism.

Myrdal's opinion is basically valid. But his passion for demystification, in which he displays an admirable singlemindedness and courage, prevents him from appreciating for what they are worth a few positive results and some soul-searching revisions of commonly accepted Europocentric theories which have come about, despite everything, under the impetus of research or that of experience. The revisions are increasingly the work of Third World economists whose original contribution continues to be underestimated, if not ignored, by Western research and education.

Background

The beginnings of development economics are commonly set, at least in the Anglo-Saxon world, in the period of the Second World War and in the studies, in England, of Rosenstein-Rodan,[16] Mandelbaum,[17] and a handful of authors particularly concerned at the time with Southeast Europe and not with the Third World proper. In their work they benefited from the discussions of Eastern European economists following the Great Depression. It is curious to note how many of the major themes of development economics, as we conceive it today, appeared at that period, for instance, in the works of Polish economists, (the only ones that I know in detail) writing about the functioning of the peasant economy and hidden unemployment,[18] or about the balance of trade between cities and rural areas, limitations imposed by foreign trade, or the possible role of government. As far as I know, no systematic analysis of this contribution, encompassing Polish, Hungarian and Russian authors writing between the two World Wars, has been done, perhaps because several of the leading protagonists subsequently settled in Western Europe and the United States and, so to speak, naturally incorporated the results of their discussions into general economic thought on underdevelopment.

Following this line, it is possible to go further back, to the writings of the Russian populists and postpopulists of the last quarter of the nineteenth century and the beginning of the twentieth and to their polemics against the Marxists. They are just beginning to be known in the West and in the Third World, thanks to Franco Venturi's work;[19] to the excellent little book by Walicki,[20] which displays all the theoretical wealth and the topicality of their discussions on each capitalism; and to the English translation of Chayanov's studies on the peasant economy.[21] And yet the questions posed by several Russian populists in the nineteenth century are almost identical to those which today preoccupy the Third World. Is it absolutely necessary to go through the stage of capitalist development? Is it possible to profit from the survival of village communities? What hidden reserves does the peasant economy hold, and what makes it different? What attitude should an "underdeveloped" country assume toward the industrialized powers? Should one count on the transfer of knowledge and of technologies and be open to foreign influences, as was advocated by the pro-Western populists, or, on the contrary, close oneself off and draw on tradition, as was suggested by the Slavophiles?

These passionate and highly instructive discussions are still waiting
to be incorporated into the body of writings on underdevelopment.
The same is true of the contributions of varying quality made by thinkers, politicians, and journalists of the Third World, in Japan and in
China, which range over about a century and which, as far as I know,
have not yet been systematically analyzed, except perhaps for India[22]
and Mexico.[23] At all events, they have not yet been assimilated by
development specialists.

It is extremely instructive in this connection to note, as early as the
nineteenth century and at the beginning of the twentieth, how well the
battles between protectionists and free trade advocates in a country
like Brazil, following the example of their European counterparts, reveal the situation of a "peripheral" producer of raw materials: how
certain more perceptive observers realized that it would be necessary
to process raw materials locally and that the wealth of a country is
measured by its output and not by its imports.[24]

In India, with Naoroji and then Ranade, Gokhale, and Dutt, a genuine school of economic thought came into being, faithful to the teach-
ings of the English classics but perfectly aware that colonial exploitation changes the rules of the game, advocating industrial protectionism
(Ranade) and doing its utmost to calculate the cost for India of English
domination. The pioneering calculations of Naoroji, then those of the
historian R. P. Dutt, are grounded in a true theory of colonial drain,
with implications that were perhaps far more radical than the authors
desired. (It is curious to note that their estimations were apparently
made independently of those that Marx had proposed in certain articles.) Gandhi, of course, was briefly discussed in the previous chapter.

While we wait for light to be shed on the background of Third
World development theories, two observations are possible. First, in
several underdeveloped countries, notably in India and China, the impact of capitalism has given rise to agrarianist doctrines akin to those
of the Russian populists; these have influenced the Chinese Marxists,
and Mao Tse-tung's thinking is far more sensitive than was that of

Lenin to the peasant problem and to the revolutionary potential of rural areas. Second, Third World thinkers have been made acutely aware of the exploitation, and even the spoliation, to which their countries are exposed by foreign trade.

Reappraisals of Foreign Trade Theories[25]

There is nothing surprising, then, in the fact that the first important theoretical battle of the postwar years was waged against the doctrines of free trade and comparative advantage. The orthodox view on the supposed advantage for the underdeveloped countries of specializing in the export of raw materials and in not becoming industrialized, an idea officially backed by the United States and the colonial powers as well as the World Bank, was refuted by Latin-American economists led by Raul Prebisch[26] and the newly created E.C.L.A.; by Indian authors and by a few Western researchers such as François Perroux (author of a famous article on the effect of domination and the asymmetric and irreversible relations between the dominators and the dominated),[27] Ragnar Nurkse,[28] Gunnar Myrdal,[29] and H. W. Singer.[30] Their conclusions on the unequal distribution of trade profits among the weak and the strong, the subordination of peripheral economies to central economies, the existence of a structural crisis in world trade, preventing most Third World countries from developing their exports at a rate sufficient to balance their imports—agree with some results of Marxist researchers based on the theory of imperialism. But they reached a wider public, including some governments in the Third World and the decision-making bodies of the United Nations. People began talking about the need to establish a more equitable system of international exchange through unilateral concessions to the underdeveloped countries. The creation of U.N.C.T.A.D. was the outcome and, sad to say, the high point of this real campaign against the sophisms of traditional foreign trade theory and the policies of domination based on it.

The Structuralist Theory of Inflation

A second, more limited, battle was waged by the Latin-American partisans of the structuralist theory of inflation against the "monetarists."[31] Whereas the International Monetary Fund persisted in advocating measures inspired by a quantitative theory of currency, budgetary restraint, and devaluations, the structuralists showed that the primary sources of inflation were to be sought in the structural rigidity of underdeveloped economies, in particular in an ossified agriculture incapable of increasing the supply of foodstuffs, and in lagging foreign trade caught in a deep-seated crisis in the international division of labor. In these circumstances, there was no point in trying to relieve the symptoms. Orthodox anti-inflationary measures could only have a negative impact on the tempo of economic activity and the standards of living and the international positions of the countries exposed to this therapy, without, however, doing anything about the causes of the inflationary upsurge. In extreme cases, one might expect paradoxical results: an inflationary deflation, that is to say, a recession accompanied by rising prices.[32] Agrarian reforms and a restructuring of the international economic order were necessary if the fight against inflation was to be effective.

Dualism Reinterpreted

From this, only one step was needed to call in question the current versions of dualism, i.e., the presentation of the structure of underdeveloped economies in the form of two juxtaposed sectors: the traditional sector and the modern sector.

Originally, the dualist model had colonialist aims; it was respectable to insist on the irrationality of economic behavior in the traditional sector, justifying the need for a trusteeship of the modern sector, established by the mother country.[33] This interpretation was abandoned when, political conditions having changed, research in economic anthropology attempted to discover how criteria of economic rationality change according to sociocultural context.

The results are still far from satisfactory, for economic anthropology is not free either from Europocentric prejudices. Some authors have even gone so far as to borrow from the capitalist economy concepts for the analysis of primitive economies.[34] But enough has been done for it to be clear that certain types of behavior, quite contrary to that of market-oriented entrepreneurs, are perfectly rational in forms of subsistence or the pursuit of social goals, once economic needs as defined by local custom have been met. Rationality always consists in choosing (where there is freedom of choice) the solution deemed to be best; this is a basic axiom of philosophical anthropology. But the criteria by which men compare the alternatives available to them are governed by the sociocultural context in which they live: in a market economy, profit is maximized; in a subsistence economy, the effort necessary to provide this subsistence is minimized. The situation becomes more complicated in a peasant economy which both provides its own subsistence and produces for the market. As the family functions here as both a unit of consumption and a unit of production, the peasant's economic calculation is not setting wages for the work performed by members of his family and figuring a theoretical profit—it would then become clear that most peasant farms have shown deficits throughout history—but comparing gross income with work performed and, more specifically, supplementary income with nonsubsistence work.[35] How is this calculation performed, and at what moment does the market mentality start to take precedence over the subsistence mentality? What material, social, and cultural conditions have to be combined to reach a threshold where behavior changes? The practical importance of such questions cannot be overestimated by the development economist.[36]

But let me get back to dualism. Although its colonialist interpretation is discredited today, the idea of two sectors juxtaposed continues to be widely accepted, particularly in certain neoclassical models which present development as the progressive siphoning out of people from the traditional sector into the modern sector, created by industrialization. This simplified and, moreover, edifying view of the process of transformation of dualist economies leading to the extinction of the traditional sector has been energetically challenged.

First, it glosses over the historical conditions in which the dualist structures were formed. Arrighi[37] has shown, with reference to Rhodesia, that the colonizers practically created of a piece the traditional sector as it exists today, by destroying the equilibrium of the tribal economy and by dispossessing the local inhabitants of the best of their lands. The whole system, and not only the modern sector, is a colonial creation accomplished in the interest of the exploiters. Undoubtedly a similar line of reasoning could be applied to many other countries.

Above all one should take into account the many benefits that the modern sector derives from the existence of the traditional sector, which, in extreme cases, is in fact an internal colony.[38] Dualism therefore puts forward a false image of the underdeveloped economy if one persists in considering the two sectors as separate entities. One should attempt, on the contrary, to demonstrate the unity of the underdeveloped economy and, within this system, the interplay of subsystems. Some Latin-American writers, whose contribution is important for the reinterpretation of dualism, have even gone so far as to reject the very concept of dualism in semantic terms. Such is the case in particular with Fernando Henrique Cardoso.[39] Others, such as Armando Cordova or Anibal Pinto, prefer to speak of heterogeneous economies. Some, such as Stavenhagen, continue to use the concept of dualism, but redefine it.[40] It is important to recognize that these are differences of terminology rather than substance.

Excess Labor Supply
There are many variations on the theme of dualism, each one setting forth pairs of opposites chosen according to the preferences and intentions of the authors. Some stress the contrast between modernism and

tradition in terms of value systems and of the attitudes they dictate.[41] Others focus primarily on the opposition between cities and rural areas, between industry and agriculture, between a market and a subsistence economy, or even between the expert sector and the domestic sector of production (which is justified in the case of ultramodern mining enclaves owned by foreign capital and having very little connection with the economy of the region). A frequent misconception consists in setting the two sectors off from each other geographically, whereas in reality they coexist in the same spaces and, in extreme cases, on the same peasant farms, which may be simultaneously subsistence and market oriented. The Marxists have tried to remove this difficulty by rightly claiming that the predominant relations of production should be the criterion of classification, but to translate this principle into practical terms poses some difficulty on account of the complexity, the heterogeneity, and the changing character of the relations of production considered in their concrete reality.

A perhaps less ambitious definition of dualism based on conditions in the labor market seems to offer a better starting point for analyzing the peculiar problems of the Third World, where the employment situation is in fact characterized by a marked contrast between the restricted group of the privileged (who have achieved stable positions in the modern sector and an advanced technology) and the rest of the population, who are forced to lead a highly precarious existence without well-paid and steady employment.[42] It is impossible to make an accurate assessment of unemployment and underemployment among agricultural workers and small farmers, subproletarians and urban craftsmen, if for reasons of a conceptual type which make this type of exercise very problematical.[43] But we can plot fairly accurately the graph for the rise of employment in the modern sector, and the figures are alarming. Very respectable rates of growth for industrial output, on the order of 8 to 9 percent yearly, create at the most an increase in employment of some 3 percent, and this does not take into account jobs eliminated in the artisanal sector, by competition with modern

industry. In Latin America, the relative shares of industrial and artisanal employment in the employed labor force has remained stable, in
spite of the spectacular rise of industrialization. It was on the order of
scarcely 13.4 percent of the working population in 1960 against 13.7
percent in 1925 (the proportion in the modern sector having increased
from 3.5 percent to 7.5 percent.[44] As for the hopes raised by the
"green revolution" and by the possibilities of intensifying agricultural
production which it was supposed to usher in, even for small farms, it
does not seem to be able to effect a substantial change in the labor
market of countries such as India.[45] A recent study shows that the increase in real wages paid to day laborers was considerable only in
Kerala, where they had political leverage; the quantity of labor employed for each unit of surface area is not increasing, except in a few
districts, and the great majority of the rural population survives as best
it can in a state of hardship which defies the European's imagination:
the percentage of persons with an income lower than 15 rupees month-
ly, according to 1960-1961 prices (taking into account disparities in
purchasing power, about 6 U.S. dollars) has increased from 38.03 percent in 1960-1961 to 73.24 percent in 1967-68 (which was in fact a
particularly bad year, but this does not alter the general picture).[46]

According to H. W. Singer, unemployment and overt underemployment affect today a quarter of the work force of the Third World, and
they are increasing at a rapid rate (on the order of 8.5 percent yearly).
There are therefore prospects of an appalling employment crisis. It is
of little importance whether the figures are perfectly accurate or not.
They show that, far from rushing toward a famine caused by insufficient agricultural production, a part of the Third World is heading
toward an even more awful disaster: a quasi-famine, produced by the
uneven distribution of employment and income, accompanied by the
overproduction of foodstuffs!

The conceptualization of dualism based on the labor market makes
it possible to move from the descriptive level of the morphology of
underdevelopment to those of pathology and of etiology. Indeed, one

of the least unsatisfactory definitions of underdevelopment is that which stresses inability to resolve simultaneously the problems of unemployment and of saturation of the economy with modern technologies, characterized by high productivity but requiring a great deal of capital. The capital available is not enough to employ everyone in activities ensuring high productivity.[47] It follows that unless technologies are found which require little capital while ensuring reasonable productivity, or unless there is access to foreign and extremely plentiful sources of capital in addition to greater frugality at home, the underdeveloped countries have no choice but to become enmeshed in an increasingly pronounced technological, occupational, and social dualism. The example of Japan proves both the persistence of the phenomenon and its immense social cost.[48]

At the theoretical level, work on problems of the labor market peculiar to Third World countries has resulted in three important developments: reconsideration of models of growth, elaboration of the concept of "human investment"* and the statement of a theory of choice techniques.

Models of growth were altered to take into account the unlimited supply of unskilled labor. The pioneering writings of Lewis[49] have had considerable repercussions in this area. The trouble is that they ignore the historical and institutional aspects of the establishment and functioning of dualist Third World economies and that they use a neoclassical apparatus which is ill-fitted to grasp the complexity of peasant economies in transition and of imperfect markets: is it possible to speak, in the Third World, of the homogeneity and the perfect mobility of labor, the substitutability of factors, and their value in terms of marginal and extramarginal productivity? It may be noted parenthetically that certain authors who are overimbued with the neoclassical theory of wages have gone so far as to cast doubt on the fundamental premise

---

*French term for labor-intensive work of the pick-and-shovel variety. (Trans.)

of Lewis's model. According to them, there is neither overt nor hidden unemployment in the rural areas of the Third World, since the wages paid to agricultural laborers continue to be greater than zero; therefore the marginal productivity of labor continues to be positive. Here is a line of reasoning which is clear, elegant, and at the same time very comforting for the governments of Third World countries, who no longer have to bother about employment for the peasant masses![50]

Two currents were responsible for the appearance of the concept of human investment. First, academic discussions focused simultaneously on the theories of hidden unemployment in rural areas; the concept of public works as an instrument not of anticyclical policy, but of development; and the idea of rural community development, originally thought to be a grass roots alternative to land reforms. Nurkse's important work on the formation of capital in underdeveloped countries[51] drew attention to the possibility of using the potential savings in the work of those in rural areas who would otherwise be unemployed. Since they must eat in any case, they could be employed in development work without giving rise to any short-term changes in consumption.

Second, the Chinese, by carrying to its logical limits the experience of the U.S.S.R. and the peoples' democracies of Eastern Europe in the field of extensive development, and with the support of the peasant masses obtained through effective agrarian reform, have decided to make human investment the mainspring of their Great Leap Forward.[52] Whatever the verdict on the results, and, in general, on the limits of the use of human investment (I shall return to this in the third part of this book) it is beyond doubt that a decisive step has been taken toward a theory of development which meets the needs of the Third World. At all events, one of its major themes has been singled out for immediate attention.[53]

The use of human investment should go hand in hand with the utilization of techniques that are conserving of capital. Here too, the Chinese have attempted to explore the idea to the full and, making a virtue out of necessity, to use rudimentary tools until those can be replaced by more sophisticated equipment. Their mishaps with the production of cast iron are well known. But it remains true that there is a need to use technologies which have already become obsolete in the industrialized countries and to find others which are labor-intensive and not very capital demanding. In short, there is a need for a sort of do-it-yourself philosophy, or for what Leiris[54] felicitously terms guerilla research, whenever these will ensure reasonable productivity. Value added should, I think, exceed the level of the minimum acceptable wage in order for "intermediate" technologies, as Schumacher[55] calls them, to be able to be used reasonably in agriculture, in construction, and certain industrial activities, as well as in the social services.

The fact that, on the one hand, the advocates of labor-intensive technologies have spoken highly of their virtues without paying sufficient attention to the necessity of simultaneously employing in certain fields (in industry in particular) capital-intensive technologies and, on the other hand, the unfortunate tendency to present the major problems of development in terms of clear-cut and exclusive dichotomies, have given rise to two kinds of reaction.

First, many Third World economists and politicians with a false concept of modernism have seen the support of labor-intensive technologies as a neocolonial maneuver to prevent the countries of the Third World from benefiting from modern scientific and technological progress.

Second, the merit of labor-intensive technologies was questioned, not without ingenuity, by proving that, in a closed economy with no inflows of external capital (apart from an initial supply), an economy, then, in which the rate of growth would depend on investment surplus, this surplus would be maximized at a level of production lower than the maximum output of available capital and labor.[56] In other words, for a given level of real wages, the maximization of surplus implies the use of capital-intensive technologies, even in underdeveloped economies, since distributing available capital over a larger number of jobs results in an increased output and increased employment, but in a lower

investment surplus. The contradiction between the maximization of
surplus and that of output is analyzed in figure 1.

On the x axis of figure 1 are shown the quantities of labor, on the
y axis the output, the quantity of available capital K being constant.
The curve OP_2 shows the output resulting from different combinations
of K with labor. It reaches its peak at P_2. The line OC_2 indicates the
portion of output assigned to wages. It is proportional to the number
of workers. The investment surplus, that is, the difference between
output and wages, reaches its maximum at point P_1 (where the tangent
to curve OP_2 is parallel to OC_2, or, where marginal productivity is
equal to the real wage).

The line OC_3 shows the level of consumption in the event that it is
decided to lower real wages in such a way as to have the same surplus
at P_2 as at P_1. In other words, C_1C_3 is parallel to P_1P_2. Individual
wages are considerably reduced, but employment increases by L_1L_2
and likewise overall consumption, the difference between C_3L_2 and
C_1L_1 being equal to $P'P''$.

output

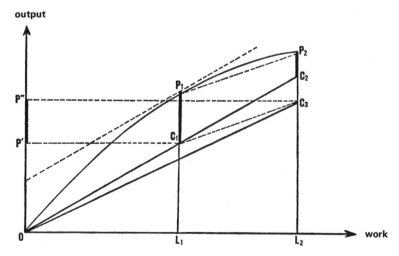

Figure 1

The argument against labor-intensive technologies is perfectly valid, provided that three rather unrealistic assumptions are accepted: that there is no inflow of external capital (for instance, taxes levied on the traditional sector); that autonomous technological progress does not exist (if it were incorporated into the argument it would reduce the opposition between the two maxima); that the manipulation of real wages is not to be taken into account.[57] At any rate, discussion provoked by the model briefly described above has made it possible better to understand what is at stake in certain development policies.

It was followed by a deluge of cost-benefit analyses and studies on the use of shadow costs for capital and labor. The planner's tendency to make these interchangeable where the choice exists is thus expressed in parameters which the planner is assumed to use in his calculations.

It is easy to express reservation, and even criticism, with regard to this literature and its inordinate claim to turn cost-benefit analyses into an instrument for choosing investment priorities. In fact it can only serve as a comparison for variants of the same plan, that is to say, for the selection of technologies in the narrow sense of the term. The false appearance of exactitude in these studies conceals arbitrary decisions about the indirect effects and the indirect costs used in the calculation; it is difficult to fix shadow prices and they have no bearing whatsoever on decisions in the private sector.[58] Be this as it may, it is nonetheless true that all these discussions have incorporated a new dimension into planning theory.

Underdevelopment in Historical Perspective
Concurrent with all these revisions of accepted economic theories, there has been a decisive attempt, on the borderline between economics and history, to study underdevelopment in its historical perspective, to build up comparative quantitative data on the real state of the Third World economies and of Europe immediately prior to the Industrial Revolution, and then on their growth in the course of the last two centuries.[59] From these, important conclusions emerge.

First, at the time of the French Revolution, the gap in terms of per capita income was fairly small, if not negligible. To convince oneself of this one has only to think of the greed aroused by the wealth of the East and sustained by the tales of European travelers and, furthermore, of the descriptions of the wretched condition of the French peasantry —from La Bruyère to Young—or of Engels's analyses and Dickens's novels, on the subject of living conditions of English industrial workers in the first part of the nineteenth century. The gap that we see today is essentially the effect of a century and a half of slow growth in Europe and of the quasi-stagnation of the Third World during the same period. The incredulous reader may consult a compound interest table to see how a capital sum invested for 150 years at 2 percent yearly multiplies and then compare these figures with those given by a rate of 2 per thousand! As, after all, there is a causal link between these two rates, the underdevelopment of the Third World appears as the counterproduct of the development of world capitalism.

Second, several studies, in particular the book by Paul Bairoch already referred to, have shown the steadily increasing cost of the investment necessary to create a job in the industrial sector. At the time of the Industrial Revolution in England, this cost amounted to a few months' wages paid to a laborer, as against 350 months today, in the Third World. Thus the impossibility of following the path of the European countries is apparent, and the argument is reinforced by the effects of the population explosion and by the impatience of the peoples of the Third World, who are conscious of the historical responsibilities involved and of standards of living in the rich countries, which extend to the local élites.

Third, Gerschenkron[60] and several other historians have applied themselves to analyzing the role of institutions in development and the correlation which might exist between the relative degree of backwardness and the degree of interventionism on the one hand, and the impact of interventionism and the rate of growth on the other. It is not necessary to follow their arguments all the way to the end to realize that this retrospective view of experience with development spells the end of laissez-faire theories.

At a quite different level, many economists and planners who think that, as Dudley Seers[61] has put it, "economics is the study of economies," and who have been influenced by Marx, have felt the need to start from scratch to analyze the socioeconomic realities in their countries, beginning by questioning history. Celse Furtado's book on the Brazilian economy[62] is probably the prototype of these works whose originality consists in their attempt to reduce economic history to a succession of operating models of the economy, abandoning history in the strict sense and indulging in anachronisms in reverse, in order to apply to past situations the analytical apparatus of the modern economist. I believe that the exploration of the border between economic history and development theory is destined to assume more and more importance in the Third World. A good example of this is Osvaldo Sunkel's work, already referred to, which seriously and successfully attempts to define development theory on the basis of the historical experience of Latin America.[63]

On the other hand, Walt Rostow's work on stages of development (whose ephomeral success derives above all from its being intended as an anticommunist manifesto and from the good-natured optimism of the doctrine of "take-off"), instead of analyzing in depth the experience of the countries of the Third World and, where possible, deducing theoretical lessons from it, straightaway proposes a dogmatic and universal model of stages of development.[64] In order better to compete with historical materialism, Rostow sets out to show that he too is a materialist and does not hesitate to state that history is abstract. But in the process, all the richness of the dialectical relations between the base and the superstructure, the means and the relations of production disappears from his work. There remains only a mechanistic materialism, interspersed with references to the social preconditions of development and promising to the élites of the Third World a path of development which is historically necessary and almost painless, without conflict and without revolution. The important thing is that they accumulate, that they invest a major part of the national income, and consequently that they deign to get rich as rapidly as possible. Rarely has a book been launched with more to-do and distributed throughout the world with such show, despite the cautious reception given to it by professionals.[65] The moral of this episode is that Marxism has a great deal of attraction for the Third World in spite of the adverse effects of dogmatism, that it continues to bring to the study and the practice of development more guidelines and more points of support than the other schools of thought while providing a unifying hypothesis.[66]

In this connection, the recent discussion on the Asian mode of production has had a twofold impact on the study of underdevelopment. It has cast new light on certain aspects of the history of a few countries of the Third World. It has also helped loosen the dogmatic grip which was paralyzing Marxism, giving it back its flexibility, its ability to benefit from contact with reality. In particular, it has well and truly helped to demolish the concept of the unilinearity of history. It has reopened the casebook of the many forms of transition from one mode of production to another and, by implication, of the many paths to socialism, corresponding to many models. This contribution is by far the most important.

The real work of putting the mechanisms of underdevelopment in historical perspective is only begun. But henceforth the simplistic hypothesis of the "development of underdevelopment"[67] solely through the action of capitalism will appear inadequate. Kula[68] counters this with a more subtle explanation by trying to show how the interests of peripheral "feudalism" adapt to the world division of labor. The periphery exports to the center, contrary to what the classical economists thought, goods for which it has no comparative advantage in productivity. Lower productivity is, however, compensated for by the even lower level of remuneration for workers. Thus world trade reinforces exploitation. Kula's essay is, however, only a starting point, and it remains to be confirmed or invalidated by concrete research. At all events, history as a discipline can only benefit from such studies, which should help it to arrive at a truly universalistic outlook.[69]

I conclude my exposition with a moderately optimistic view of the evolution of development economics over the last twenty years, if only because, at the outset, total Europocentrism was the rule and is gradually giving way to a growing sense of realism. This progress is of consequence.

It is possible to foresee three advances: recognition of the special problems of the Third World is taking the place of a Europocentric view; the concept of development is becoming richer and growing multidimensional, whereas at the beginning it was seen in terms of the growth of the economy alone; barriers between disciplines, in spite of the weight of academic traditions, are yielding to the demands for a multidisciplinary approach. With the elements which we already have at our disposal, it seems possible to construct an all-embracing hypothesis. This is what I propose to establish in the third part of this work, even if it involves budening the reader with a few unavoidable repetitions.

Notes to Chapter 7

1. O. Sunkel and P. Paz, among others, have done this in their very interesting work, *El subdesarrollo latinoamericano y la teoria del desarrollo,* Mexico, 1970.

2. See the chapter on economics in the UNESCO report, *Main Trends of Research in the Social and Human Sciences,* part 1 (The Hague, 1970).

3. Karl Marx, *Capital,* vol. 1 (Paris, 1969), introduction to the German edition, pp. 17-30.

4. See *Sur les sociétés précapitalistes. Textes choisis de Marx, Engels, Lénine* (Centre d'Etude et de Recherches Marxistes; Paris, 1970), pp. 318-342.

5. The expression is W. Kula's, from "Secteurs et régions arriérés dans l'économie du capitalisme naissant," *Studi Storici,* 1.3 (April-June 1960), 569-585.

6. For the differences between developed and underdeveloped capitalist countries on the one hand, and capitalist and socialist countries on the other, see two essays by M. Kalecki, "The Difference between Crucial Economic Problems of Developed and Underdeveloped Non-Socialist Economics," in *Essays on Planning and Economic Development,* vol. 3 (Warsaw, 1968), pp. 9-18, and "Theories of Growth in Different Social Systems," *Scientia* (May-June 1970).

7. I am indebted to Gunnar Myrdal for several very pertinent analyses of the Europocentrism and opportunism of the economic sciences; see in particular *Asian Drama* (New York, 1968), *Objectivity in Social Research* (New York, 1969) and *The Challenge of World Poverty* (New York, 1970).

8. Indian authors above all are to be given the credit for having questioned the applicability of Keynes to an underdeveloped economy (see, in particular A. K. Das Gupta, "Keynesian Economics and Underdeveloped Countries, in *Keynesian Economics, A Symposium* (Delhi, 1956); *Tendencies in Economic Theory* (Chandigarh, 1960); "Marx and Keynes," in *Social and Economic Change, Essays in Honour of Prof. D. P. Mukerji* (Bombay, 1967), pp. 351-358. See also V. B. Singh, "Keynesian Economics in Relation to Under-Developed Countries," in *Keynesian Economics.* V. K. R. V. Rao, "Deficit Financing, Capital Formation and Price Behaviour in an Underdeveloped Economy," *Indian Economic Review,* no. 3/1953, 1-17.

9. See Kari Levitt, *Silent Surrender: The Multinational Corporation in Canada* (Toronto, 1970), pp. 25-26.

10. For a recent discussion of centers of development, see M. Penouil, "Poles de développement et régions sous-développées et en pays sous-développés," *Information sur les sciences sociales,* June 1970, pp. 41-69.

11. M. S. Khan's work entitled *Schumpeter's Theory of Capitalist Development* (Aligarh, 1957), provides a typical example of this. Despite its title, it makes no reference to the specific problems of the Third World. The implication is therefore that Schumpeter's theory has a universal field of application.

12. This operation is described in detail by one of its organizers, D. C. McClelland, "The Impulse to Modernization," in *Modernization: The Dynamics of Growth* (Voice of America Forum Lectures, ed. M. Weiner; Washington, D.C., n.d.).

13. I refer the reader once again to Gunner Myrdal's works, already cited, and to M. Kalecki's articles.

14. See in this connection P. Streeten, "Economic Models and Their Usefulness for Planning in South Asia," in *Myrdal, Asian Drama,* vol. 3, appendix 3, pp. 1,941-2,004.

15. Gunnar Myrdal, "Cleansing the Approach from Biases in the Study of Under-developed Countries," in *Information sur les sciences sociales,* June 1969, pp. 9-26. (This article is a draft of the first chapter of *The Challenge of World Poverty.*)

16. P. N. Rosenstein-Rodan, "Problems of Industrialization of Eastern and South-Eastern Europe," *Economic Journal* 53 (June-September 1943).

17. K. Mandelbaum, *The Industrialization of Backward Areas* (Oxford, 1945).

18. Doreen Warriner deals with this topic in *The Economics of Peasant Farming* (London, 1939).

19. Franco Venturi, *Roots of Revolution* (London, 1960).

20. A. Walicki, *The Controversy over Capitalism. A Study in the Social Philosophy of the Russian Populists* (Oxford, 1969); see, by the same author, the excellent long introduction to an anthology of Russian populist writings published in a Polish translation in Warsaw in 1965, under the title *Filozofia spoleczna narodnictwa rosyjskiego* (The social philosophy of the Russian populists).

21. A. V. Chayanov, *The Theory of Peasant Economy,* ed. D. Thorner, B. Kerblay, and R. E. F. Smith (Honewood, Illinois, 1966); see also D. Thorner, "Une théorie néo-populiste de l'économie paysanne: l'école de A. V. Cajanov," in *Annales,* no. 6/1966.

22. See in particular P. K. Gopalakrishnan, *Development of Economic Ideas in India (1880-1950)* (New Delhi, 1959), and B. Chandra, *The Rise and Growth of Economic Nationalism in India* (New Delhi, 1966).

23. J. W. Herzog, *Antología del pensamiento economico-social,* Mexico, Fondo de Cultura Economica, 1963.

24. See H. Bastos, *O pensamento industrial no Brasil* (São Paulo, 1952).

25. I examine this problem in detail in my work *Foreign Trade and Economic Development of Underdeveloped Countries* (Bombay, 1965).

26. See in particular his "Commercial Policy in the Underdeveloped Country," *American Economic Review,* 49.2 (May 1959), 251-273, and his reports to UNCTAD for the years 1964 and 1968: *Toward a New Trade Policy for Development* (United Nations; Paris, 1964), and *Towards a Global Strategy of Development* (United Nations; New York, 1968).

27. F. Perroux, "Esquisse d'une théorie de l'économie dominante," *Economie Appliquée,* nos. 2-3/1948.

28. R. Nurkse, "Patterns of Trade and Development," in *Equilibrium and Growth in the World Economy* (Cambridge, Mass., 1961).

29. Gunnar Myrdal, *An International Economy: Problems and Prospects* (New York, 1956).

30. H. W. Singer, "The Distribution of Gains between Investing and Borrowing Countries," in *American Economic Review*, 40.2 (May 1950).

31. See in particular O. Sunkel, "La inflación chilena: Un enfoque heterodoxo," *El Trimestre Económico*, no. 100 (October-December 1958); D. Seers, "A Theory of Inflation and Growth in Underdeveloped Economies based on the Experience of Latin America," *Oxford Economic Papers*, June 1962; and J. Grunwald, "The 'Structuralist' School on Price Stability and Development: The Chilean Case," in *Latin American Issues*, ed. A. O. Hirschmann (New York, 1961).

32. R. Thorp and E. Eshag, "Economic and Social Consequences of Orthodox Economic Policies in Argentina in the Postwar Years," in *Bulletin of the Oxford Institute of Statistics*, 27.1 (February 1965), 3-44.

33. This is the interpretation that can be given to J. M. Bocke's work, *Economics and Economic Policy of Dual Societies* (New York, 1953).

34. See, for instance, some of the contributions to the work edited *Capital, Savings and Credit in Peasant Societies*, ed. R. Firth and E. S. Yamey (London, 1964).

35. See in this connection J. Tepicht's recent article, "Les complexités de l'économie paysanne," *Information sur les sciences sociales*, 1969, pp. 51-68.

36. See in this connection my article, "La notion de surplus et son application aux économies primitives," in *L'Homme* (July-September 1966).

37. G. Arrighi, *Sviluppo Economico e sovrastruttura in Africa* (Turin, 1969).

38. This term was used in connection with northeast Brazil by Josné de Castro; see also R. Stavenhagen's stirring article, "Seven Fallacies about Latin America," in *Latin America, Reform or Revolution?* (New York, 1968), pp. 15-34.

39. F. H. Cardoso, *Sociologie du developpement en Amerique Latine* (Paris, 1969).

40. R. Stavenhagen, *Classes sociales.*

41. It is not possible to refer the reader to one specific work: a bibliography compiled by John Brode under the title *The Process of Modernization* (Cambridge, Mass., 1969) lists 12,304 titles, without claiming to be complete.

42. See in this connection H. W. Singer, *Dualism Revisited.* Working Paper of the Institute of Development Studies at the University of Sussex, England, October 1969.

43. See on this problem in particular Myrdal, *Asian Drama,* vol. 3, appendix 6, pp. 2,203-2,221; and P. Streeten, "An Institutional Critique of Development Concepts," in *Archives européennes de sociologie,* 9.1 (1970); see also a recent report published by the Indian Planning Commission (*Report of the Committee of Exports on Unemployment Estimates;* New Delhi, 1970) which points out the impossibility of using the Europocentric concept of employment in a country such as India, where wage earners constitute only 31 percent of the rural working population and 51.4 percent of city dwellers, whereas self-employed workers make up respectively 36.6 percent and 35.6 percent, the proportion of members of the family working without receiving any remuneration being 24.8 percent and 11.3 percent (p. 15). It is to be noted in passing that this report puts forward less alarming unemployment estimates than those that we have quoted, but emphasizes one of the characteristic features of development: the transformation of hidden unemployment into open unemployment. The authors very reasonably propose that instead of endeavoring to calculate the number of persons affected by hidden unemployment, one should estimate rather the number of work-days available.

44. Z. Slawinski, "La structure de la main-d'oeuvre en Amérique Latine," in *Problèmes de planification des ressources humaines en Amérique Latine et dans le projet Régional Méditerranéen* (OECD; Paris, 1967), p. 182. In the same study the author gives the following figures on productivity in dollars, per worker and branch, for the year 1960:

factories	2,795
crafts	348
building	720
agricultural sector	482
trade and finances	2,084.

45. See J. P. Lewis, "Wanted in India: A Relevant Radicalism," in *Economic and Political Weekly,* special issue, vol. 5, 29-31 (1970), pp. 1217-1220.

46. P. Bardhan, " 'Green Revolution' and Agricultural Labourers," ibid., pp. 1,239-1,246.

47. O. Lange, "Alcuni problemi riguardanti la planificazione economica nei paesi sottosviluppati," in *Critica Economica,* no. 3/1956, pp. 43-51.

48. This fact is implicitly acknowledged in S. Okita's study, "La croissance rapide du Japon d'après-guerre," in *Analyse et prévision,* 5 (1968), 1-28. See also "La dualité du développement industriel au Japon," in *Industrialisation et productivité,* United Nations, no. 8 (New York, 1964), pp. 43-55; and above all S. Ishikawa's very important book, *Economic Development in Asian Perspective* (Tokyo, 1967), pp. 357-468.

49. W. A. Lewis, "Economic Development with Unlimited Supplies of Labour," in *The Manchester School of Economic and Social Studies,* May 1954; *Theory of Economic Growth* (Homewood, Ill., 1965); and *Development Planning: The Essentials of Economic Policy* (New York, 1968). A more sophisticated version of this model, but one which also has a neoclassical frame of reference, somewhat modified in the area of wage theory, is the work of J. C. H. Fei and G. Ranis, *Development of the Labor Surplus Economy, Theory and Policy* (New Haven, Conn., 1964).

50. B. Hanson, *Marginal Productivity Wage Theory and Subsistence Wage Theory in Egyptian Agriculture,* Memorandum 547, Institute of National Planning, Cairo, March 1965; B. Hanson and G. A. Marzeuk, *Development and Economic Policy in the U.A.R.* (Amsterdam, 1965).

51. Ragnar Nurkse, *Problems of Capital Formation in Underdeveloped Countries* (New York, 1957).

52. C. Bettelheim, J. Charière, and H. Marchisio, *La construction du socialisme on Chine* (Paris, 1965).

53. For a discussion of other experiments in human investment, see E. Raynaud, *Investissements humains, illusions et réalités* (Paris and The Hague, 1969).

54. M. Leiris, *Cinq études d'ethnologie* (Paris, 1969).

55. See in particular E. F. Schumacher, "Social and Economic Problems Calling for the Development of Intermediate Technology," duplicated text, distributed by the Intermediate Technology Group, London, July 1965.

56. See in particular A. K. Sen, *Choice of Techniques* (Oxford, 1960); H. Leibenstein, *Economic Backwardness and Economic Growth* (New York, 1957); and Z. Dobrska, *Wyber technik producji w krajach gospodarczo zacofanych* (Choice of production techniques in economically backward countries), Warsaw, 1963.

57. See Z. Dobrska, *Wyber technik producji,* and M. Kalecki, *Introduction to the Theory of Growth in a Socialist Economy* (London, 1970).

58. For a frontal attack on the use of shadow prices, see Myrdal, *Asian Drama,* vol. 3, appendix 5, pp. 2,031-2,039.

59. See the pioneering work of Simon Kuznets, in particular "Quantitative Aspects of the Economic Growth of Nations," *Economic Development and Cultural Change,* vol. 5, 1/17 (October 1956), vol. 6, 3, part 1 (April 1957); and also S. J. Patel, *Essays en Economic Transition* (London, 1966) and P. Bairoch, *Révolution industrielle et sous-développement* (Paris, 1967). See also E. J. Hobsbawm's penetrating remarks on the differences between the

English Industrial Revolution and that of the Third World countries, *Industry and Empire* (Harmondsworth, 1969), pp. 34-55.

60. Alexander Gerschenkron, *Economic Backwardness in Historical Perspective: A Book of Essays* (Cambridge, Mass., 1962).

61. D. Seers, "The Limitation of the Special Case," in *Bulletin of the Oxford University Institute of Statistics,* 25.2 (May 1963), 77-98.

62. C. Furtado, *Formação econômica do Brasil* (Rio de Janeiro, 1963).

63. O. Sunkel and P. Paz, *El subdesarrollo;* see also for a valid attempt at interpreting the special Asian conditions, S. Ishikawa, *Economic Development in Asian Perspective.*

64. W. Rostow, *States of Economic Growth* (Cambridge, England, 1960).

65. The conference held at Cambridge to discuss Rostow's theory, the proceedings of which have been published under the editorship of Rostow himself (*The Economics of Take-off into Sustained Growth,* Proceedings of a Conference held by the International Economic Association; London, 1963) clearly shows that this American economist does not appear convincing to his historian colleagues.

66. E. J. Hobsbawm, *Introduction to Karl Marx: Precapitalist Economic Formations* (London, 1964); and, by the same author, "Karl Marx' Contribution to Historiography," in *Marx and Contemporary Scientific Thought* (The Hague, 1969), pp. 197-221.

67. G. Frank, *Le développement du sous-développement: L'Amérique Latine* (Paris, 1970).

68. W. Kula, "Il sottosviluppo economico in una prospettiva storica," *Annali della Fondazione Luigi Einaudi* (Turin), vol. 3 (1969), pp. 23-36.

69. While accepting in all its implications the criticism of the colonial and postcolonial history of the Third World, written from the outside looking in, I am not sure that the right approach, for a truly universal history, consists in restricting oneself to an insider's perspective, as is postulated by J. Chesnaux in his interesting article, "Pour une histoire asiatique de l'Asie moderne," *Diogène,* no. 55 (1966), pp. 110-126.

III Toward an Operational Theory
of Development

8   Why a Development Theory?

After pointing out so many of the distortions of the social sciences, their Europocentric limitations, and the tenacity of barriers between disciplines, have I the right to propose a general development theory, one which claims, moreover, to be operational? Should I not, on the contrary, abandon any attempt to be all-encompassing and, with realistic modesty, set the social sciences the thankless task of accumulating specialized knowledge and developing analytical tools for limited use, catering to the peculiarities of each individual case?

I do not think so, and I shall state my case in two ways: By trying, first of all, to show the central position occupied by development theory in the structure of the social sciences, and, second, by defining the particular features of an operational theory.

My explanation will be based on economics, but it applies, I believe, to all of the social sciences, especially since the concept of development extends far beyond the specific sphere of economics. Over and above the diversity of schools, it seems possible to make out in contemporary economic thought three major areas of concern (if one discounts all that relates to the apparatus, the "toolbox" which is drawn upon and added to according to the requirements of theoretical work.[1] In each of these areas, different paradigms (which amount to conceptual models) are used.[2]

First, economists are concerned with describing, with analyzing *the functioning of economies.* They do so at various levels, ranging from socioeconomic systems and the ways in which they individually function all the way through to the enterprise. And they attach a great deal of importance to the interlocking of these levels, which is why, in their writings, they make such a distinction between *macroeconomics* and *microeconomics.* The basic paradigm that they use is *organicist,* or if one prefers, *functionalist.* The socioeconomic structure is characterized on the basis of the mechanisms by which the system functions and on that of institutions, which, for the requirements of analysis, are assumed to be unchanging, so long as the model is in use. Feedbacks are considered only to the extent that they reestablish equilibrium, thereby ensuring the unchangeability of the model. This is certainly true of the theory of business cycles in capitalist systems; it always presupposes a return to the initial position, after more or less dramatic reversals.[3] Likewise, discussions of the different organizational models of the socialist economy do not introduce, in reality, any dynamic element capable of altering the paradigm. They are concerned, in fact, with the way in which certain mechanisms can be substituted for others, thus modifying the importance attributed to the market and to administrative decision making; but once established, the new model is supposed to stay as it is, until the next modification. As a matter of fact, it should be possible to conceive, in the manner of cybernetics, dynamic models of functioning in which an initial equilibrium between input and output and the resulting interplay of feedbacks would cause a change in the actual structure. Oskar Lange has attempted to do this, but his explanation is too general to be applied to a theory of economic function.[4]

Second, economists study *phenomena of growth,* which we may roughly describe as the increase of wealth as a result of the allocation of the product between investment and consumption. The paradigm applied here is mechanistic insofar as the growth of the product depends mostly on investment and it is possible, in principle, to quantify this relation.

The introduction of nonmaterial factors of growth, for instance, the training of the labor force, does not alter the paradigm, and a great deal of useless effort has been devoted to quantifying the impact of these other factors on the growth of the product. Economic activity is of course based on various forms of complementarity, the most important of which is that of capital and labor. As Paul Streeten recently pointed out, it is as daft to expect a violin to produce a melody without the collaboration of a violinist as it is to expect a violinist to play without a violin.[5] But it is the nature of growth theory to study the consequences of investment and to pursue its optimization, while allowing for the

constraints imposed by complementarity and the characteristic functioning of the economy under study. A satisfactory model of growth must
therefore take as its parameters the essential data provided by the
theory of economic function, or else fall prey to ahistoricity, limited to
a logical exercise devoid of social content. Growth theory in an advanced capitalist system must thus consider effective demand as a strategic variable, whereas in a socialist system it should, on the contrary,
attempt to explain limitations and bottlenecks in supply, since in
theory the problem of effective demand does not arise where there is
wage and price control.[6] Last, there should be a composite model for
underdeveloped mixed economies, showing, on the one hand, bottlenecks caused by underdevelopment of the means of production, and,
on the other, overproduction in specific sectors resulting both from
hypertrophy of certain industries and from underconsumption among
the greater part of the population caused by a very inequitable distribution of output.[7]

A close relationship is thus established between the theory of function and the theory of growth. The paradigms of these theories are
complementary. Growth is studied within structures the functioning
of which determines, to a great extent, the pace and the rate of quantitative change. It is possible to analyze modifications in the functioning of an economy resulting from its growth rate, and especially from
acceleration, and to ask what modifications become possible at a certain stage of growth. We thus touch on dynamics and at the same time
refer to a component of the process of development each time that we
speak of growth, that is to say, of a movement of the economy which
changes the volume of economic activity.

But is growth enough to explain development, a process which encompasses it and, at the same time, changes structures? To claim that
would be to take the part for the whole, or to postulate a crudely ma-
terialistic development theory in which qualitative changes would be
seen as strictly dependent on quantitative fluctuations; this is, basically,
the conception of Rostow and of authors, too many to mention, who

try to make laws of development out of laboriously calculated correlations between the level of per capita income and the most diverse variables, ranging from industrial production to newspaper consumption of newsprint.[8]

Economists have consequently been led to venture into a third field, that of *development theory,* which, as it were, encompasses and places within the same general framework theories of function and of growth and legitimizes them as incomplete but valid. This is not, strictly speaking, their field, since what is involved here is indeed world history.

One cannot have it both ways. History may be a science which can support all-embracing hypotheses on the functioning of societies. In this case the partial hypotheses of economists can be more or less ingeniously brought into line with an overall view of society and of the historical process. The choice of development goals is made on the basis of a scientific analysis of possible actions, which, moreover, in no way changes the political character of the choice itself; strict optimization of the development process is impossible when it comes up against the multiplicity of heterogeneous goals, against the absence of criteria of uniformity which would make it possible to scale calculations,[9] against the number of variables and the laws of development, which are tendentious at best.

Or perhaps history is not subject to laws, not even biased ones, and all forecasting becomes impossible. Economics and the social sciences would collapse, since they deal only with fragments of a reality which eludes scientific analysis and, ultimately, determines the future of these fragments, which are part of a global historical process. More precisely, our models for forecasting would be valid only insofar as it would be possible to isolate the fragment subjected to analysis, assuming the interplay of environmental variables and parameters to be negligible.[10] This would mean reducing the social sciences to very little: they could even be considered redundant in terms of action, either because they are seen to have no grasp of reality or because historical agnosticism is interpreted as an invitation to unbridled willfulness in political action.

Thus the social sciences have need of a development theory which can serve as their mainstay (at the very least, as their strongest theory in the sense that logicians give to this term) until growth, functioning, and development can be explained by a single set of equations, as is postulated, at an extremely abstract level, by systems theory.[11]

In view of the difficulty of the undertaking, it is not surprising that the most diverse hypotheses have been put forward, based on extremely different paradigms. In this connection, we should note the undeniable attraction of the dialectical paradigm as constructed by Marx. Although the Marxian theory of modes of production does not manage to resolve all the major problems of development and, in particular, to explain completely the transitions from one form to another, the explosion caused by contradictions in the system and their transformation into new contradictions at a specific moment,[12] it has the merit of posing those problems, by stressing the complex interplay of the different economic, social, and cultural variables. The narrow economic determinism which has so often been attributed to Marx (and which some Marxists have practiced) is but a crude distortion of his thinking, which is characterized by the refusal to divide the economic off from the social and by an attempt to apprehend the concrete social totality.[13]

The theory of modes of production, then, is merely a starting point for the more concrete study of development with these modes serving as categories of analysis and not as convenient pigeonholes for various historical cases.[14] Its paradigm is Marx's *Das Kapital,* interpreted as a model of the genesis and functioning of the capitalism of free competition, in Western Europe. It is at this level, or even at a level of greater specificity, that more and more studies of concrete models of development should be undertaken in order to arrive at a historical typology. This, I believe, would be the right path to follow.

First, because development theory cannot rise above the level of historical specificity, even by embracing historical materialism: the reason is that the laws with which the latter is concerned are, as I have already pointed out, tendentious, stochastic laws, based on the law of large numbers; but I am concerned with a very limited number of discrete cases and, consequently, it is impossible to deduce directly from such laws.

Second, the value of a rigorously applied and well-conceived comparative method should be stressed, since, for research workers in the social sciences, the only substitute for laboratory experiment is that afforded by journeys through time and space.

In short, development theory could take the form of a typology of the various paths of development, abstracted to models based on concrete situations, halfway between the excessive abstraction of the theory of socioeconomic systems and the total empiricism of case studies. It goes without saying that, conceived in this way, it should continually be changed, revising models as every day experience and the critical reflection to which it gives rise accumulate, grouping them together or splitting them off from each other according to requirements. What I am describing is a long and exacting program whose first stage seems to be historical study, carried out according to a methodology as uniform as possible and inspired by the desire to understand the process of development in global terms.

To what use could such a theory be put once it has been sketched out?

At the theoretical level, it would function as the mainstay of the social science system. At the operational level, its role would consist in inspiring the practitioner, not by supplying him with prescriptions for action, but by enriching his imagination and by helping him to ask the right questions, to see beyond the appearances of phenomena, and to define more clearly the possible instruments and the field of action. It is, moreover, the purpose of economic and social theories to call forth the right questions, to train research workers and practitioners in a mode of reasoning rather than to provide them with ready-made answers. At the most these theories may aspire to lay down certain standards for action, to judge of certain choices in advance, in the name of a social and ethical axiology that the theoretician should always endeavor to make explicit, if only for his own sake. That the right solution should be based on the specific character of each case in no way implies an excessive empiricism. A good number of failures in the application of the social sciences and their subsequent falling into disrepute are due to the unfortunate confusion between this faculty of the theory to provide an overall intellectual approach and the attempt to force an infinitely rich and sometimes baffling reality into the narrow framework of a pre-established model.

The use to which development theory may be put will consist in extracting from it—after it has been enriched by facts reduced to models— a consistent and complete set of questions useful in analyzing specific situations and in elaborating a strategy of structural change which may reasonably be carried out, with the means available. Comparative analysis will prove useful in enriching the sociological imagination, in defining the field of "likely possibilities" and the efficiency of the instruments used. In other words, development theory becomes operational by way of the methodology which underlies it and which it puts into practice. At the outset, the provisional synthesis based on scraps of knowledge and the elaboration of a methodology for the typological studies proposed above merge with each other.

Notes to Chapter 8

1. See the chapter on economics in the work already referred to, *Main Trends of Research in the Social and Human Sciences,* part 1 (The Hague, 1970).

2. I use the concept of "paradigm" in a sense fairly similar to that given it by Thomas Kuhn, in *The Structure of Scientific Revolutions* (Chicago, 1962).

3. There are few dynamic models which are also concerned with growth. Kalecki's is one of the best known; see M. Kalecki, *Theory of Economic Dynamics: An Essay on Cyclical and Long-Run Changes in the Capitalistic Economy* (London: 1956).

4. See Oskar Lange, *Wholes and Parts: A General Theory of Systems Behavior* (Warsaw, 1962).

5. P. Streeten in Myrdal, *Asian Drama* (New York, 1968), vol. 3, appendix 3, pp. 1953-1954.

6. See M. Kalecki's article already cited, "Theories of Growth in Different Social Systems," *Scientia* (May-June 1970).

7. See in this connection my study "Development Planning and Policies for Increasing Domestic Resources for Investment (with special reference to Latin America)," in United Nations, *Report on the Third Interregional Seminar on Development Planning,* Santiago, Chili, March 1968, pp. 154-186.

8. See, for a particularly preposterous example of this procedure, L. Zimmerman's article, "Are There Laws of Progress?" in *On Political Economy and Econometrics: Essays in Honour of Oskar Lange* (Warsaw, 1969), pp. 641-649.

9. In reading works on economic and social anthropology one realizes how difficult it is to formulate a homogeneous goal function, even in a "primitive" society.

10. See in this connection H. Liebenstein's very interesting article, "What Can We Expect from a Theory of Development," *Kyklos,* 19.1 (1966), p. 122.

11. See in this connection A. Rapoport, "Mathematical Aspects of General Systems Analysis," in UNESCO, *The Social Sciences, Problems and Orientations,* (Paris and The Hague, 1968), pp. 320-334.

12. W. Kula refers to this problem in the conclusion to his work, *Théorie économique du système féodal* (Paris, 1970).

13. See, among others, K. Kosik, *La Dialectique du Concret,* Paris 1970, and *L'explication dans les Sciences,* (Paris, 1973).

14. I refer the reader once again to the works by Hobsbawm already cited.

The Concept of Surplus and Its Applications

Surplus is not easily defined. When considered as the difference between production and consumption it becomes banal. If subsistence is substituted for consumption, that is to say, the consumption deemed necessary for maintaining the labor force, surplus becomes the measure of freedom in the allocation of the product. But subsistence does not lend itself very well to quantification, as the level of subsistence is a cultural concept, variable in space and time, implying value judgments in addition to physiological norms. This is especially true when the society is rich. In primitive and peasant societies, one can equate subsistence with the part of the product which is deducted by the direct producer to provide for his family, but the evaluation of "necessary" consumption in affluent societies can only be arbitrary. Moreover, a distinction should be drawn between the product which is actually produced and the potential product, which could be obtained if all the labor force and the idle capacities of production were used to the full.[1] Practically insurmountable difficulties stand in the way of calculating the potential surplus, since it can have any meaning only in the context of a detailed analysis of potential supply and actual demand, which implies the existence of efficient planning.

All the same, as Joan Robinson has observed, people generally know the difference between the necessary and the superfluous,[2] between bread and butter. From the classical writers right up to the neo-Marxists, the concept of surplus owes its heuristic value and indeed its career to this simple and fundamental distinction between that which is necessarily earmarked for consumption by the producers, to ensure their survival, and that which remains for various uses: between the part of the product whose fate has been predetermined and the part which ensures (and at the same time measures) freedom of choice between conspicuous individual consumption, mass consumption, investment, which is a way of expanding future choices, or leisure.

This distinction should not be taken too literally. There is a margin of choice implied in the very concept of subsistence and, for class societies, the balance of power between those who govern and those who are governed has often led to fluctuations in the level of subsistence, those who are governed endeavoring to raise it and those who govern being divided between the desire to corner a large surplus and the fear of compromising the productivity of the system. Furthermore, choices among conspicuous individual consumption, mass consumption, investment, or leisure rarely take the form of clear choices on account of their complexity: the mediation of the whole social organization is involved and, what is more, the comparing of present and future advantages is always a risky enterprise. Ultimately, these options reflect the deep-seated characteristics of the social system and are backed by cultural and even religious sanction. That is why the study of the allocation surplus is so valuable. Without being a determinant of the system in the strict sense, it is a very good index of it and—in spite of the imprecision mentioned above—surplus thus becomes a central category of economic history[3] and anthropology and, of course, of development theory. For development can in fact be defined as a transformation of structures making it possible for surplus to be used for purposes consciously chosen by society.

I think that the simplest way to define the concept of surplus more clearly is to begin with the case of a "primitive" and classless economy.[4]

Let us take the example of a society providing L_1 working days yearly and producing, by means of a given technique, T_1 product units. We shall assume this society to have only simple tools and limited access to natural resources. Consequently, additional quantities of work L performed according to the same technique and with the same equipment will yield diminishing returns until production reaches a maximum T_m. Thus, for instance, we may assume that the cultivation of marginal land produces increasingly smaller crops, on account of the increasingly poor quality of the land available; in other words, we accept the praxeological explanation of the law of diminishing returns according to which rationality consists in cultivating the most fertile land until it is exhausted and then going on to less fertile land (this line of reasoning presupposes,

however, a minimal knowledge of soil science for the result to correspond to the intention).[5]

We shall consider variations in climatic conditions in the same way
as changes of techniques. Thus, L_1 days of work will produce T'_1 units
in an exceptionally good year and T''_1 units in an exceptionally bad
year. We shall assume, finally, that "subsistence" consumption C is proportional to the number of days of work put in and that at any moment
it is lower than the product, that is to say that there is a surplus; this
hypothesis is in accordance with the results of a great deal of anthropological research. These assumptions are represented graphically by
figure 2.

In the course of a normal year, we have a surplus in the form of the
material product $T_1 C_1$. It is to be observed that, in order to provide
for subsistence consumption $L_1 C_1$ it would have been enough for our

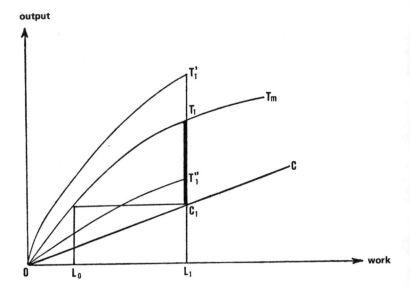

Figure 2

society to put in OL_0 days of work. It would thereby have gained L_0L_1 days of "leisure." This is the first choice possible between surplus in the form of product and a certain quantity of free time. Michael Sahlins has described as the first affluent society certain populations of hunters and food-gatherers for whom a few hours of daily work on the part of the adult men are enough to provide amply for the food requirements of the community.[6] At first glance, these populations are already confronted by the Veblenian alternative of choosing between "conspicuous leisure" and "conspicuous consumption."[7]

This, however, is to judge by appearances. The nomadic life style imposes leisure rather than the production of "durable" consumer goods, which it is difficult for men to transport on their backs as they follow the wild animals they hunt. But it so happens that we are dealing with a case where living conditions are particularly restrictive. The choice between the material product and leisure may, on the other hand, arise in fact in all situations where the production techniques employed do not univocally determine the ways in which the surplus is allocated, especially when the product is undiversified and exchange with the outside world of surpluses of local products for goods of a different kind is not easy. The option of voluntarily limiting material consumption in order to mete out the maximum available time for other activities—which we wrongly call "leisure activities" (wrongly since they often have great social significance)—may perhaps shock our "acquisitive" mentality, but it merely prefigures a fundamental choice for the society of tomorrow. Strictly speaking, there is no choice for leisure but for an allocation of surplus in the form of time for activities other than work which is directly productive of material assets.

This said, what are the main uses to which surplus is put in a primitive society?

First of all, a considerable proportion of free time and material surplus is devoted to the different ceremonies   and community events whose purpose is to reinforce the social fabric and to ensure the functioning of the system. The importance accorded to ceremonial observances in which goods which have been accumulated over a long period are destroyed (potlatch) has been well studied.

Then, mention should be made of expenditure on religion and magic which are all the more esteemed in that they are considered to be a component of, if not a substitute for, production techniques.[8] Artistic activity is closely bound up with magic. The material means necessary for artistic production are rudimentary, but it so happens that entire populations indulge in this activity, devoting a great deal of time to it. The amazing achievements of so-called primitive art are to be explained by the conjunction of three factors: the nonexistence of specifically material barriers to the expansion of artistic activity; the importance enjoyed by such activity in primitive societies; the selection of talent made possible by the widespread practice of the arts. No modern society can be compared, from this point of view, with certain tribes where practically all children and adults indulge in artistic creation and take a keen pleasure in aesthetic discussions; nowhere else is such a relatively large and "expert" public to be found.[9]

What remains of surplus in material form is: (1) stored for use in times of possible shortage (amounting to a redistribution of consumption over time); (2) exchanged for goods not produced by the society and therefore consumed, invested, or hoarded after having been physically transformed; (3) hoarded, be it as objects or animals the possession of which confers a particular status and the ceremonial exchange of which is provided for on certain occasions (kula, but also marriage dowry)—another way of using surplus in order to ensure social cohesiveness; or (4) invested.

This list of different possible uses suggests—and this is confirmed by anthropological studies—that net investment, narrowly defined as a change in technology resulting in greater labor productivity and, consequently, in an increase in per capita surplus, other conditions remaining equal, is of only marginal importance in primitive economies. If investment does take place, it is as a means of coping with demographic pressure, which gives rise in the long run to important changes in the techniques used. In particular, hunting, food-gathering and nomadic burning of cultivation require a high land/population ratio. Once population density goes beyond a certain threshold, techniques of sedentary agricultural production must be used, characterized by lower productivity *of labor* but enabling a larger population to be accommodated within a territory by means of a higher productivity *per acre.*[10]

The next stage may involve moving on to irrigated farming. This ensures both higher land and labor productivity but it calls for an initial investment involving a whole valley and therefore entails going beyond a threshold of demographic density and social organization. The three techniques are compared in figure 3, where T_1 = nomadic burning cultivation, T_2 = nonirrigated farming, T_3 = irrigated farming.

In opposition to the *accumulative* model which assigns a large part of the surplus to net investment and thus gives rise to a cumulative process of growth, ultimately taking the form of an increase in all the ways of enjoying the product, we shall say that our model is *dissipative,* without giving any ethical value to this adjective. Accelerated growth, which does not subsume development in the broad sense of the word, but underlies it and constitutes the necessary condition for it, presupposes the transition from the *dissipative* model to the *accumulative* model. This is an extremely difficult process in that it implies changing the entire behavior of the society, reflected in the very way in which the surplus is used.

What conditions are necessary to channel a more substantial part of the surplus into investment and to start a cumulative process that would allow surplus to snowball? Is it enough to provide access to the market, by setting up the infrastructure, and to ensure reasonable terms of trade while presenting the population with the model of consumption in acquisitive societies? Or is there a psychological threshold to be crossed, a cultural transformation to be made?

I am touching here on the central problem of development policies. Consequently, I do not want to abandon my model of primitive economies without raising a question, an ethical one this time: do we have

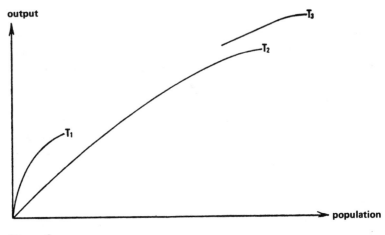

Figure 3

the right to impose from outside—or even to induce—this change in the system of surplus allocation?

Many anthropologists reply in the negative, in the name of cultural equality and on account of the impossibility of constructing a uniform scale of comparison to show the direction of "progress," and, *a fortiori,* to quantify it. While I recognize the generosity of this attitude, my position is more subtle. I believe that henceforth it will no longer be possible to avoid the ascendancy of a universal system of material values, with regard to certain of man's basic needs in the areas of health, nutrition, housing, and education. In these basic areas, rational consumer norms must be applied to mankind as a whole. These standards may vary within certain limits, according to local requirements and traditions.[11] But it is all too easy to use the respect that ethnologists recommend as an excuse for perpetrating blatant inequalities in the distribution of the world's wealth. However, the study of primitive societies and of the extreme variety of their organizational forms should at the same time convince us of the limitations of the acquisitive society. The latter transforms a means into an end; accumulation becomes the supreme principle of rationality. For the variety of social forms are substituted standardization and one-dimensionality, concealed by the apparent sovereignty of the consumer and the allurements of conspicuous consumption, which goes hand in hand with an immense wasting of public resources, armaments being accorded pride of place in the long-term economic policies of the big powers. But development should have other aims and in particular that of constructing a richer and more balanced civilization in which surplus would be used for purposes other than that of simply increasing wealth and overfeeding individual spending power, which is often inequitably distributed. These are the two prevalent features of the *accumulative-dissipative* model of affluent societies.

Will socialism be capable of one day transcending this model and offering a real and attractive solution, combining well-being with common sense? The question is posed in practical terms by both the invasion of Czechoslovakia and by the Chinese schism, which constitutes a basic censure of a Soviet society heading toward the acquisitive model of individual consumption, accompanied by the wasting of public funds for the sake of prestige, for instance, in the race to the moon (from which sin, moreover, China is not exempt, while the superpowers seem irremediably attached to it). But until such time as China becomes more wealthy and less regimented and can aspire to put itself forward as a model, we must say that the Chinese, by advocating egalitarian frugality, are turning necessity into a virtue and trying to make the best of their economic underdevelopment.

Let us now tackle one of the initial hypotheses of our model, the nonexistence of social classes. The capacity of direct producers to provide for their own consumption and still to produce a surplus (or to provide a certain additional quantity of labor) is indeed at the basis of the social division into classes of producers and nonproducers. How do

the latter acquire the right to benefit from the surplus? Was it originally a payment for the protection provided by the warriors against attack
from neighboring tribes, or for the services of priests and magicians
(who possessed what we see as a pseudo-technique but which, in the
eyes of those concerned, truly constituted a component of the techniques of production), or for the administration of communal activities
by the chiefs of the community? Or was it a tribute paid to conquerors? All these hypotheses have been put forward at one time or
another by historians and anthropologists and all are accurate, probably, for there is no reason to believe that the transition from a classless society to a differentiated society occurs everywhere in the same
way. The processes are sometimes sudden, sometimes gradual, unfold-
ing within the very varied framework of so-called primitive social organizations. What they all have in common is that they use the surplus for
consumption by one or several classes of nonproducers. Insofar as this
right is legitimized by services rendered, what is involved is a social division of labor. If, on the contrary, appropriation takes place in the
name of a divine right, or of a birthright, or of the right of the strongest,
taking the form of extortion to benefit a parasitic class (in the form of
taxes, forced or menial labor or booty) we are looking at different
forms of regimes based on social inequality. The way in which the allocation of surplus is organized and the uses to which it is put by the
dominant class and the state which it manages, are a characteristic index, and the economic history of class societies may therefore begin
with the analysis of the surplus production, appropriation, and uses.
The further away we get from primitive society, the more our model
becomes dissipative, this time in the pejorative sense of the word, because a large part of the surplus is set apart to be lavishly consumed by
the overlords and for prestige investments—pyramids, palaces, cathedrals. The efficiency of the system of extortion is paralleled by the
wretchedness of the producers and the ostentation of the courts, the
splendor of monuments to the glory of monarchs and gods.

   After the change brought about by incipient capitalism, the model becomes accumulative. The surplus accumulates in the hands of the owners of the means of production and not in those of the direct producers, who have become proletarians: extortion takes the form of the gain in value, that is to say, the difference between added value and the wages of the workers who create that value. The central position of the concept of gain in value in Marx's analysis of capitalism is too well known for me to have to dwell on it. Socialist regimes have not broken with the accumulative model, but surplus, instead of accumulating in the form of profit in the hands of the capitalists, remains at the government's disposal and therefore at the disposal of the community insofar as the government represents it.

With regard to development theory, the foregoing considerations underline the importance of the income distribution. But it is not enough to propose, as do numerous economists and politicians in the Third World, that surplus be tapped to serve development. There is a need, at the same time, to analyze the implications of the social cost of development as it affects different classes of society and to clarify assumptions about the allocation of surplus among the established social classes and the government. There cannot be a neutral program here. Not to change anything in the existing mechanisms of distribution amounts in fact, in mixed economies, to bestowing further privileges on those who are already privileged, to favoring the concentration of wealth in their hands. The often-advanced thesis according to which one should wait for the poor countries to become richer before taking steps to ensure a more equitable distribution of income is not very convincing: it is based on the idea that the unequal distribution of income favors accumulation and investments by capitalists and, consequently, acceleration of the growth rate. This point of view is not confirmed by the facts: an increase in profits does not necessarily incite capitalists to invest rather than to consume, nor, when they decide to invest, to do so in their own countries; nor, above all, to finance priority projects. As Myrdal has shown, egalitarianism could, on the contrary, become a powerful springboard for development.[12]

The role of various classes and of the state in the distribution and use of surplus, in an underdeveloped mixed economy, may be subjected to a detailed empirical analysis, based on a composite model of the relations of production. Here are the general guidelines of such an analysis.

I shall distinguish between two sectors: the traditional, t, and the modern, m, itself divided into three subsectors: domestic capitalist *(mc)*, foreign capitalist *(me)* and public capitalist *(mg)*. My division of the economy into t and m does not signify acceptance of a mechanistic version of the dualism which sees juxtaposed independent entities as two sectors. I wish, on the contrary, to stress the relations of dependency between t and m. I shall consequently define t as the part of the economy in which precapitalist relations of production still prevail (including small-scale peasant and artisanal production). The dividing line will therefore not be between agriculture and industry, between rural areas and towns, between production for export or for the domestic market, although the great majority of traditional producers live in the country and in small towns. Nor can this line be marked out on a map, for elements of t and m coexist, as I have already pointed out, within the same village and even within the same peasant farm, where a cash crop produced with the help of paid laborers and using industrial inputs and advanced techniques (therefore forming part of m) may exist alongside traditional farming, oriented primarily toward private consumption and based on family labor. Doubtless this peasant agriculture will in the end be integrated into the capitalist economy, but it has not been yet, and my analytical ability would be reduced if I were at this early stage to cast aside the distinctions proposed here. The specific characteristic of the capitalist system is that it places under its control, in order to exploit them, precapitalist modes of production; ossifies them and perpetuates them; and sometimes even creates them from scratch.

A typology of colonialism could be constructed on such considerations, without, however, giving way to the exaggerated view which sees everywhere in the Third World, right from the origin of colonization, the world capitalist system in operation. The sugar produced in Brazil in the sixteenth and seventeenth centuries was already incorporated into the system of world capitalist trade. But the mode of production, in the strict sense, was based on slavery, whereas the superstructure transplanted from Portugal was distinctly "feudal." Similarly, it is in the transplantation of the Spanish feudal structure into Argentina, for instance, that one should probably seek one of the reasons for this country's dropping behind after the Second World War, in relation to such countries as Australia or Canada. It should be pointed out, finally, that, in the colonial countries, capitalism developed most rapidly not in places where it was introduced in enclaves, but wherever the small-scale local producers were given the opportunity to be integrated into the world market by the mechanism of a very unequal trade that was admittedly unequal and resulted in substantial profits for European traders, but sufficiently attractive to bring about a capitalist transformation of the rural areas, when feudal structures did not stand in the way. This could be said, in particular, of Nigeria or Ghana.

What occurs when landowners are confronted with the following choices: to consume, to buy additional lands, to improve agricultural production, to invest in the cities, to use their money abroad, to hoard it in jewels or gold? Conspicuous consumption among the great absentee landowners is commonly observed in the countries of the Third World. There is purchase of new lands. In overpopulated countries it is often the indebted peasant who is forced to sell his land. In this case, the sum that he receives goes into the hands of another landowner, or of a moneylender, if those are not one and the same person. Sometimes the property deed is simply changed in order to make good a debt, in which case the surplus formerly loaned by the lord to the peasant and increased by the interest charged on it returns to him in the form of land. There are, of course, cases of land being sold by the lord to the peasants in plots, generally at very favorable prices, before the big landowner invests in industry or real estate and the construction business in town, or more rarely in the modernization of agriculture. The money used for these purchases comes then from rural people with some savings (the few wealthier peasants who buy lands) and from city people when the land is used for suburban housing tracts.

The major landowners rarely invest in agriculture, and this may be explained by the conjunction of two factors: the comfortable level of income provided by traditional farming (based more often than is suggested by statistics on de facto sharecropping, without security of tenure for the peasant) and the higher yield of investments such as real estate speculation, the building of apartments in cities, or foreign trade. In short, there is little chance that the modernization of agriculture will be achieved by what Lenin called the Prussian way, meaning the transformation of the major traditional landowners into capitalist entrepreneurs. While it is possible today to observe an undeniable rise of agrarian capitalism in the Third World[13]—from the combined effect of the outlets created by urbanization and inflationary prices, of the many favors bestowed on agriculture by the governments of the Third World, and of the supply of industrial inputs and new technologies made possible by the progress of industrialization—this rural revolution seems to be taking place above all to the advantage of a small minority of rich peasants, capable of shaking themselves free of the grip of the moneylending tradesman, or of people from the cities: immigrants, retired civil servants, retired officials. For these people it is more profitable to invest in agriculture than in trade, property, or small industry. One's attention is drawn to isolated cases, in the vicinity of large towns, where the operation becomes even more profitable than moneylending, provided that one specializes in poultry production, vegetable gardening, and fruit crops. To this list of promoters and beneficiaries of the "green revolution" should be added powerful capitalist enterprises, generally connected with the food industry. But the major traditional landowners seem to be the last to perceive these new opportunities. Psychologically, this is understandable, for their way of looking at things is still dominated by the traditional framework, and the high level of their income acts as a screen.

However, in spite of a basic structural relationship which is unfavorable to agricultural prices (rarely attaining world averages in the Third World, while industrial prices are usually higher by a margin of 100 percent and more), it is not all sure that the profitability of industrial investment is greater than that of modern agriculture, especially in periods of inflation when agricultural prices rise more quickly than industrial prices. But there is a certain prestige attached to industry. This provides an opportunity to give an economic foundation and a pretext to the permanent presence in the city of the absentee landowner. Above all, the wide-ranging social contacts maintained by the members of the landowning oligarchies and their influence over governments enable them to call on large public funds for all industrial investment. And as these funds are obtained under preferential conditions, the profit rate skyrockets in relation to the fraction of capital proper. Investments abroad, which entail a transfer of economic resources, are, sad to say, frequent, for the traditional oligarchies fear political changes which would be unfavorable to them.

Finally, hoarding is a common phenomenon in many Third World countries. Insofar as this involves the purchase of gold produced abroad (and often smuggled in, thereby doubling its local price in relation to world rates, as is the case in India), once again there is a transfer of surplus to foreign countries, with the difference, theoretical as it may be, that the hoarded gold may at any moment create a demand on the market, whereas the withdrawal of capital illegally invested abroad is more complicated and less probable.

Thus, the part of the surplus which goes to the landowners is to a large extent wasted and used in a way which does not serve the development of the national economy. A certain amount of investment in the urban economy and in industry especially does, however, take place, and its importance cannot be underestimated for the political analysis of class relations. Indeed, the rigid view which holds that landowners oppose the bourgeoisie does not correspond, in the majority of cases, to anything real; in fact, firmly established personal alliances exist between these categories.

Another part of the surplus produced by the peasant is cornered by the moneylender or the local tradesman, often one and the same person, not to mention the case, frequent in Latin America, where the landowner supervises commercial operations, since the plantation hands and sharecroppers are forced to get their supplies in the shop which he runs. The local dealer has to transfer a part of what he charges to the major commercial companies, situated in the modern sector. He is in fact their agent, and they are the ones who benefit most from exchanges between t and m, to such an extent that it is possible to speak of a veritable domestic colonial pact. In my opinion, accumulated profits in the m sector, at the expense of t, partly explain the apparently very high rate of surplus in m. There remains, however, enough for the moneylender-*cum*-dealer to enlarge his inventory and his lending capital. Peasants, in general, resort to borrowing only in distress or in delicate ceremonial situations such as marriages or funerals. For no investment, except perhaps the purchase of livestock without which the farm cannot function and, of course, of seed, can warrant the paying of the interest rate demanded by the moneylender. Furthermore, this rate is not fixed and is adjusted, from year to year, according to the prospects of the person in debt, it usually being in the moneylender's interest to ensure that his debtor does not actually die of hunger (unless he decides to force him off his land in payment for his debts). This flexibility and the total absence of other forms of social assistance in the event of famine or other misfortunes explain the persistence of the phenomenon of moneylending in the t sector.[14] The part of the surplus which remains in the hands of the moneylender is, by and large, lost to investment, and the flexibility of moneylending rates explains why, in the end, the peasant is left year after year without any resources to invest—apart from investment in the form of labor, an impact which may acquire a certain importance although, generally, it is not included in statistics.

Finally, for the sake of completeness, I should mention the part of the surplus which accrues to the state in taxes. In most Third World countries, state revenues deriving from taxes paid by the t sector are small and are not sufficient to pay for public investment in the economic and social infrastructure of the rural areas.

I shall now go on to the m sector. The private capitalist sector mc uses the surplus which it produces and which it appropriates to finance the capitalists' conspicuous consumption and for investment. The lifestyle model proposed by the rich countries in conjunction with the tradition of lavish consumption subscribed to by the landowning oligarchies results in consumer patterns which are diametrically opposed to the model of frugality and thrift peculiar to European (and American) capitalism in its early days. What remains to be invested, after this expenditure, goes in part toward unbridled property speculation, toward import and export business (and therefore to an increase of working capital) and toward investments abroad. Accumulation actually translated into industrial and agricultural investment is therefore fairly restricted and, what is more, is filtered through the open market, which favors investments with a high profit-earning profile: it is rare, as we shall see, for these to coincide with social priorities. It is often said that the countries of the Third World accumulate little because they are poor. In absolute terms, this is a banal statement. In relative terms, it does not correspond to reality. Accumulation rates are sometimes fairly high; the trouble is that the accumulated resources are badly used. If my analysis is correct, to claim that it should be made easier for capitalists to make profits so as to speed up growth is truly an act of faith in the virtues of the abstract model of capitalism of free competition. This is to disregard completely the reality which surrounds us, for it is possible to criticize the functioning of mc solely from the point of view of the mechanism of accumulation and the subsequent utilization of resources—that is to say, without even bringing principles of social justice into it.

The *me* sector presents a serious dilemma. Two mutually exclusive choices confront it: either it transfers its profits abroad, which is equivalent to a net loss of resources for the country; or it reinvests them, in which case there is a danger, in view of the unequal relations of power between *mc* and *me,* that *mc* will become subordinated to *me* and then become progressively denationalized. This phenomenon is beginning to concern public opinion in the Third World. The conglomerates and foreign companies generally, indoctrinated in new management techniques which tend to diversify activities, are presently buying many enterprises belonging to capitalists in the Third World. In extreme cases none of the benefits which are supposed to result from the investing of foreign capital materialize: production techniques are not modernized, access to foreign markets is not obtained, the initial risk and the promotional effort are borne by the local capitalists. On the other hand, the modern industrial sector is increasingly dominated by foreigners. Insofar as transactions are made with profits already accumulated locally by foreign capital, at the outset a part of the surplus of *me* is therefore transferred into the hands of the local capitalists (which brings us back to the possibilities examined for *mc*); *me* acquires in exchange a permanent right to repatriate (or to reinvest) more profits subsequently. The effect of this steady accumulation of rights by *me* over the meager foreign exchange available in the Third World countries can only be disastrous in the long run, unless foreign investment gives rise to exports that make substantial earnings in foreign exchange. And this argument is valid even when there is, at the starting point, an inflow of foreign capital. It is often said that direct investments are good for business in the countries which receive them since they do not have to pay back the capital, as is the case with credit. This argument is fallacious on two counts. It overlooks the fact that credit creates liabilities only for a determined period of time. Moreover, all the calculations show that the annual servicing of direct foreign investments is more onerous than that of the debt contracted in credit, for the profit margins are established at a higher level than that of interest rates for international loans.

From this short discussion three conclusions may be drawn.

1. The expansion of the subsector *me* should be limited and subordinated to other forms of recourse to foreign capital—loans from multilateral sources; if need be, bilateral loans; and finally, participation of foreign capital in joint ventures for a limited time period, repayable from the profits (or in products) of the enterprises thus created. Arrangements such as these, often discussed by U.N.C.T.A.D., are being applied in the relations between industrialized countries and socialist countries of Eastern Europe. It is difficult to see why the industrial powers should discriminate between the countries of the Third World and the socialist countries.

2. The expropriation of foreign capital should limit it to sums which have actually come into the country, increased by a legally fixed profit. In compensation, additional profits should be treated on an equal footing with domestic private capital, thus guaranteeing property rights for foreign capitalists but limiting the volume of transfers abroad. Measures such as these have been attempted at various times in Argentina and Brazil without much effect; the idea is, however, a good one, and if it were applied at the same time by several Third World countries, the chances are that foreign firms would have to adapt to such measures.

3. Finally, at the political level, enterprises in *me,* as indeed in *mc,* should be taxed at the highest acceptable rate, for this implies a transfer of surplus *mg,* which may, at least in theory, use it in such a way as to promote the desired development policy. Indeed, *mg* has at its disposal the surplus produced by public enterprises and small quantities of surplus transferred from *t, mc,* and *me* by fiscal mechanisms, and these resources finance both the current expenditure of the administration and the public investment. But there is also the possibility of creating a surplus by deficit financing of investments, which should not cause inflation as long as there are idle capacities in the economy, and insofar as supply adapts itself to increased demand within a short period. This is the case in certain countries of the Third World, and the "green

revolution" should enable them to make use more and more frequently of public works and to expand social services by resorting to deficit financing.

Those who are opposed to the expansion of *mg* claim that the public funds are eaten up by an overstaffed administration. This is doubtless so, but is the private sector more efficient? The argument that the private entrepreneurs make large profits from their operations is not in itself very convincing since the system of imperfect competition and of price control makes it possible to pass high costs on to the consumer. One could say that the entrepreneur who is satisfied with a "fair" make-up makes more the more inefficient he is and the higher his costs are. Furthermore, the profit earning capacity of the private sector is increased by tax fraud and by transfers (inadequately studied and difficult to comprehend through statistics) of public funds to *mc* and *me*, in the form of bank loans under preferential conditions, not to mention other advantages granted to private industrialists by the government. All these factors make the private sector appear more efficient than it is in reality.

Nor can one conclude anything from the frequent deficits of public enterprises, for often what is involved here is a policy of subsidies to the rest of the economy, implemented by a low price for public services. In short, the bureaucratic obstacles and the inadequate organization of the public sector constitute a barrier to development; but once the administrative difficulties have been overcome, it can be run according to plan. In the confrontation with private capitalism, all that the government has at its disposal are various means of persuasion and discussion, the effect of which is never certain.

I shall now return once again to the concept of surplus, but this time in a different context. I shall take the case of a closed economy: the surplus of foodstuffs extorted or purchased from the peasants determines the size of the urban population. The division of labor between rural areas and cities, and more generally between agriculture and nonagricultural professions, is determined by this agricultural surplus. In this sense, the rate of progress of agriculture has determined the appearance and the development of other, often more productive, activities, which are held back by the shortage of provisions for nonagricultural workers. The bottleneck in the supply of foodstuffs can be eliminated by foreign trade, but I have chosen the hypothesis of a closed economy in order to grasp more clearly the importance of available agricultural surplus in development strategy.

Certainly, this surplus should find its way to the cities and to the building sites of public works, assuming that the development program entails a certain amount of human investment. But it is in no way necessary for it to correspond to an economic surplus taken away from the peasants. Food supplies can very easily take the form of sales, the economic counterpart of which is the supply of artisanal and industrial goods sought by the peasants. An element of taxation could still be incorporated in this exchange—by taking advantage of the ratio of industrial prices to agricultural prices, if the former were raised by means of a high value-added tax on all consumer goods considered nonessential.

However, there has often been an unfortunate confusion between these two types of surplus, there still being a great temptation to kill two birds with one stone and to burden the peasants with a large tax in kind. Socialist theoreticians such as Preobrazhensky,[15] as well as those who advocate the Japanese capitalist model for the Third World, stress the need for capital accumulation at the expense of the peasants, who form the overwhelming majority of the populations of underdeveloped countries. This, in my opinion, is a dangerous thesis on account of its social consequences; and, what is more, it is theoretically false. History seems to have shown Bukharin to have been in the right when he opposed the ideas of Preobrazhensky. Soviet agriculture was ruined for a long time by hasty collectivization, whereas it could probably have developed fairly well through commercial exchange between cities and rural areas, directed by a government with a monopsony on the purchase of important agricultural products, exercising direct control over the prices of goods bought by the peasants, and endowed with means of action in the form of advance purchase contracts drawn up with producers, credit for production and investment, and a network of trade and service cooperatives. The peasant family farms would have been gradually led toward socialist forms of agriculture—the way being paved for collectivization by the experience of association with the government and the cooperatives and made both possible and necessary beforehand by the industrialization of agricultural production. The placing of the land under common ownership would then have occurred as the last and not the first step toward the socialization of agriculture.[16]

As to the supposed applicability of the Japanese model, reference should be made once again to Ishikawa's important study,[17] in which he has endeavored to show that in the countries of Southeast Asia there is no way of providing an economic boost without a flow of exogenous investments in agriculture, on top of what the peasants might be able to invest by themselves. At the beginning of the Meiji era, Japan was in a quite different situation, as it had already accomplished a great deal of work on its agricultural infrastructure. Furthermore, Ishikawa considers that the net contribution of agriculture to the financing of Japanese industrialization has not attained the proportions commonly attributed to it.

Moreover, may one not cast doubt on the very idea of the need for a preliminary capital accumulation, in the context of a development program directed by the government? There is no reason to extrapolate in this way on the basis of the historical model of capitalist accumulation. The government can easily create at least a part of savings, as it invests, by juggling with prices and taxes and by resorting, if necessary, to deficit financing whenever there are savings made unproductive by hoarding or whenever there are idle capacities of production capable of meeting the additional demand thus created. In particular, the only limit to the rise of employment is the supply of essential goods, and as Kalecki has shown, the problems of financing development amount to adequate supply of these goods and to the availability of foreign exchange to pay for the necessary imports.[18]

In short, we may conclude that the agricultural surplus should be seen as playing an important part in development strategy, apart, however, from the problem of mobilizing the economic surplus.

Notes to Chapter 9

1. The concept of potential surplus was first suggested by P. Baran in *The Political Economy of Growth* (New York, 1954).

2. Joan Robinson, *Freedom and Necessity* (London, 1970), p. 25.

3. It was Engels above all who insisted on the importance of this concept; see *Anti-Dühring* (French edition; Paris, 1950), pp. 214, 225.

4. I have dwelt on this problem at greater length in the article already cited, "La notion de surplus et son application aux économies primitives," *L'Homme,* July-September 1966.

5. For a behavioral interpretation of the law of diminishing returns, see Oskar Lange, *Political Economy* (London, 1963).

6. Michael Sahlins, *Stone-Age Economies* (Chicago, 1972).

7. See Thorstein Veblen, *Theory of the Leisure Class* (French edition; Paris, 1970).

8. See, for instance, B. Malinowski, *Argonauts of the Western Pacific* (London, 1922), and Raymond Firth, *Human Types: An Introduction to Social Anthropology* (New York, 1958).

9. I deal briefly with this subject in the essay entitled "L'Art primitif: Le point de vue de l'économiste," in *Echanges et Communications: Mélanges offerts à Claude Lévi-Strauss à l'occasion de son 60e anniversaire* (The Hague, 1970).

10. See Esther Boserup, *Conditions of Agricultural Growth: The Economics of Agrarian Change under Population Pressure* (Chicago, 1965).

11. The normative approach to environmental problems is recommended in K. W. Kapp, "Environmental Disruption: General Issues and Methodological Problems," in *Environmental Disruption*, pp. 3-22). This point of view can easily be given a more general application. See also, for a clarification of the

choices of services considered essential in a given society, J. M. Colette, *Etude sur les systèmes de décision* (United Nations; Geneva, 1970).

12. See Gunnar Myrdal, *Asian Drama* (New York, 1968), vol. 2, chapt. 16, and *The Challenge of World Poverty* (New York, 1970).

13. This phenomenon has even been observed in India; see D. Thorner, "New Class Rises in Rural India," *The Statesman* (New Delhi, 1-4 (November 1967).

14. I have already referred to this phenomenon; chapter 6, note 16.

15. E. Preobrazhensky, *New Economics* (New York, 1965); consulted in the French edition, *La nouvelle economique* (Paris, 1966). For the debate between Preobrazhensky and Bukharin, see W. Brus, *The Market in a Socialist Economy* (London, 1972).

16. This is a summary of the main points of J. Tepicht's analysis, *Doswiadozenia i perspektywy rolnictwa* (Warsaw, 1961); see also, by the same author, "L'agriculture paysanne et le développement de l'économie polonaise," *Etudes rurales,* nos. 25-26 (January-June, 1967), pp. 41-49, and *Marxisme et agriculture: Le paysan polonais* (Paris, 1973).

17. See S. Ishikawa, *Economic Development in Asian Perspective* (New York, 1967).

18. M. Kalecki, "Problems of Financing Economic Development in a Mixed Economy," in *Essays on Planning and Economic Development* (Warsaw, 1965), vol. 2, pp. 37-50.

10   The Illusion of Spontaneous Development

The distribution and the use of surplus in underdeveloped mixed economies reveal the enormous social wastage involved in their functioning and provide *a contrario* justification for planning backed by vigorous interventionism. And yet there are many who still believe in the virtues of development through the free play of market forces, aided, at the very most, here and there, by half-hearted and, as it were, hobbled government intervention.

Planning, it is true, experienced a great vogue some time ago in the countries of the Third World under the combined influence of the Soviet model, the French *plans indicatifs,* and the publicity given to India's second five-year plan. The Kennedy administration went so far as to impose the hasty formulation of pseudoplans on Latin-American governments wishing to obtain aid from the United States, within the framework of the Alliance for Progress. This represented quite a shift from official American doctrine in the first decade after the war, when planning and agrarian reform were almost synonyms of Communism.

Since then, pseudoplans have met with a large number of failures, doubtless because several leaders of the newly-independent countries made them into an instrument of ideology, a declaration of intent promising here and now the realization of all hopes. Was this not a sort of magical incantation? It was enough to write something down on paper for all wishes to be granted. The formulation of unreal plans has even become in some cases an excuse for not tackling those thorny problems of economics which should be the main concern of all planning worthy of the name.[1]

Formalization, the sophistication of methods, the mirage of easy planning where all that one has to do is push the button of the computer—the "thinking machine"—have added to the confusion. And all this has been aided and abetted by Soviet planners, who, for political reasons, have pretended to believe in the pseudoplans drawn up in the friendly capitals of the Third World. The doctrine proclaiming the lack of viability of any attempt at economic progress, outside of an economy entirely under government control, was put into cold storage. But as the orthodox Marxists continued to affirm that it was impossible for the countries of the Third World to develop in the capitalist ways, it became necessary, in order to remove the contradiction, to invent the "noncapitalist way." This ill-defined and purposely vague concept took in various hybrid forms of state capitalism which went arm in arm with bureaucratic capitalism and which were grouped under the banner of socialism, generally accompanied by a "national" adjective.

When several regimes which were considered to be left-wing collapsed, the right, in the Third World countries and in the West, seized the opportunity to discredit at one and the same time socialism and planning. The situation was compounded by the fact that India, for a long time considered to be a laboratory of planning, found itself confronted with a difficult economic situation,[2] contrasting with the economic growth of a country like Mexico, which had never embarked on planning to such a far-ranging extent. Of course, such comparisons never take into account the differences between the initial situations and available resources. They nonetheless capture the public imagination. Despite these failures, a decisive stage in making the very idea of planning respectable seems to have been reached. But those in charge of the economy, in most of the Third World countries, consider it today to be of no more than secondary importance, looking rather toward the example of the extraordinary growth of Japan, presented as the result of the government's effective and discreet cooperation with the private sector, whose dynamism is the basis for success.

Without any doubt, Japan affords an example for the Third World: that of a model of interventionism, put into practice since the beginning of the Meiji era. The feudal vassals of the court were transformed into capitalists by the government itself, which played the role of an industrial pioneer, then subsequently sold the newly established enterprises, once they had become viable, to private capitalists at rock-bottom prices. At the same time, it set about promoting a policy of "catching up with" Western science and technology, by temporarily importing teachers and specialists and by sending Japanese abroad to be educated.[3] To judge by the 1884 plan, the Japanese were the first nation in the world to implement an overall scientific and technological policy—one which was, moreover, extremely well conceived.

This Japanese model of the interventionism of a government which acts in fact as a nursery to private capitalists and finances them, has been taken up by many countries in the Third World, the industrial development firms and the different development banks being its main instrument.[4] It is easy to show that at the very basis of this model—whatever its numerous technical variants in the areas of administration and financing—there is a flagrant contradiction to which I have already referred in connection with the applications of Schumpeter's theory to the Third World. First of all, the government takes on the function of innovator and runs the risks attached to this. It thus takes the place of the private capitalist in his avowedly most important functions, the one which justifies his very existence and his right to the appropriation of surplus. But at the very moment when the government has proved itself as an innovator, it renounces the reward which should fall to it as a result of this success and delivers the newly created enterprise over to the private capitalist in conditions which are usually very advantageous for the latter, on the pretext that the government does not have the managerial capacity necessary (although it has just proved the opposite) and that the talents of the private entrepreneur are called for (whereas he has shown himself incapable of doing without government aid). But this criticism on strictly logical grounds does not take into consideration the essential political option inherent in the Japanese model: the desire to promote capitalism as such, to provide it with a firm base.

For its modernization, the Japanese Empire chose, then, the socio-economic system which, at that time, appeared to be the only one capable of producing military, technological, and material progress and which, furthermore, could absorb the traditional superstructure. It provided the feudal system with a way out, a "Prussian way," based not simply on agriculture but on the whole of the economy. By placing the model in its historical context, it is possible to measure its immense social cost for the toiling masses of Japan, subjected to un-bridled exploitation (the wretched wages paid to them explain the competitiveness of the products of Japanese light industry during its industrial revolution), made accomplices to the exploitation of colo-nized peoples and then sacrificed in the wars unleashed by the mili-tarist regime. The outcome was the 1945 defeat, the holocaust of Hiroshima.

Furthermore, one should not overlook the favorable factors which benefited Japan toward the end of the nineteenth century and which are lacking today in the Third World. These were a situation extremely favorable to the exportation of silk, since the mulberry bush had been struck by an epidemic in Europe; the indifference of foreign private capital, which saw little on which to fasten its greed in Japan, incom-parably poorer in natural resources than its important neighbor China, not to mention the opportunities for investment afforded by the American continent; lastly, the remarkable development, for that time, of the rural infrastructure and of education just when Japan was em-barking on industrialization.

If we now take a look at the last twenty years, as do those who are keen on the Japanese model, forgetting to take the Japan of the previ-ous period (1900-1945) as a basis of comparison, we should seriously raise the question as to whether, at a qualitative level, over and above the impressive indexes of growth, Japan truly constituted and con-tinues to constitute a model worthy of emulation by the Third World.

Before giving a reply, we should note that the "spiral of growth" in the postwar years[5] may very well be explained by the combination of several factors: the existence of a plentiful supply of skilled labor, ac-customed to shabby wages and subjected to a system of industrial and trade-union organization making it possible for capitalist accumulation to attain rates unprecedented in history (in other words, causing the Japanese to be the people with the lowest level of consumption in the world, in relation to the level of the GNP); the success of an agrarian

reform implemented from above; the advantage of complete modernization founded on the last word in technology, made possible by vast
destruction; keeping military expenditure at an extremely low level;
the extra boost given by the wars in Korea and Vietnam, and the expenditure of the American army; then, at the psychological level, the
stubborn desire of a vanquished nation to have its revenge on its van-
quishers by taking the lead in scientific and technological progress
throughout the world. However, most of these factors are in the
process of disappearing.

Will Japan be capable, all the same, of maintaining its extraordinarily
high rate of growth? The sensitive spot of its economy is foreign trade.
Not having any natural resources, Japan is in a position where it has to
import almost all of the raw materials which it needs for its industries—
as well as a substantial part of its foodstuffs. According to Japan's projections, this will necessitate a tenfold increase in exports in the thirty
years to come, accompanied by increasing specialization. I must confess that I lack the imagination to conceive of outlets for 130 billion
dollars worth of equipment, software, advanced industrial products, and
gradually abandonment of traditional exports—products of the textile,
optical, and electronics industry and even ship hulls—unless Japan wishes
once again to take the political stance of an imperial power. The government's economic adviser at this writing, Saburo Okita, foresaw that
Japan's relations with the countries of Southeast Asia could resemble,
in certain respects, the relations of the United States with Latin America,[6] and the resumption of arms production is increasingly being considered, for political and probably economic reasons, since the Japanese
economy cannot offer itself the luxury of a recession without running
the risk of a very serious crisis.

But, and here I touch on the main issue, is the apparent prosperity
of Japan bringing about a real rise in the standard of living?

On the basis of statistics of consumption, I should reply in the affirmative. But what a crude simplification! Japan, proud of its technological successes and its powerful industries, is also the country

where environmental disruption has reached unheard-of proportions, beyond comparison with what is occurring elsewhere. Pollution, urban congestion, bad housing conditions all affect the life of the average Japanese and, a fortiori, of the poor Japanese, seriously restricting the advantages of fast-growing individual consumption. What is more, the future seems to be gravely compromised, since those in charge of economic life have displayed a lack of social imagination contrasting with the boldness of their technological views. Only fifteen years ago, all or almost all could have been saved, provided that a minimum of social planning had been introduced, that the corporations had been regulated, and that the race for profits had been checked.

The social costs of the postwar Japanese expansion are sometimes compared with those of the industrial revolution in Europe. The analogy is false. The Japanese were familiar with the social record of the industrial revolutions of the past, if only through their own experience, and they could have drawn lessons from them. They had at their disposal, from the outset, an incomparably superior material, scientific, and human base, which they put, however, solely in the service of the partial rationality of the corporation, renouncing overall rationality, except for the coordination of the interests of corporations. In the last analysis, the Japanese way relies essentially on the spontaneous generation of development from economic expansion, and sets up as a supreme principle the internalization of profits by the enterprise and the externalization of its costs. The interventionism of the government in the economic sphere, more pronounced than is often admitted, conforms to this rule.

If the intention of the American army of occupation was to provide for resuscitated Japanese capitalism the best starting conditions for an unrestrained race toward expansion, considered as a goal in itself, their efforts have been crowned with success: Japan's rogue capitalism has given its proofs of vitality by beating all records of productivity, but also of destructiveness and social cost. We may perhaps say that, fortunately for most of the Third World countries, the Japanese model will not be applied there, as they lack the starting conditions present in Japan.

But let there be no mistake. Far from considering Japan as an anti-model, many Third World countries are embarking on the path of spontaneous development, supported by government intervention which is intended to have only a regulating effect and which, as we shall show, aggravates the distortions instead of correcting them.

The reason is that faith in the virtues of the theory of spontaneous development, in the self-regulating capacity of the market economy, remains the chief characteristic of the capitalist ideology, despite the nasty tricks that life goes on playing on the principles of free enterprise and despite the violations of those principles continually committed by the main parties concerned—the capitalists themselves—and the governments wishing to help them. There is no doubt that the model of a market economy based on perfect competition has an impeccable logic about it, provided that we accept the validity of its premises concerning the atomization of supply and demand, the perfect mobility of factors, and the system's miraculous faculty of adapting instantaneously to changes in conditions. In this sense, it has been said that the market was the first computer in the service of the optimization of economic activity.[7] It is not surprising that, confronted with the failures of a distribution system centralized to the utmost, certain socialist reformers of Eastern Europe have also been seduced by its effectiveness. It would still have to be possible to ensure its functioning in conditions close to the theoretical model. Paradoxically, this might not be unthinkable (certain limits being well-defined in advance) within the framework of a socialist economy,[8] whereas in the capitalist system of so-called free competition, the premises of this model are, so to speak, *never* achieved.

The market is indeed imperfect. The concentrations of power appear on the side of both supply and demand; J. B. Say's *loi des débouchés* turns out to be a myth; the government has to intervene in order to re-establish the equilibriums which have been upset and to aid the capitalists in their task of accumulating profits. In fact, capitalism of free competition was but a brief interlude in the succession of the different forms of interventionism. But then, profit—the expression of the rationality of the enterprise—ceases to have the social significance attributed to it by classical theory. It represents a balance of power favorable to the enterprise, and not necessarily efficient production, if the mechanism of competition is not brought into play. How can one say that profitable production meets a demand expressing social needs, at a period when individual consumption is geared and manipulated by advertising and when public expenditure creates an outlet for industries by purchasing weapons and maintaining armies? To limit the goal of economic activity to meeting demand is to evade the main issue.

Indeed, in the economic process, production and income distribution are tangled up together and take place in a historical sequence. This is poles apart from the theories of static equilibrium, and the real problem is to know what kind of sequence is established by the free play of market forces. Setting aside the now well-elucidated problems of the dynamics of the capitalist economy, governed for the main part by capitalists' ideas of their future profits and the decisions concerning investment their ideas cause them to make,[9] I shall endeavor to show that the model of spontaneous development in an underdeveloped mixed economy, far from having the harmonious effects attributed to it by its supporters, gives rise to increasingly deep-seated imbalances at three different levels: that of regions, that of social classes, and that of nations.[10]

Inequalities between regions, more or less everywhere in the world, reflect certain "objective" differences in natural resources, in climate, in geographical situation, and sometimes certain historical accidents. But these initial differences are often magnified, in the course of development, by a cumulative process involving the concentration of

secondary and tertiary activities, which can be explained quite well by
the concept of external economies. People prefer to invest wherever
they find a developed infrastructure, skills, and other enterprises to co-
operate, at least until such time as the concentration becomes excessive
and the external economies change sign and become negative. Such has
been the experience of industrial revolutions up to the present time, in
spite of the mounting inconveniences caused by urban congestion. No
serious effort has yet been made to rethink the concept of external
economies in the light of the technological progress achieved in the field
of communications. This progress should make it possible to re-deploy
certain activities (research, education, modern services, pollution-free
industries) within the rural framework and to create a sort of nonagricultural rural civilization so as to try to check the present trend toward
an ecumenopolis.[11] Several countries of the Third World are well
placed to avoid the excesses of an overurbanized civilization. But to
my knowledge, China and North Korea are the only countries to be
seriously concerned about this problem.

The mechanism of differentiation between "advanced" and "backward" regions exercises a very powerful effect in most Third World
countries, especially those that cover a large geographical arch. There
is a historical explanation for this. The enclaves of modernity and the
pockets of industrialization—which are in fact extensions of the former
mother countries and of the industrial nations—had, as soon as they
were established, such an advantage over the rest of the country, both
at the material and at the cultural levels, that further differentiation
and a progressive alienation of the advanced region became inevitable,
sometimes causing a successionist impulse in politics. Certain *paulista*
still say that São Paulo is the locomotive pulling the empty cars, the
other states of Brazil.

This advanced, insular sector is, however, too weak and wasteful to
integrate the backward regions with itself by modernizing them. Its
fascination for imported technologies requires a large amount of capital,
so it is incapable of solving unemployment and underemployment

problems in the traditional sector. In contrast, it is quite up to imposing on the traditional sector a relationship of domination which, in extreme cases, becomes a veritable internal colonization, a systematic exaction of the economic substance of the backward regions. In the previous chapter we saw the mechanisms whereby surplus is transferred and we observed that the balance of trade involving agricultural products from the backward regions and industrial products from the advanced region are structurally very advantageous for the latter, at least in comparison with the terms of trade in the developed countries. To be convinced of this, one has only to recall that the prices of agricultural products, in most of the Third World, are lower than world prices; on the other hand, industrial prices are higher. Galloping inflation slightly corrects this balance of trade, but without changing it essentially. We are therefore confronted with an "unequal exchange"—a term which I hesitate to use on account of the fruitless controversies to which it has given rise, but which nevertheless retains an undeniable intuitive value.[12]

But undoubtedly the heaviest tribute which the backward sector pays to the advanced sector is the social cost of raising the labor force which, once adult, migrates to the major cities in great numbers, but not without incurring the hostility of the working class already provided with steady industrial employment; the latter fears, not without reason, the competition of cheap labor. The shantytowns of the large cities of the Third World are an extension of the backward regions, and the urban subproletariat is but another form of the jobless or underemployed agricultural proletariat.

What actually happens, then, contradicts the theory that capital flows to wherever there is a plentiful and cheap supply of manpower. If ever this phase of colonialism existed, it is no more. Capital prefers to take its bearings from external economies and to bring cheap labor to industrial concentrations, either from the backward regions or, if need be, from outside its own frontiers. The Europe of "metics" which is being built before our eyes, with the massive immigration of

South European and African workers, provides substantial proof of what I have just said. This is why all attempts to promote the development of backward regions by merely introducing "centers of development" have been unsuccessful. They were dependent on a spontaneous development which does not exist and assumed that the creation of the infrastructure would be enough to arouse a pioneering spirit in the capitalists. But capitalists are gregarious, as a matter of self-interest.

How does spontaneous development affect the distribution of income?

The situation in the traditional sector does not call for lengthy commentary: it is scarcely affected by the process except for being automatically plundered to the advantage of the modern sector, for which it is partly compensated by major government investment in public works or that of private enterprise interested in exploiting natural resources, which, in contrast with cheap labor, always attracts investments. In this sector, the disparities in income distribution are enormous; the rich are sometimes just as rich as the wealthiest industrialists, while the masses are poorer and relatively more numerous than in the modern sector. This explains why the average per capita income in the poorest states of Brazil, Mexico, or India is no more than a fraction of the average income in the richest states.

In the modern sector, there is a rapid concentration of wealth to the advantage of (local and foreign) capitalists, hardly bothered by the political pressure of trade unions and of people's parties which, from time to time, manage to have a few social measures introduced. These measures affect only the stabilized industrial proletariat and the "white collar workers"—a minority which is likewise privileged in relation to the masses of the urban subproletariat and the poor peasantry. The concentration of wealth is to be explained by the combination of closely connected factors: initial income distribution and the resulting pattern of demand; chronic difficulties with regard to foreign trade; imperfection of the market; the use of capital-intensive technologies; the complicity and ineptitude of the government; tax fraud; and finally, inflation.

Initially, we are confronted with a restricted but wealthy group of consumers of imported industrial goods whose life style reflects a curious mixture of local traditions of feudal ostentation and bourgeois behavior, imitated from the rich countries. The rest of the population of course consumes certain goods turned out by the light and food processing industries, but in limited quantities, since the poor of the traditional sector and the urban subproletariat living on the fringe of society have, on an average, only a few dollars a year for the purchase of such products.[13]

The first step toward industrialization usually consists in establishing industries producing everyday goods (textiles, shoes, beer, soap, matches, and so on) as a response to difficulties with foreign trade, which may have been caused by a temporary break in the import networks during the two world wars, the consequence of the Great Crash of 1929 or the shortage of foreign exchange.

But these industries reach their ceilings fairly quickly if a more reasonable policy of income distribution is not undertaken to broaden their outlets. Moreover, they are sometimes exposed, once the acute crisis in foreign trade has passed, to the competition of their foreign counterparts. Very quickly, then, the focal point of industrialization shifts toward consumer goods of a higher order, to durable goods, automobiles in particular. This involves using production techniques imported from the developed countries, even when production is in the hands of a local firm and not a subsidiary of a foreign firm. These technologies are capital intensive and therefore generally ensure fairly high productivity. But the level of wages is not established in relation to this productivity. It is geared to the wages paid in other activities, particularly in that it is subject to the pressure of high unemployment and the effects of the rural exodus. As industrialization based on imported technologies creates few jobs in relation to the volume of investment, it is frequent in many Third World towns for the

announcement of a major industrial project to produce such an inflow
of immigration that, all in all, there is a rise in urban unemployment.
It is true that the presence of an excessive supply of unskilled labor
contrasts with the lack of skilled workers, who enjoy considerably
higher wages. For entrepreneurs, this is one more reason (we shall see
that there are several others) to prefer capital-intensive technologies,
even if technological alternatives exist.

In fact, the high profits of the industrialist derive both from the absence of real competition and from a sort of complicity, voluntary or
not, on the part of the government.

Why does our industrialist not have to fear the competition of
another entrepreneur who would use more rudimentary techniques
and would be satisfied with lower productivity, for which he would
compensate by the considerably lower expenditure on equipment, the
price of which is always very high in the Third World?

The reason is that, first, goods of a certain sophistication are involved, and, in default of local industrial research, technologies from
the developed countries have to be used, all of which are based on the
substitution of capital for labor. Furthermore, with a foreign license
it is possible to market the product under a prestigious brand name and
to sell it at a higher price than a local substitute.

Moreover, as the market is limited, there is a good chance that our
producer will be able to enjoy what is in fact a monopolistic or oligopolistic situation, especially if he succeeds, through his choice of the
models he is putting on the market and by advertising, in individualiz-
ing his product. One of the most dangerous illusions for the Third
World is the belief that its economy is passing through the historical
stages of capitalism and, at the present time, is at the stage of capitalism of free competition. In fact, the intervention of new producers
gives rise to the fragmentation of the market and to increased costs for
all producers,[14] without, however, resulting in the elimination of the
least efficient; on the contrary, they all profit, since prices are based,
I have said, on the cost plus a "fair" markup, which the government

controls occasionally without being able or without wishing to take its supervision too far. In these conditions, the greater the immobilization of capital, the higher the costs and the more considerable the profits. Hence the apparent paradox, observed in Latin America during the last twenty years, that the chronic underutilization of productive capacities in no way prevents new industrial investments.[15] This is because business is profitable despite partly idle production capacities, not to mention the profits deriving from investment activity and the obtaining to this end, of credit from the government on concessionary terms. Of course, the list prices are thus far higher than would have to be paid for imported equivalents, but the industrialists have nothing to fear; they enjoy a great deal of protection, set up to aid the establishment of local industries.

Last, the high price of equipment does not affect the entrepreneur's calculation of his profit-earning capacity for as long as he is able to obtain loans at a low rate of interest. In most Third World countries, the industrialist, with his prestige, has access to public sources of capital through the agency of so-called industrial development corporations and development banks. In certain cases, with the help of inflation, the rates of interest on loans granted to industrialists have turned out to be negative.[16]

On the other hand, the government is incapable of putting an effective tax on the profits accumulated by the capitalist. And for several reasons.

First of all, one must reckon with the inefficiency of corrupt tax collection, aggravated by the widespread opinion that only direct taxes are equitable. This would undoubtedly be the case if it were not so easy for capitalists to dodge income taxes. Indirect taxes, which considerably raise the cost of luxuries such as foreign exchange for travel abroad, or taxes on real and personal property, would be a surer way of taxing them.

On top of this there are the different forms of government assistance to the capitalist, in the name of the doctrine of promoting private capitalism as the surest path to development and the necessity of placing at his disposal the resources for investment. We have seen that this policy has none of the results anticipated: instead of promoting development in such a way as to create jobs, it encourages the industrialist to use techniques which replace labor by capital. And this is especially so in that the facility with which any person belonging to the local élite can obtain loans for industrial investment or for property speculation contrasts with the shortage of working capital: anti-inflationary policy results in fact in the curtailing of short-term bank credit. Meanwhile, the building of luxury apartments and of vacation homes goes on uninterrupted and does a brisk trade, many people seeing in the purchasing of property a way of protecting themselves against inflation. Foreign loans for the purchase of equipment act in the same way.

In addition, the capitalist is aided by social measures which were originally intended to be progressive. Labor legislation, taken literally, obliges the employer to pay for a large part of the worker's social security and protects the latter against arbitrary dismissals. The practical effects of such legislation, however, are often contrary to its apparent intentions. Employers' contributions to social security rarely result in a real increase in the welfare of the workers. At best, they benefit only the restricted group of the stabilized industrial proletariat, introducing one more division between this group and the mass of urban subproletarians and the poor peasantry. But who could not cite many cases in which these funds have been misappropriated for political ends or for property speculation under the guise of loans for the construction of low-cost housing? At the same time, if the cost of labor rises in relation to wages paid (in some cases it may double), this, for the employer, is an additional reason to proceed with mechanization. The more firmly established the trade union movement becomes, the more rigorous social legislation is, the more the employer attempts to reduce the number of workers to the minimum. Rather than hiring new workers in periods when there is great demand, he will prefer to pay overtime to fewer personnel. The number of jobs created by industrialization is thus lower than what it could be and, at the same time that wealth is concentrated in the hands of the capitalists, income is distributed in a decreasingly uniform manner among the different categories of workers.

Finally, inflation, which is rife in most of the Third World countries, can only accentuate the tendency toward the rise of capitalist profits' relative share in income.

These mechanisms of uneven development at the national level repeat themselves at the level of the world economy. The countries of the Third World feature here as backward regions, lined up against the great multinational corporations, which are the main beneficiaries. Here, too, the doctrine of spontaneous development and free trade serves as an ideological screen for the operation. A polarization of wealth thus takes place on the world scale, which does not mean that the economy of the Third World does not grow, but that it grows less quickly than it might have. The crux of the problem, moreover, does not reside so much in the differences of growth rates or in the gap between rich countries and poor countries as in the slowing down of the growth rate of Third World economies, due to the skimming off of economic resources, formerly as taxes and tribute which had to be paid by the colonies, nowadays as profits repatriated by foreign firms and of profits the rich countries make from commercial and financial operations.

Undoubtedly the sum total of colonial drain and repatriated profits has never been more than a fraction of the national incomes of Third World countries. But Baran is right in thinking that it should be compared not with the income of these countries but with the surplus available for investment. The same observation holds good for the way of evaluating the impact of transfers on metropolitan economies.[17] Taking the analysis further than Baran, we shall say that what is involved is a tax on both surplus and available foreign exchange, and therefore on the resources for importing the equipment necessary for investment. As most of the Third World countries experience chronic difficulties in this area, the drain on the economy has an extremely debilitating effect and, insofar as it causes the sacrifice of potential investments, its cumulative effects are considerable.

With regard to unequal exchange in international trade which must now be discussed, I should say straightaway that the study of fluctuations in the balance of trade, which in recent times has come so much into vogue, does not tell us much about the crux of the problem. At best it makes it possible to grasp fluctuations in relation to a base year, the choice of which opens the door to manipulations sometimes far removed from scientific objectivity. Of course, any deterioration in the balance of trade will, in order for equilibrium to be re-established, have to be compensated for by inflows of capital each year equaling the initial loss. Reciprocally, any improvement is equivalent to an annual inflow of capital equal to the initial gain, therefore a windfall. But it should not be forgotten that the balance of trade measures fluctuations in the purchasing power of exports, calculated in terms of imports, assuming that price fluctuations have given rise to no change either in the amount or in the composition of exports and imports, which is an unlikely hypothesis. Were we all the same to accept it, we would be overlooking the whole matter of price structures in transactions and the real distribution of gains. The same multinational firm may find itself on both sides of a transaction at the same time, and when this happens it becomes almost impossible to see how it intends to maximize its global profits. And it is this which is important, if we really want to measure the inequality of exchange.

I do not think that such a measurement can be checked by means of a general theoretical line of reasoning, although Marx's observations have inspired attempts. To tell the truth, if we take Marx as our starting point, we end up with two concepts of unequal exchange, neither of which is operative.

The first insists on the unequal exchange of labor, an obvious observation which can be applied to any exchange of products between two enterprises of different technological levels, under no matter what system. At a greater level of sophistication, this perspective poses the problem of weighing the quantity of labor exchanged by its quality. This question was raised by Marx, but to my knowledge, there is no satisfactory operative solution to it, except to claim, like certain authors of the neoclassical school, that differences in wages adequately reflect differences in skills.[18]

The second concept would consist in saying that the underdeveloped country has no choice but to sell its products below their real value and to purchase products from the industrialized countries at a price higher than their value. But this is to assume that we know how to calculate the value of a product directly, on the basis of the amount of labor socially necessary to produce it. As far as I know, however this problem has not met with a satisfactory operative solution either.

All the same, the second variant presents certain advantages over the first. It affords an interesting starting point for concrete studies of prices (and not of values). Indeed, it is possible to find examples where, for certain imported goods, the Third World countries pay more than purchasers in the developed countries, and where they find themselves obliged to sell their exports at reduced prices. But above all, this explanation places emphasis on the balance of power between the partners in the transaction, on the basis of which it may be suggested that unequal exchange be seen in the same light as the distribution of income between profits and wages in the capitalist system.[19] This idea ties in with Myrdal, according to whom equity in international trade can never be ensured by formal equality between partners possessing different degrees of power.

Nor do I think that the Third World countries should seek, first and foremost, an improvement in the balance of trade. In making this their battle cry at the United Nations and in U.N.C.T.A.D., they have fallen prey to their own tactics. For the great industrial powers could ask for no better than to engage in long and fruitless arguments about the evolution of the balance of trade, sometimes between rich countries and poor countries, at other times between industrial products and raw materials (quite different from each other). The disease is not cured by treating one or another of its symptoms. In order to demonstrate convincingly the deterioration of the balance of trade in Third World countries, it should be seen instead as a manifestation of a structural crisis in the international division of labor that has been established on the world scale by the capitalist industrial revolution.

Most Third World countries—not counting the producers of oil or of strategic raw materials and a few other exceptions—are not able to finance a satisfactory flow of imports by means of their traditional exports.[20] The time is no more when one could claim that foreign trade would stimulate their growth and thereby justify monoculture or the mono-exploitation of mineral wealth (accompanied by a colonial or "feudal" superstructure) by the doctrine of comparative advantage, another form of faith in spontaneous development.

The conclusion, following on the unquestionable progress achieved by several Third World countries at the end of the nineteenth century and the beginning of the twentieth, is that these initial short and medium-term successes hastened their downfall, since specialization was increasingly forced upon them, with the common consent of the dominating powers and the élites of the dominated countries. From this there resulted an unbalanced economic and social structure. So long as exports brought in foreign exchange, despite the loss resulting from unequal exchange and foreign investment, the expansion of mono-exportation was all that mattered. Then, with the collapse following the Crash of 1929, the call went out for the needed diversification of the economy, but the foreign exchange necessary for the importing of capital goods was cruelly lacking at the time. Thus the model of growth based on mono-exportation bore within it the seeds of its own destruction and of its transformation into the model of an import-sensitive economy in which foreign trade became the chief bottleneck.[21] At the present time the prospects for the traditional exports of the Third World continue to appear unfavorable for reasons of which some are objective and others a result of the organization of the world capitalist economy.

The former include the difference between the rates of population growth of the countries producing raw materials and the consumer countries, the relative saturation of the markets of rich countries with products of tropical origin, technological progress characterized both by a more efficient use of raw materials and by their replacement by synthetics, and finally the importance assumed by precision industries, which require little in the way of material inputs for each product unit.

Among the latter, one should take into account the different protectionist policies of the developed countries; the role played on several markets by giant conglomerates which pursue their own strategies on the world scale, scarcely concerned about their impact on the national economies of different Third World countries;[22] the virtual nonexistence of research into a better use of the natural resources of the Third World; the insincerity of the industrial powers in the UN and U.N.C.T.A.D. whenever the problem of a serious reorganization of world trade is addressed. Although the very creation of the U.N.C.T.A.D. could be interpreted as a victory for the Third World, it has since proved to be incapable of imposing an effective program of action on that body. Many Third World governments have even rallied to the principles of free trade, that is to say, to the most powerful means of action at the disposal of the industrial countries to ensure their economic domination over the Third World and to paralyze any serious attempt at planned development.

The increasingly obvious failure of the model of growth actuated by foreign trade caused the doctrine of comparative advantage to be abandoned, at least for a while. Until that time it was invoked in a superficial manner to justify the division of labor between industrialized countries and the Third World, without a thorough examination of the possibilities of development of each country and from a completely static viewpoint, as though, in the long run, the initial advantage enjoyed by those who were the first to build factories was never going to disappear. The choice, possible in principle, between the diversification of the economy (aiming at decreasing the relative share of imports) and the specialization of production (aiming at increasing traditional exports in order to balance out increased imports) had become purely theoretical, since the second term could not be applied without the risk of a disastrous collapse of prices. So the Third World began to build factories and to defend them against foreign competition by often excessive forms of protectionism, going hand in hand with increased government interventionism.

By a curious paradox of history, it was the far-ranging repercussions of the Crash of 1929 which brought about this positive change of position in several Latin American countries; and the impact of the Second World War would only accentuate the movement. It was also furthered, at least in Brazil, by the involuntarily Keynesian policy of the government, which continued, in the middle of the crisis, to buy from the planters coffee which could not be sold.[23] The purpose of this policy was to protect the immediate interests of the landed oligarchy; its effect was to transform it into a class of industrialists.

For a good twenty years industrialization, carried out with the objective of restricting imports, enjoyed some success—sometimes more apparent than real, since it led to increased imports in equipment, inputs, technical services, and so on. Euphoria overtook the élites in power. And yet, at the basis of this protectionist policy, there was an error in perspective which subsequently turned out to be very costly. As government intervention was being employed indiscriminately in favor of all import-substituting production, leaving the allocation of investments to the market, the industrialists first of all fell back on easy substitutions, and therefore on the production of consumer goods for which there was a wide market. This was not necessarily a bad choice, although it would perhaps have been a good idea to give more attention to producer goods. Then came the turn of building materials (necessary to a building industry which was thriving on property speculation) and finally that of consumer goods of a higher order, durable goods and automobiles. This was definitely a very bad choice. Doubtless the entrepreneurs were not to blame: they merely followed the indications of the market, which were themselves determined by the unequal distribution of income.[24] This was nonetheless an economic mistake, for several obvious reasons:

1. Because these industries cannot be accorded social priority in countries where a major part of the population lives in very precarious conditions

2. Because, as I have said, these industries were based on a technology which was wasteful of capital

3. Because foreign capital can find its way into these industries in order, it is claimed, to promote efficiency (which cannot be achieved in a narrow and fragmented market), and because it has thus turned to its own advantage the protectionist legislation which was originally designed to protect emerging industry from foreign competition

4. Last, because the excessive development of this sector of production devoted to luxury consumer goods (including the building of villas and lavish apartments) in the long run interferes with the country's possibilities of development.

To see all this, it is enough to use a simplified model of interindustrial relations, halfway between Marx's models and Leontief's input-output tables.[25] I shall use a model of a closed economy with four sectors, represented in figure 4 in diagrammatic form. The arrows represent the flows; the sectors are represented by E (capital goods), M (raw materials and intermediate products), C_1 (essential consumer goods), and C_2 (nonpriority consumer goods).

The reader will object that the distinction between C_1 and C_2 is arbitrary. I admit it; it is nevertheless essential to any serious discussion of priorities in development policy and, furthermore, it is operational, since, for an economy and a given period, it should not be difficult to list the main products to be included in C_1.

It is easy to see that C_2 competes with C_1, M, and E as far as the

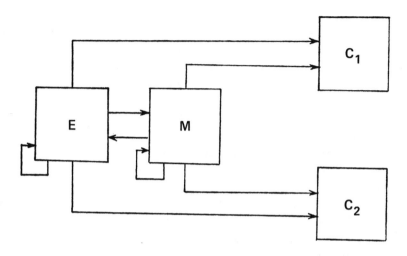

Figure 4

distribution of capital goods and intermediate goods is concerned. The same is true with regard to foreign exchange and skilled personnel. If these factors, of which there is a limited supply, are drained toward C_2, they will not be available for the expansion of C_1, M, or E. Harmonious long-term development can be achieved, however, only by ensuring the expansion of E, in order to provide the equipment necessary for the setting up and repair of production machinery, of C_1 in order to produce the real counterpart of wages (for we assume that growth takes place in such a way as to increase both employment and real wages); and of M in order to meet the requirements of E and of C_1. In this process of expanded reproduction (in which I have been careful to include C_1 while introducing a minimum of social postulates), C_2 is the only sector not to participate directly.[26] Logically, its growth should be strictly regulated, in the interests of accelerated growth. However, the interplay of market mechanisms produces exactly the opposite result, under the combined effect of the increasingly unequal distribution of income and a clumsy and incomplete policy of protectionism, incapable of seeing beyond the immediate and apparent effects of restriction of imports on the balance of payments. All the same, as I have said, initially this policy produces results. But this type of growth is quickly exhausted; it is a *perverse growth.* Argentina, which over the last twenty years has stepped back down to the rank of an underdeveloped country, in spite of the head start which it possessed immediately after the Second World War, is undoubtedly the most complete illustration of my model. But there is no lack of other examples.

Nevertheless, the protectionist policy was necessary. If it missed the mark, it was because it did not dare interfere with the spontaneous determination of investment priorities. The most frequent diagnosis for the failure of the first phase of import substitution[27] casts doubt on the very usefulness of protectionism and praises the virtues of foreign trade and free competition. Such an unrealistic view merely proves with what tenacity economists become attached to simplifying dichotomies. The durability of the paradigm of spontaneous development is not at all surprising: introduced by the classical economists, it is supported ideologically by capitalism, even when its survival calls for a more energetic interventionism.

But has anyone really thought about the social cost which should ensue, in underdeveloped countries, from the opening up of the market, in the name of the hypothetical rationalization of an inefficient industry? Its inevitable consequences would be bankruptcies, greater unemployment, and an even more pronounced dependence on the centers which dominate the world economy. And which countries of the Third World can bear the burden of necessarily increased imports, over a long period, witout definitively compromising their balance of payments? At all events, the cure seems more dangerous than the disease, as grave as the latter may be. And this is especially so in that it is perfectly possible to conceive of a corrective policy of

practicing, in quite the opposite way, increased interventionism, based
on an overall analysis of the process of growth.

As for the promotion of industrial exports from Third World countries, it would certainly be welcome, and no effort should be spared in
this direction. But here too the remedies put forward seem to me to
be ill-chosen. Efforts are made to convince the Third World countries
that, in order to become competitive, they should import the most advanced equipment from the industrialized countries. It is an illusion to
think that competitiveness can be achieved through measures introduced within the isolated enterprise; in my opinion, the sources of non-
competitiveness should be sought elsewhere, in the effects of ill-conceived economic, fiscal, and social policies, in the general inefficiency
of the system which gives rise to the high price of inputs.[28]

And if excessively high costs were the only obstacle, why not introduce a policy of export subsidies? No objections are raised, when it
comes to import substitution, to allowing subsidies which may double
or treble the price of the local product in relation to world prices, but
by a curious asymmetry (which can be explained only by a blind respect for the rules of free trade), there is a refusal to do the same for
certain exports. At the very most, there is a grudging acceptance of
the idea of successive devaluations, which do not have the same selective capacity as subsidies and which raise the prices of all imports
across the board. In reality, access to the markets of developed countries is jealously guarded by a series of *de facto* protectionist measures,
and the crux of the problem is institutional and political. As is proved
by measures considered in the United States to regulate imports of
textiles and shoes, this is true even of the famous "cheap-labor goods,"
the production of which is recommended to all the Third World countries, without allowing for the real absorptive capacity of the world
markets. The few recent successes in this field—South Korea, Taiwan,
Hong Kong, Puerto Rico—are all very small countries, being used as
stakes in large-scale political operations and, what is essential, accepting a satellite position in relation to a dominant economy.

The new division of labor differs from the traditional relations between advanced countries and producers of raw materials in the sense that certain manufactured articles take the place of raw materials; but it prolongs them in respect of unequal exchange and fixed rules. The Third World countries need to broaden their export structure. They would be more successful in this if a well-conceived cooperation were to be established between the three underdeveloped continents, a cooperation in no way restricted to "cheap-labor goods" but audaciously tackling the production and exchange of capital goods. Once again, this entails planning and implementation through series of long-term mutual agreements, guaranteed by governments,[29] that is, reducing the uncertainty inherent in free trade by increased interventionism, not by abandoning the most vulnerable part of the national economy to the spontaneous forces of the market.

Notes to Chapter 10

1. For the concept of "pseudoplan," see C. Bobrowski, *Planowanie gospodarcze: Problemy podstawowe.* (Economic planning: Basic problems; Warsaw, 1965), and also the papers for a symposium on the theme "Crisis in Planning," organized by the Institute of Development Studies of the University of Sussex, June-July 1969. The document prepared by D. Seers bore the significant title "The Prevalence of Pseudoplanning." For a recent overall view of planning in the Third World, see, in the *Archives européennes de sociologie,* 11.1 (1970), the articles by C. Furtado, "Planification et réforme de structure en Amérique Latine" (pp. 81-93) and C. Bobrowski, "Dix ans de planification dans les pays sous-développés" (pp. 94-104).

2. See P. Streeten, *The Crisis of Indian Planning* (New York, 1968).

3. See H. Tuge, *Historical Development of Science and Technology in Japan* (Tokyo, 1968).

4. I have done an analysis of this model in *Patterns of Public Sector in Underdeveloped Economies* (Bombay, 1964).

5. I borrow this term from S. Okita, *Essays in Japan and Asia* (Tokyo 1970), pp. 21-38.

6. Ibid., pp. 73-79.

7. Oskar Lange, "Maszyna liczaca i rynek" (The computer and the market), in *O socjalizmie i gospodarce socjalistycznej* (Socialism and socialist economics; Warsaw, 1966), pp. 448-454, a posthumous article, also published in the collection of essays in memory of P. Baran.

8. This idea seems to have strongly influenced the Czech reformers, such as O. Sik, in his *Plan and Market under Socialism* (Prague, 1967), and also *La vérité sur l'économie tchécoslovaque* (Paris, 1969). For a more subtle discussion of the relations between plan and market, see especially the work already referred to by W. Brus, *The Market in a Socialist Economy* (London, 1972).

9. See M. Kalecki, *Theory of Economic Dynamics* (London, 1956), and the important article by the same author, "Trend and Business Cycles Reconsidered," in *The Economic Journal,* 78.310 (June 1968), pp. 263-276.

10. What is involved then is "uneven development" in a broader sense than Lenin gave it in applying it above all to the unequal rate of development of various countries.

11. I borrowed this term from C. A. Dioxadis, *Ekistics: An Introduction to the Science of Human Settlements* (London, 1968).

12. I do not share the views of A. Emmanuel, the author of a work entitled *L'échange inégal: Essai sur les antagonismes dans les rapports économiques internationaux* (Paris, 1969). The discussions which followed on the publication of this book revived controversies which the economists of Eastern Europe have carried on for several years, and without much result.

13. According to estimates of the United Nations Economic Commission for Latin America, in 1960, the poorest half of the population of Latin America spent on consumer goods less than 130 dollars a head, including 7 dollars for textiles, shoes, and clothing and 10 for all other industrial goods, including drink and tobacco (U.N., ECLA, *The Process of Industrial Development in Latin America;* New York, 1966, p. 126).

14. See T. Scitovsky's contribution to a conference held by the Inter-American Development Bank: *El Processo de Industrialización en America Latina,* Guatemala, April 1969, pp. 31-51.

15. According to the estimates of the Latin American Institute of Economic and Social Planning, at Santiago, Latin American industries were working at 58.2 percent of their capacity during the period 1960-1963 (ILPES, Santiago, July 24, 1969; Working paper entitled "Elementos para la elaboración de una politica de desarrollo con integratión para America Latina," p. 49).

16. Thus, for instance, M. Mamalakis points out that in the past the Chilean Development Corporation was reimbursed only a fraction of the real value of the loans distributed to Chilean enterprises. The reason was that these loans contained no clause guaranteeing them against devaluation, not to mention the fact that the operations of the Chilean Development Corporation have often consisted in changing money borrowed in foreign exchange into loans payable in local currency. (See "An Analysis of the Financial and Investment Activities of the Chilean Development Corporation: 1939-1964," in *The Journal of Development Studies* (January 1969), p. 122.

17. P. Baran, *The Political Economy of Growth* (New York, 1954).

18. This is the procedure that Schultz uses for the economics of education. (See "Education and Economic Growth," in *Social Forces Influencing American Education;* Chicago, 1961). E. F. Denison also uses it (see *The Residual Factor and Economic Growth;* Paris, 1964, text followed by a critical discussion). The same method is used by the Soviet economist S. G. Strumilin, in "The Economic Significance of National Education," in *Textes choisis sur l'économie de l'éducation* (Paris, 1968), pp. 413-450.

19. Once again I refer the reader to M. Kalecki's fundamental *Theory of Economic Dynamics.*

20. See in this connection Ragnar Nurkse's very important work, *Patterns of Trade and Development* (New York, 1961).

21. I have attempted to describe this dialectical transformation in my work *Foreign Trade and Economic Development of Underdeveloped Countries* (Bombay, 1965).

22. C. Furtado, "La concentration du pouvoir économique aux Etats-Unis et ses projections en Amérique Latine," in *Esprit,* April 1969.

23. C. Furtado, *Formação econômica do Brasil* (Rio de Janeiro, 1963), and A. B. de Castro, "Una tentativa de interpretación del modelo histórico latino-americano," in *America Latina: Ensayos de interpretación económica* (Santiago, 1969), pp. 79-119.

24. This is emphasized in connection with India by J. Mirlees, "Targets and Investment in Industry" Streeten, in *The Crisis of Indian Planning,* p. 76.

25. Concerning the relations between Leontief's tables and Marx's models of reproduction, see Oskar Lange, *Leçons d'économétrie* (Paris, 1970), pp. 150-156.

26. P. Sraffa (*Production of Commodities by Means of Commodities;* Cambridge, 1960, pp. 7-8) defines luxury (or nonessential) goods as those which do not enter into the production of other goods. Certain luxury commodities, on

the other hand, participate in their own reproduction, such as racehorses.

27. See in particular R. Prebisch's report to the United Nations Economic Commission for Latin America, *Towards a Dynamic Development Policy for Latin America* (New York, 1964), and M. da Tavares' study, "El processo de substitución de importationes como modelo de desarrollo reciente en America Latina," in *America Latina,* pp. 150-179.

28. Thus it was possible to see in Chili that the relative inefficiency of certain local enterprises in relation to their European counterparts was far less pronounced when production costs were calculated on the basis of the prices of West European factors.

29. See M. Kalecki and I. Sachs, "Forms of Foreign Aid: An Economic Analysis," in *Information sur les sciences sociales* (March 1966), pp. 21-44 and in particular pp. 40-44.

11   The Choice of Goals

I must now take up again the main thread of my essay: the problem of development goals. How are they to be chosen?

One might think that the defining of goals is the necessary prelude to all serious planning. However, it is often regarded as enough to state a few undeniable and vague platitudes expressing a desire to promote popular welfare, to provide full employment as soon as possible, to offer more social and cultural services, and to reduce the asymmetry in the distribution of income. The United Nations sets the example by contrasting unified development—economic, social, and cultural—with the quantitative growth of the economy.[1] Then, when the time comes to lend a hand, the problem is reduced simply to the growth rate of the economy or, at best, to that of consumption. The aberrations of the Stalinist five-year plans should, however, serve as an object lesson on the danger of making growth of the national product the supreme goal of economic activity. In fact it should be seen merely as a means of increasing consumption, understood in its broadest sense. Indeed, beyond a certain limit the rate of investment necessary to support the accelerated expansion of the economy increases to such an extent that the absolute level of consumption remains lower in the accelerated variant of growth than in the slower variant, pursued over an excessively long period.

By way of illustration, figures 5, 6, and 7 compare three hypothetical cases of growth (note that the scale is semilogarithmic). The first and second variants both ensure stable growth of output and of consumption. The growth rate is higher in the second, but this advantage requires income devoted to investments to be relatively greater (difference between P and C) and, consequently, a sacrifice in consumption from the outset. It will be necessary to wait m years for C_2 to equal and subsequently overtake C_1. The third variant (Stalinist) ensures an even faster growth of the product than the second. But for p years, the relative share in income of investments continues to increase, and it is therefore only at the end of n years that C_3 overtakes C_2. (To simplify the presentation I have assumed that for p years C_3 grows at the

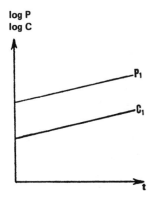

Figure 5

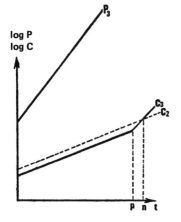

Figure 7

same rate as C_2, but initially, the proportion of C_3 to income is lower than that of C_2, which explains the faster growth of P_3).

These examples clearly show the kind of decisions which have to be made in planning for growth: more consumption in the immediate future signifies less consumption subsequently and, reciprocally, greater austerity in the initial stage results in affluence after a certain time. Everything depends, then, on the choice of time horizon and on the relative value accorded to future consumption in relation to consumption here and now. However, this comparison between the present and the future is impossible or, at the very least, immoral, as Joan Robinson has pointed out;[2] for the consumers of today and those of tomorrow will not be the same if n stretches out over the life span of a generation. Have we the right to sacrifice a generation for the sake of the prosperity of generations to come? This question is all the more dramatic in that planning entails another, which is exactly the opposite: have we the right to mortgage the future by the misuse of natural resources and the environmental disruption which for some time now have accompanied industrialization and urbanization? In short, the rates of increase of consumption, which planners use as though they were a technical and objectified instrument, in fact conceal fundamental political decisions, implying a judgment on the endurance of the population or, in more poetic terms, on its willingness to sacrifice itself to a brighter future.

Of course, there are physical and biological limits to the acceleration of growth. The former reveal themselves in the impossibility of carrying through certain investment projects on account of a lack of equipment and qualified personnel (in extreme cases, the resources intended for investment are wasted, which increases the disparity between the growth rates of P and C). As for the latter, they derive from the fact that, in order to work, men—like animals—need to consume a minimum in order to maintain their strength. This consideration is more than rhetorical when one thinks of the living conditions of rural populations and of the urban subproletariat in many Third World countries. At all events, it stresses the importance of a rigorous study of the effects of planning on the distribution of income. The options represented in figures 4, 5, and 6 apply as they stand only in the case of a perfectly egalitarian society.

On the other hand, when a minority monopolizes a large part of the national income, it is possible to imagine a process of accelerated growth which does not take place at the expense of working-class consumption. It would be enough to limit the growth rate of the consumption of the elites. Of course, this is easier to do on paper than to achieve at the political level, but it proves the fallacy of general appeals for austerity made so often in the Third World in the name of development.

By way of example[3] I compare, in tables 3 and 4, two alternatives of growth for an economy where, initially, the distribution of income Y is the following: investment $I = 10$, consumption of the elites $C_e = 40$, mass consumption $C_m = 50$. In hypothesis A this distribution is maintained, and as the capital/output ratio is 2.5 a rate of uniform growth r of 4 percent yearly is ensured. In hypothesis B we assume that the capital/output ratio is the same, but, because of an appropriate tax policy the consumption of the elites C_e initially grows at a rate equal to one fourth of the growth rate r, the proportion of mass consumption in income Y always remaining equal to 50 percent of the income. The saving thus obtained is transferred to investment. The rate reaches 6.5 percent after 6 years and subsequently becomes stabilized. It seems to me that hypothesis B offers a reasonable program for the acceleration of growth, conceived as a compromise between the social datum of redistributing income and the particular interests of the elites in power, of whom no sacrifice in the absolute sense is required except for the temporary reduction of the rate of *increase* of their consumption.[4]

Over and above this simple arithmetical exercise, it is of course necessary to see the balance of political forces which, in the last analysis, determines the distribution of income and the complex interplay of physical constraints; foreign trade; accessible production techniques, the choice of which will influence the distribution of income and

Table 3. Hypothesis A: Growth of an Economy with No Change in the Distribution of Income and with a Capital/Output Ratio of 2.5

	t_0	t_1	t_2	t_3
National income Y	100	104.0	108.2	112.5
Mass consumption C_m	50	52.0	54.1	56.2
Consumption of the elites C_e	40	41.6	43.3	45.0
Investments I	10	10.4	10.8	11.2
Growth rate r		4.0	4.0	4.0

Table 4. Hypothesis B: Growth of an Economy with Some Change in Distribution of Income and with a Capital/Output Ratio of 2.5

	t_0	t_1	t_2	t_3
National income Y	100	104.0	108.6	114.0
Mass consumption C_m	50	52.0	54.3	57.0
Consumption of the elites C_e	40	40.4	40.8	41.3
Investments I	10	11.6	13.4	15.6
Growth rate r		4.0	4.38	4.95

t_4	t_5	t_6	t_7	t_8	t_9	t_{10}
117.0	121.7	126.5	131.6	136.9	142.4	148.1
58.5	60.8	63.3	65.8	68.4	71.2	74.0
46.8	48.7	50.6	52.6	54.8	57.0	59.3
11.7	12.2	12.6	13.2	13.7	14.2	14.8
4.0	4.0	4.0	4.0	4.0	4.0	4.0

t_4	t_5	t_6	t_7	t_8	t_9	t_{10}
120.2	127.5	136.0	145.0	154.4	164.4	175.1
60.1	63.7	68.0	72.5	77.2	82.2	87.5
41.9	42.5	45.9	48.9	52.1	55.5	59.1
18.2	21.2	22.1	23.6	25.1	26.7	28.5
5.48	6.04	6.5	6.5	6.5	6.5	6.5

determine the amount of employment created; and so on.

But if one postulates a given distribution of income between individual and mass consumption, profit-making and social investments, it is possible, in principle, to construct a fairly rigorous plan by the iterative method. This consists in exploring the effects of the hypothetical growth rate resulting from a postulated distribution of income between investment and consumption and from an initial assumption about the capital/output ratio (which will be subsequently refined, in the light of detailed assumptions about the structure of consumption, the operations of foreign trade, the resulting investment projects, and the production techniques chosen). Drafting a plan conceived in this way entails a certain number of partial optimizations of foreign trade and the choice of investment projects as well as production techniques, but the essential procedure—determining the structure of consumption—is performed empirically, by projecting the trends observed, by using analogy with other countries, and by trying to introduce certain more or less scientifically established norms, relating to land area covered by housing, calculations of calorie and protein intake, and so on. Thus conceived, the exercise makes it possible to identify bottlenecks, which are reduced in the last analysis to problems with the balance of payments, for, in principle, it is always possible to use imports to make up for inadequate supply on the domestic market, provided that they are offset by exports. As the best opportunities for exporting and finding substitutes for imports are exhausted, however, each additional effort in this area results in increasingly large investments. In extreme cases, the gains resulting from the increased availability of foreign exchange do not seem to be sufficiently attractive to justify the increased burden of investments, and it becomes preferable to limit the growth rate of the economy, taking into account the limitations imposed by the balance of payments.

The method which I have just described and for which I am indebted to Kalecki[5] has the advantage of being simple. It clarifies the choices and paves the way for a dialogue between planners and politicians. It does not demand of the latter any far-ranging technological knowledge, and it requires repeated transitions from the level of macroeconomic abstraction to that of actual projects. Last, it makes it possible, to a certain extent, to match the goals of growth with that of creating jobs, through choice of techniques and products intended for export (the maneuver of choosing output mix being limited, as far as the domestic market is concerned, by the structure of demand). It does not aspire, however, to posing the problem as a homogeneous goal function in which the different goals are set in harmony with each other by weighting them, which gives a fallacious elegance and an apparent exactitude to a procedure which in reality throws back on the politician the main part of the work involved in planning by requesting him to supply the relative weights.[6]

In short, this method has marked an important stage in the theory and practice of long-term planning, and it continues to offer more attractive (and, above all, more realistic) possibilities of application than many prescriptions for planning made by computers, which a number of academics in Western universities would be happy to experiment with at the expense of the Third World. But it remains attached to the perspective of growth, which may be explained historically in two ways.

First, in the mind of the planner in an underdeveloped country (be it socialist or not), growth necessarily occupies a central place, both as a goal in itself, to increase basic consumption, and as a necessary condition for the attaining of all other goals. It is fashionable today to call growth into question and to set qualitative goals in opposition to it. But this opposition is often false, for a higher quality of life can be obtained only by a quantitative process of growth; moreover, having enough to eat, being busy at a job rather than enduring a forced idleness which in no way resembles leisure, and having decent housing are goals which must indisputably be accorded priority by underdeveloped countries, and so much so that any discussion about the quantitative and qualitative goals of development becomes (for the time being, at least) purely academic. The only way of providing an outlet for social

tensions is by surging forward. The alternative of slow growth with a
larger measure of social justice does not exist,[7] just as it is false to
claim that growth must first of all be achieved in order for social justice to follow.[8] The transition from the morphological description of
underdevelopment to the setting of immediate goals of action is therefore effected naturally. This makes it seem easy to determine the priorities of initial plans when requirements are obvious and possibilities
still limited; and, at bottom, it matters little what way one sets about
this task.[9] This also makes such plans dangerous, for it is absolutely
necessary to take the analysis beyond the morphological level and deal
with the pathology and the etiology of underdevelopment.

Second, long-term planning came into existence, essentially, through
the extrapolation of five-year plans as they were conceived and put into
practice in the U.S.S.R. It is therefore geared to general and sectorial
growth rates and to production goals and the investments necessary to
achieve them, all considered in light of the real possibilities of the
economy and, consequently, bogged down in everyday concerns.

Paradoxically, there is little room here for structural change, because
of a belief in the virtues of basic reforms affecting the pattern of ownership and because management problems and their relation with political
structures are underestimated. Yet socialism implies, at one and the
same time, the collective ownership of the basic means of production,
a high degree of egalitarianism in the distribution of income, and a very
broad citizen participation in the political and economic management
of the country. The first term of this trinomial is of course necessary
but not sufficient to define a socialist regime.

That fact is generally forgotten, and such a view reduces the field of
possibilities. It treats as data certain strategic variables; it outlaws the
imagination; it results, in extreme cases, in the making of veritable social metadecisions (such as choosing between the growth of the material
product and leisure, the structure of wages and incomes, the ratio between individual and overall consumption) without making them explicit, so to speak, as a byproduct of a certain number of everyday

decisions. This happens in socialist countries, which are naturally pre-disposed to long-term planning, and, a fortiori, in countries with mixed economies. When an interdisciplinary group in Poland, led by S. Zol-kiewski,[10] set about formulating a long-term model of culture and consumption, a veritable exercise in futurology, they soon realized that they would have to make a very important preliminary theoretical attempt to identify the determinants of such a model, its variants and strategic variables, the weight of the living past and of social structures, the influence of foreign models of culture and consumption, the range of possibilities resulting from this complex interplay of basic economic and social facts and from the elements of an axiology. Likewise, it was necessary to clarify the decisions to be made, by classifying them according to their time scale and their degree of flexibility and by attempting to see the ways in which they related to each other. In the end, the fragility of the customary distinction between ends and means, effects and costs, became clear. Finally, the question arose as to the institutional framework within which to discuss options and proceed with the conscious choice of a real design for civilization, conceived both as a supreme goal and as a frame of reference for economic planning proper.

To these difficulties are added the urgent problems presented by the increasingly destructive exploitation of natural resources and by the deterioration of the quality of urban life. What is involved are the "standard" forms of pollution (air, water, noise), and also the psychological repercussions, inadequately studied hitherto, of excessive urban concentration, of the ugliness of cities, of the different forms of alienation caused by industrial civilization. It is often claimed that these are problems peculiar to rich countries. This is false, and for many reasons.[11]

For one, colonization has often been responsible for environmental disruption within the colonized territory, the exploitation of this or that natural resource with no consideration of physical, biological, or social consequences. Then, ill-conceived development projects have often resulted in destruction. Sometimes, by interfering with ecosystems without taking into account all the possible consequences (sometimes difficult to detect in the present state of knowledge); sometimes by thinking it desirable, in order to limit investment, to give up conservation projects by irrigating without draining, by cutting down the forests without regard for the changes in climate which would result, and in the end destroying more than was created. So long as we remain dominated by the rationality of the enterprise, by the idea that, whenever possible, profits must be internalized and costs externalized, such accidents or misdeeds will continue to occur.

What is more, the terrible pollution and the frightful living conditions to which many cities in the Third World are subject are especially serious in that the resources necessary to remedy them are entirely lacking. One of the consequences of the insular development of modern towns and the nuclei of industrialization modeled on the European (or American) examples is the introduction of pollution, in advance of the other benefits of industrial civilization. Action to avert the most dramatic effects of environmental disruption is therefore also necessary in the Third World, provided that it is not made into an additional barrier to development, or a pretext for abandoning industrialization, as some neo-Malthusians fiercely opposed to the development of the Third World would urge.[12] It should be seen, on the contrary, as an additional dimension to be taken into consideration in long-term planning, especially since a large number of environmental control operations require only "human investment" and therefore could even be achieved in the poor countries, with considerable social and economic consequences in the long run.

But we should think above all of prevention, wherever it is not already too late. We thus come to the problems covered by a blueprint for society in its broadest sense, in which economics, sociology, ethics, and aesthetics merge in the overall consideration of development goals neglected by familiar European models, be they capitalist or socialist. Over and above the political schism, it is this effort to rethink society and to give it a new egalitarian, nonalienating, nonurban, nonbureaucratic, and modern form which should be seen in the

Chinese dispute[13] with Soviet socialism. The only true advantage of the latecomers in the race for development might well be the possibility that they still have of rejecting existing models and of defining themselves by opposing them, of creating, in other words, original blueprints.

Unfortunately, the present trend is in completely the opposite direction: the Third World is modeling itself on the industrial societies. While perfectly aware of the impossibility of creating from nothing a blueprint that can be based only on social experience, I think that a theoretical effort is necessary, one which could be given the special designation of long-term planning. The paradigm for such activity should be different from that for medium-range planning. City planning, which subordinates its visionary aspect and its interdisciplinary approach to the unity of its subject, probably offers a good starting point. But long-term planning should lead to a strategy of structural change, that is to say, a systemic analysis of goals in relation to material and technical means, of policies considered as instruments both of change and of management, and of timetables, since scheduling is crucial to the theory of planning and can produce distinctly varied strategies.

Notes to Chapter 11

1. See in particular the important report entitled *Social Policy and Planning in National Development* (E/CN.5/445, December 11, 1969).

2. Joan Robinson, *Economic Philosophy* (London, 1962), p. 113.

3. I take this example from my study: "Development Planning and Policies for Increasing Domestic Resources for Investment (with Special Reference to Latin America)," in *Policies of Plan Implementation,* Report of the Third Interregional Seminar on Development Planning, Santiago, March 1968, pp. 178-179.

4. The whole exercise could be complicated by introducing the rates of population growth of the elites and the masses. It might then be necessary to spread over a longer period the phase of accelerating the economy, if it were decided to make a political condition of nonreduction at all times, in absolute terms, of the

the per capita consumption of the elites. Personally I do not think that such a condition should be set. But in any case the example cited above is only a methodological guideline.

5. See in particular M. Kalecki, "An Outline of a Method of Constructing a Perspective Plan," in *Essays on Planning and Economic Development,* vol. 1 (Warsaw, 1963), pp. 9-22, and, for a diagrammatic presentation, the appendix to my study "The Determination of Targets for Domestic Saving and the Inflow of External Resources," in *Planning Domestic and External Resources for Investment,* Report of the Second Interregional Seminar on Development Planning, United Nations, Amsterdam, September 1966, pp. 70-72.

6. For a very clear and elementary description of this procedure, see Jan Tinbergen, *Central Planning* (New Haven, Conn., 1964).

7. See in this connection the already mentioned article by J.-P. Lewis, "Wanted in India: A Relevant Radicalism," *Economic and Political Weekly,* special issue, 5.29-31 (1970), pp. 1217-1220. But the alternative of trading off some growth for more social justice from the outset should not be ruled out, as would be indicated by the Chinese example.

8. I refer once again to Myrdal's point of view on this subject.

9. C. Brobowski has stressed this point on many occasions.

10. An unfortunately incomplete report on the work undertaken by this group has been published in two successive issues of *Kultura i Spoleczenstwo,* no. 4/ 1967 and no. 1/1968.

11. I dealt with this problem in "Development Planning and Environment: The Case of the Countries of the Third World," in *Environmental Disruption: A Challenge to Social Scientists,* pp. 275-285.

12. Thus P. R. Ehrlich, whose work enjoys a certain prestige in the United States, does not hesitate to write: "We will have to recognize the fact that most countries can never industrialize and that giving them industrialization aid is wasteful. We will have to accept the fact (already shown by theory, computer simulation, and practice) that it is pointless to help any country with a rapidly growing population unless the aid is very largely for population control, or at least unless such population control is included." P. R. Ehrlich, "Famine 1975: Fact or Fallacy," in *The Environmental Crisis,* ed. H. W. Helfrich (New Haven, Conn., 1970).

13. This effort by the Chinese is described sympathetically, but sometimes too naively for my taste, by Han Suyin, *China in the Year 2001* (Harmondsworth, 1970).

Underdevelopment is characterized, and even defined, by the rigidity of structures, by the difficulty of getting out of ruts, by bottlenecks in the flow of goods. This situation is poles apart from that marvelous flexibility postulated by the theory of the market of perfect competition and which the developed economies possess to a certain extent. As it is impossible to build up a development strategy on the paradigm of pragmatic solutions, the planner must explore in advance the obstacles to be overcome in the race to development. Care must be taken to avoid the snare of a fragmentary approach and the illusion that the problems can be tackled one by one. Analysis must result in an overall view of the different obstacles and the ways in which they reinforce each other. A diagram such as that in figure 8, where the arrows show the direction of interactions, aids this process.

Let us first of all focus our attention on the center. A backward agriculture acts in such a way as to curb the development of industries and, generally speaking, of all secondary and tertiary activities, since it does not supply the surplus of foodstuffs necessary for the urban population, nor the raw materials for certain industries. This difficulty will be aggravated by the country's poverty—which gives rise to a high income-elasticity in demand for foodstuffs—and by considerable demographic pressure. (As demographic pressure affects the entire system, I have placed it outside the diagram, for greater simplicity). The galloping inflation to which most Third World countries are subject may be explained to a large extent by the inadequacy of agricultural production. And, reciprocally, an underdeveloped industry checks the progress of agricultural production, for which fertilizers, insecticides, tools, and machines are necessary. Both agriculture and industry are handicapped by the absence of an adequate infrastructure: industries come to a halt for lack of electrical power and crops rot in the fields on account of breakdowns in transport.

The shortage of skilled personnel is an additional handicap; the overabundant supply of nonqualified labor cannot offset the lack of specialists, which is further aggravated by the structure of higher

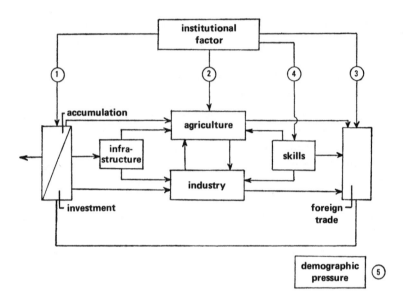

Figure 8

education in the Third World. Humanities and law occupy first place there, reflecting a scale of values inherited from the colonial period and corresponding also to the opportunities for commercial and administrative careers, which have increased since the departure of the colonizers.

In short, there is a closed circle of underdeveloped forces of production. To what should we attribute this situation as it relates to agriculture, industry, and the infrastructure? A part of the answer is provided by the inadequate level of productive investments, which in turn is to be explained by the low level of accumulation, a substantial part of which, moreover, goes abroad as return on foreign capital.

Let us now consider foreign trade. Its function is of the greatest importance, for the physical and human weaknesses of the system can be offset by importation. The more underdeveloped an economy is, the more it depends on foreign trade, even when that constitutes only a tiny fraction of the national income. Paradoxically, it is when superfluous imports have already been eliminated (and therefore when available foreign exchange is used solely for the purchase of the products and services necessary to ease the bottlenecks) that this dependence is most felt. In other words, foreign trade makes it possible to transform a given and poorly differentiated structure of production into a different structure of supply, one adapted to the requirements of the plan. But this maneuver has narrow limits, for it depends on the existence of outlets for exports. And if these are lacking, as is the case for the great majority of the traditional export products of the Third World, foreign trade, instead of easing the bottlenecks, creates one which turns out to be fundamental and ends by curbing the rate of investments. The reason for this is that, once superfluous imports have been eliminated, it is impossible not to meet a rigid demand for imports of intermediate products, raw materials, and, in certain cases, the foodstuffs necessary for the functioning of the economy and the prevention of famine. If this is not done, the existing machinery of production will stand idle and social disaster will soon follow. Consequently, any reduction in available foreign exchange, if it is not offset by credit, causes a contraction of capital goods imports. In extreme cases, the financial resources earmarked for investment are underutilized, because the essential foreign exchange component is lacking; we are confronted with a paralyzing feedback from foreign trade on the national economy.

In the model just described one might see yet another version of the "vicious circle of underdevelopment," restricted to a concern with the forces of production alone, if we did not bring into play the institutional factor in the broadest sense of the word, that is, encompassing the relations of production, the political system, and even custom. It is only at this level of analysis, which has become political, that it is possible to find answers to the following fundamental questions: why is the accumulation insufficient and why is it squandered?

In what way do the ossified agrarian structures prevent agriculture from advancing? To what use are the possibilities of foreign trade put? What is the government's attitude toward problems of professional training, technological progress, and scientific research?

As a result, it seems possible, if not easy, to break out of the vicious circle, by means of a coherent set of policies to effect (1) the redistribution of income; (2) agrarian reforms; (3) the control of foreign trade; (4) cultural development (education, science and technology); and (5) a demographic policy. I should stress once again the systemic character which all development strategy should have. Action must be directed toward the five weak points at the same time, and the intervention of government in all these fields is the minimum condition for effective planning. It should always be borne in mind that, in the last analysis, it is the most constricting bottleneck which will impose its limit on the growth rate. If, therefore, these policies are not implemented in harmony with each other—and consequently realized in different degrees according to the requirements of specific cases—there will always be idle production capacities. Now, it is precisely this social wastage that planning sets out to avert. It is aimed at balanced growth—if by this term one understands the elimination of bottlenecks and a better use of all available resources; on the other hand, it is always unbalanced, in the sense that policies are implemented to different degrees, that the equilibriums existing from the outset are disturbed (which follows naturally from all development), and that a choice is made of clearly determined points of attack, within the framework of a strategy. I should therefore say that discussion of the respective merits of balanced and unbalanced growth (I am thinking especially of the writings of Nurkse and Hirschman)[1] are largely based on a semantic misunderstanding.

Note to Chapter 12

1. See Ragnar Nurkse, *Problems of Capital Formation in Underdeveloped Countries* (New York, 1957) and A. O. Hirschman, *Strategy of Economic Development* (New Haven, Conn., 1958).

13   The Range of Policies

The will—and the power—to upset equilibriums are therefore a precondition of all accelerated development, organized and directed according to a plan. For many countries in the Third World, this entails, from the outset, a far-ranging transformation of existing political relations. Without this radical transformation they can embark only on pseudoplanning, which is ineffective in practice and conservative ideologically and, in the long run, compromises the very idea of planning. Far from being a politically neutral instrument of modernization, planning, in order to be effective, must be radical, in the etymological sense of the word, must attack structures themselves. And in order to avoid bureaucratic degeneracy, it must also, as is more than abundantly proven *a contrario* by the Soviet and East European experience, be democratic, again in the etymological sense of the term, that is to say, must be achieved by real and not formal popular participation. At first sight, these seem restrictive conditions and ones indeed that are hard to meet. Some interpret them quite simply to mean that all planning is impossible outside revolutionary regimes of the extreme left. I do not share this peremptory point of view.

First, we do not have enough information to know for certain whether the most important concrete experiment to date—that of the Chinese cultural revolution—has been truly effective as far as economic and social planning are concerned. Furthermore, political radicalism, by itself, is not enough, as is clearly proven by the Cuban failure.

Second, it is all too easy, and even naive, to wait, in the Latin Quarter of Paris, for world revolution to occur as a precondition for all effective action in the Third World. Until such time as more radical measures can be adopted, reformism—while certainly not offering any ultimate solutions—imposes itself as a moral obligation, if only as an attempt to improve the lot of the wretched peoples of the Third World right away, while working for the adoption of more radical positions when the limits of reformism become obvious. If only too in order to obtain more concrete knowledge of economic and social mechanisms, which can be acquired only through action.

Moreover, an often effective way of discrediting the conservative elites in power is to confront them thus with compromise reformist programs. They would accept them if they took their own talk seriously, or if they had a modicum of foresight. But usually they reject them.

In short, I do not think that this problem can be discussed in terms of a dichotomy: one cannot pinpoint any political threshold which suddenly opens the way to effective planning, any strait and narrow way leading to revolution outside of which planning has no place. In reality there are different degrees of effectiveness according to the degree of boldness with which governments[1] promote policies of structural change and obtain popular support for such policies. As we have already seen, it is not possible to reduce the complex political realities of the Third World to the capitalism-socialism dichotomy; intermediate regimes and even, in certain cases, neocapitalist regimes are capable of grappling here and there with the existing structures. In each of the key areas covered by development policies, a wide choice of possibilities presents itself, ranging from the ultraconservative status quo to the most radical basic reforms. It is this that I shall attempt to explain in this chapter.

Income Distribution

In a mixed economy, nonintervention in the distribution of income implies the increasing concentration of wealth in the hands of an elite and a subsidiary process, benefiting the working-class aristocracies in relation to the disinherited rural masses and the urban subproletariat. Confiscating private capitalist enterprises affords of course the surest means of effecting, once and for all, a change in the distribution of income and of setting the process of development on a firm basis, that of accumulation within the public sector. But this should not stop one from seeing that profits made within the country by government enterprises ultimately amount to a levy (identical to taxes) on the national income that is distributed. The high prices of industrial consumer goods in the socialist countries are tantamount to an indirect tax system, the fairness of which is sometimes very debatable.

In any case, this is a measure which clearly depends on a revolutionary situation. Furthermore, the nationalization of foreign firms may result in international reprisals, morally inadmissible and damaging to the sovereignty of the revolutionary country, but nevertheless very real. This sometimes makes it necessary for even countries of anti-imperialist persuasion to hedge. They have to make do with half-measures, which reduce the amount of expropriated profits, but are acceptable *in extremis* to foreign firms, so long as their real profit margin is not reduced to zero. The changes in regulations governing distribution of profits between concessionary enterprises and petroleum-producing countries is a good example of these procedures, which will doubtless multiply if the countries of the Third World learn to act together. All the same, what the oil companies have managed to impose for a long time on the countries of the Third World as a basis for discussion is the percentage distribution of net profit. What would really be of consequence is supervision of the way in which the net profit is calculated, without which profits may flow out of the country, disguised as payments for fictitious services and costs.

Likewise, massive reinvestment of the return on foreign capital is a snare which should be avoided. At first sight, it is a more attractive solution than the expropriation of profits. In reality it causes foreign ascendancy in the national economy to become steadily more powerful and this, in the long run, has negative repercussions on the balance of payments, except in the case where reinvestments are treated as local private capital, without any right to the expropriation of profits.

For domestic firms and individuals, tax measures offer undeniable possibilities, which most of the time are not exploited or are compromised by the venality of the administration. Corruption is a fact whose importance cannot be underestimated, although its paralyzing effects on the economy have sometimes been exaggerated,[2] or, more serious, invoked as an excuse for not reforming the tax system. On the other hand, it is necessary, in the name of realism, to abandon the superficial conception of direct taxes as the only form of equitable taxation, according to which indirect taxes are always attacked as though a salt tax or a tax on matches were under discussion. In most of the Third World countries, the only ones to pay direct taxes in full are the wage earners, as their taxes are withheld. The wealthy find a thousand ways of doging taxes. The penalties which, from time to time, right-wing governments inflict on a few tax dodgers by way of example, in no way constitute an effective solution; the sole purpose of their spectacular and demagogic character is to conceal the ultraconservatism of these governments. In order to make those who should be the first to support the cost of development pay taxes, there should be a heavy tax on conspicuous wealth,[3] and draconian and highly progressive indirect taxes should be imposed on superfluous consumption, luxury goods above all, while the few essential goods consumed by the impoverished masses should be completely tax free.

A tax reform of this kind is not achieved without difficulties. First of all, there must be agreement on the list of essential consumer goods, even if this entails fairly complicated procedures[4] and periodically reviewing of the lists. Above all, a consistent tax policy must be pursued. Thus, while it is reasonable to establish a heavy tax on private cars—assuming that it is too late to limit their use—users should not be subsidized by excessively reducing the price of gasoline, by not collecting highway tolls on tourist routes, and by using funds which should be used for public transport to improve traffic conditions for private cars in cities. It is necessary, finally, to have the courage to reject the democratic pretenses of the welfare state and to stop making available to the elites, who are practically the only ones to benefit from them, free public services, in the field of higher education, for instance. Real democracy consists in opening the doors of the university to those of modest means and in providing them with scholarships so that they can pursue their studies. It is a joke in the worst possible taste to claim that free higher education is a social victory, when 75 percent of students, or more, drive to the university in private cars and belong to the small circle of families who are sufficiently rich to pay for their children's studies.

Last, a highly progressive tax on land should be considered as an instrument for the promotion of agricultural productivity and the redistribution of marginal land. Landowners who are incapable of sufficiently increasing production in order to pay taxes are thus forced to sell their marginal lands, preferably to the government, which would then be able to set aside land to be used as a basis for agrarian reform.[5]

A well-conceived and selective taxation system makes it possible not only to transfer a part of the available resources to the government, but also to influence private expenditure, encouraging certain investments for which the government offers tax benefits and credits. But in order for this policy to be effective, it is necessary to set up machinery for the control of investments. The advantages offered to persuade the private sector to invest in ways which tally with the goals of the plan can fully play their role only when the capitalists are at the same time dissuaded, by administrative means, from making investments which, although they have a very high profit-earning capacity, deserve only small social priority. At all events, the government must be prepared to make priority investments itself, if the incentives used do not convince the private capitalists. The public sector thus appears as the pillar of planned development, even in a mixed economy; its power of persuasion and dissuasion over the private sector depends on its size and even more on its dynamism in investment.

Over and above tax reform and the role assigned to the public sector, what is therefore being challenged is the entire model of interventionism. The range of possibilities, still within the context of mixed economies, lies between two opposing models. Of course, neither of the two exists anywhere in pure form, but they afford useful guidelines for the analysis of concrete situations. I am referring first to the Japanese model, already analyzed, and second to the Indian model.[6] The latter, proposed rather than achieved by the Congress

party immediately after Indian independence, assigns a steadily growing role to the public sector, as holder of monopolies and privileged
positions in several industries which, undoubtedly, have the faculty of
transforming economic structures. Whereas the Japanese model makes
the public sector an instrument of the private and results in the privati-
zation of successful public investments, the "Indian" model proposes
that the private sector be limited for the benefit of the public and that
private enterprise be subordinated to the requirements of the plan.
The failure of the Indian model, in India itself, and the increasing importance assumed in that country by the Japanese model in no way
changes, in my opinion, the theoretical significance of the Indian
model, which other intermediate regimes, such as Algeria, Egypt, or
Syria, are at present trying to put into practice.

Apart from these standard considerations, there remains the field of
human investment, which has not been very well explored hitherto. It
may be considered the simultaneous creation of investment and the
savings necessary to finance it, which pre-exist in semiunemployed
rural societies in the form of free working time (this is clearly one of
the two forms of surplus that I have distinguished). The idea is tempt-
ing, so much so that care must be taken not to exagerrate its importance, as was the case, it seems, at the time of China's first Great Leap
Forward. Indeed, the use of voluntary and unpaid peasant labor (and
why not of the urban subproletariat?) requires the fulfillment of a certain number of preliminary conditions.

First of all, labor must be given completely voluntarily. There is
therefore no room for human investment wherever social inequalities
persist, since voluntary labor is then transformed into forced labor
with its unfortunate connotations from the past; the failures of the
"shramdan" in India and similar campaigns in North Africa prove it.
There must also be available means of financing, if only in the form of
rudimentary tools and foodstuffs, for the additional expenditure of
energy must be compensated for if one wishes to attain reasonable

standards of productivity. To count exclusively on enthusiasm is dangerous for two reasons: enthusiasm does not fill stomachs and it has a tendency to be quickly exhausted. Finally, one must realize that the number of tasks that can be performed by "human investment" is limited and that these amount, roughly speaking, to certain types of rural work, often with a long gestation period and calling for a high level of concentrated effort, posing thorny problems of organization and, even more, problems relating to level of awareness, to the amount of confidence inspired by the leaders, and to the ability to appreciate the benefits of activities whose results will not be seen for a very long time. The paradox of the situation of the underdeveloped countries is indeed that they are better placed to devote their energies to long-term goals than to activities with immediate effects, while the pressure of hardship and the reminder of the levels of consumption attained in rich countries naturally encourage them to adopt the opposite attitude.

In this context, I should like to state a fundamental objection to the blueprint of the Chinese revolution: either frugality will one day have to give way to a more open attitude toward consumption (meaning that this frugality has a tactical and transitory character, despite the attempt to set it up as a moral principle); or else the mobilization of energies and resources for the modernization and economic expansion of the country is redundant. However, it is quite possible to conceive of the future model of consumption in China deviating from the Western or Soviet models.

At a more immediate level, many countries of the Third World, even in mixed economic systems, could speed up their grwoth rate and obtain advantageous results from the social point of view by deciding to introduce into their plans an additional component for building of low-price housing and controlling pollution by reducing to a minimum the use of mechanized equipment, both for the work itself and for the manufacturing of building materials. The same remark applies to social services. Even if these works are financed by the government and cease to be a "human investment" in the strict sense, based on labor given

voluntarily, their effects could be substantial. This is especially so in
that they do not pose any insurmountable financial problems provided
the difficulties arising from the limited supply of agricultural produce
are overcome.

Agrarian Reform

The two extremes of the range of agrarian reform policies may easily
be defined: on the one hand total and immediate expropriation, without compensation for the landowners, followed by collectivization; on
the other hand the legal and economic status quo, implying the con-
tinuation of precapitalist relations of production, since sharecropping
in its most extreme form is similar to bondage. In contrast, the variety
of intermediate solutions reflects the multiplicity of situations, in the
political and legal as well as the economic realms, in an area which is
ultrasusceptible to special cases, so much so that many countries have
made agrarian legislation and policy an area reserved for the provincial
administration. But this desire to avoid dogmatism is sometimes dearly
paid for, since the influence of the reactionary landowners makes itself
felt to a greater degree in local administration than in the central government. A few general points stand out, nevertheless, from this mass
of particularities.

First of all it should be pointed out that there has been a twofold
evolution of ideas in the course of the last twenty years. Immediately
after the Second World War, opinions were polarized. The supporters
of a reform of the property laws, as radical as possible, believed in the
magic virtues of the redistribution of land: the peasants, having become the owners of their small plots or members of cooperatives,
would set about steadily producing an overabundant supply of provisions. The opponents of the reform dismissed it as fanciful and insisted on the advantages of an investment policy aimed at the clearing
of new lands, irrigation, and the production (or the purchase outside)
of chemical fertilizers. In short, social engineering and economic action were presented, politically, as mutually exclusive options. Today,

the two parties have made amends and everyone is more or less agreed
that land reform, in order to be effective, must be accompanied by a
policy of active support for agriculture in the form of guaranteed
prices, loans, public investments, and technical assistance, and that,
reciprocally, this policy of support would miss the mark if attention
were not given at the same time to property structures and the status
of the farmer.

However, a fundamental opposition still remains: some simply want
growth in agricultural production, and, more precisely, a more plentiful
marketable surplus to meet the foreign and urban demand; others are
set on the reform of property structures as an end in itself, aimed at
improving the lot of millions of landless peasants, of sharecroppers, of
farmhands, of luckless people without steady employment, living from
day to day, or of owners of tiny plots of land who are almost as badly
off. What is at stake is the life and the dignity of the greater part of the
present world population and, to speak less emotionally, the equilibrium
of the economic and social structure of the Third World.

The inadequacy of agricultural production has been, for many countries of the Third World and for a sufficiently long period to justify
generalization, the most acutely felt physical constraint. The growth
rate of the demand for foodstuffs a is determined by the growth rate of
the population p and by the increase in per capita income y multiplied
by the income-elasticity of demand e,[7] as expressed by the following
equation:

$a = p + ey.$

If p = 2.5 percent, y = 2 percent, and e = 0.5 (figures which are low
and fairly probable), a = 3.5 percent. However, except in cases where
there are considerable reserves of fallow land and the initial level of
productivity is very low, an average rate of growth for agricultural production of 3.5 percent yearly is difficult, if not impossible, to attain
regularly.[8] This is all the more true because this calculation must be
made not for the total product but for the part of it which is marketed

and for the demand which is met through the market. Now, in this case, *a* grows far more quickly on account of the rural exodus to the cities, since the reduction of the peasant population does not cause an increase in the marketable surplus of food produced, but rather a slight improvement in peasant food consumption.[9] Moreover, *e* varies according to the food supply and population groups, the income-elasticity of the demand for meat being far higher than the figure 0.5 used above.

As for the effects of agrarian reform on the marketable surplus, they may be negative at the present, since the peasant is no longer forced to sell a part of his produce to pay land rent and taxes, thus sacrificing his level of consumption. The opponents of agrarian reforms take advantage of this to say that the reform is counterproductive, in which they are wrong, for they forget that raising the peasant's standard of living is one of the immediate goals of development, even if supplies for the cities suffer. But this, I agree, presents the planners with a difficult problem. It may be said in passing that more often than not the arguments against dividing up large land holdings are not valid either, since the land is then not cultivated according to the economically advantageous rules of large-scale farming. They are farmed as plots, rented out to sharecroppers or placed under the responsibility of "colons" (whose status is halfway between farmhand and sharecropper). The continued existence of large coffee, cocoa, or sugar plantations in certain countries is often justified by suggesting that these crops cannot be profitably farmed by small farmers. But the experience of other countries proves the contrary.

Moreover, the pessimism of many experts as to the chances of increasing the food production of the Third World—with the exception of a few disaster areas—is no longer in such a great danger of famine, although the amount and the nutritional value of the food consumed by a large majority of its inhabitants remain unsatisfactory. Statistics provide abundant proof of this.[10]

Only ten years ago at this writing, it seemd that the ability to overcome the problem of food supply could, by a tragic paradox, be obtained only at a high level of general development. Therefore, at a time when, so to speak, the problem no longer exists, since development has been accompanied by a deceleration, and even a falling off, of the demand for foodstuffs, the peasants are in fact faced with the threat of overproduction. In the light of more recent data, we must revise our position.

The possibility of rapidly increasing agricultural production seems truly to exist today, in several countries of the Third World, under the combined effect of urban demand, of a balance of trade more favorable to agriculture owing to inflation, of the supply of intermediate industrial products, of the availability of new technologies developed by the "green revolution," of the aid lavishly provided by governments in the form of investments (in irrigation and the infrastructure), of loans and a tax system favorable to farmers. But what has generally happened is a capitalist infiltration into agriculture, effected by a limited number of entrepreneurs, of major companies connected with the food-processing industry, sometimes of former landowners or a minority of rich peasants, and usually involving newcomers to agriculture: immigrants, military veterans who have become smallholders, retired administrators, and other city dwellers, beginning with those who, having gained their wealth illegally, seek the respectability which is afforded by the status of a modern farmer, coddled by a government that wants to be sure of food supplies for the country and is prepared to turn a blind eye to the origins of the fortunes acquired. The great majority of peasants do not participate in this new prosperity, except to the extent that there is slightly more often a day's work available wherever the effects of mechanization are not too pronounced. All in all, this kind of agricultural development is destined to accentuate the technological, economic, and social dualism in rural areas and to make more unsolvable than ever the problem of employment and a decent standard of living for the peasants. I therefore refute the hopes for the "green revolution" so long as it is implemented by a capitalist revolution.

Unfortunately, the experience of many countries proves that it is possible to turn even agrarian reforms which are fairly radical on paper to the advantage of rural capitalists, either because the legislation contains clauses exempting so-called modern and well-cultivated forms, or else because the laws have been wrongly interpreted, with the connivance of the authorities. In certain Indian states, sharecroppers abandon land willingly, so it is said, to the owners (these are, of course, forced evictions). There is too much inequality in the balance of power between the poor and illiterate peasant, hedged in by the need to earn a living from day to day, and the landowner, who is sufficiently rich and influential to acquiesce if need be in shady dealings and the possibility of having to answer in court. True agrarian reform must be based on an executive power which is resolved to carry it out, either because it represents the peasants or else because it fears mass movements.

I should say agrarian reforms, in the plural, for it is not certain that the redistribution of land is the most important task. In a pinch, confirming sharecropper status might be enough, if rents were actually reduced, if the debts of the peasants were abolished or reduced, a decent system of cooperative or government marketing established, and water, industrial inputs, and technical assistance effectively made available to small farmers. But in these areas, corruption and nepotism may distort the best-intentioned reforms, not to mention cases where such good will is lacking.[11]

As for the limits of individual land holdings, the amount of compensation for expropriated landowners, the conditions of accession to land under the agrarian reforms, these are questions which, once again, depend on the balance of political power. Certain reforms, such as the Egyptian, directed against a minority of major landowners, do not dare touch the average and small landowners, who live off the exploitation of sharecroppers and farm workers; and such reforms, despite a radical terminology, merely serve to reinforce capitalist relationships, which, historically speaking, is perhaps a step forward in relation to the precapitalist relationships, but which continues to place the great mass of laborers and sharecroppers in a marginal economic and political situation.

On the other hand, I do not think that small family ownership, not involving the use of paid labor, must necessarily lead to agrarian capitalism;[12] it is enough for the government to provide it with an adequate framework and to be responsible for the marketing of the chief products and for credit for agriculture and, where the case arises, for the cooperative network (of which the small peasants would be the effective managers), along with technical assistance. Family ownership offers the undeniable advantages of adaptability to a policy for promoting agricultural production through the intensive use of labor and non-monetary investment—an adaptability which collective farms cannot have. They become superior only when it is possible to provide them with modern equipment and management, while providing other occupations for surplus manpower. Premature collectivization, far from removing obstacles, may, on the contrary, slow down the transformation of agriculture, even when it attempts to legitimize itself by referring to a still living tradition of precapitalist collectivist practices. Which does not mean that I condemn a priori resorting to cooperative solutions, or to government farms self-managed by agricultural laborers. But the specifics of the situation must provide an impetus in this direction.

Foreign Trade

I have dwelt at length on the cardinal role of foreign trade in the process of development, even when the process is based on import substitution. It does not necessarily follow that the government should take responsibility for all foreign trade operations, it being often too cumbersome for the public sector to manage them directly, especially when a large number of specialized transactions relating to a varied range of products are involved. On the other hand, a monopoly on the sale of the chief export goods, which is easier to achieve, affords undeniable advantages for both negotiations on the international market and the organization of the tax system. It enables the government to set the margin between the prices paid to producers and world prices, or, if the need arises, to put into effect a system of subsidies for productions sold abroad. For other products, it is possible to conceive of different procedures for the administrative control of imports or the more or less automatic allocation of foreign exchange (for instance, through systems of multiple exchange rates), and support for exports through direct promotion, selective taxation or, quite simply, by means of subsidies. I do not see why export subsidies should be excluded, while the subsidy of local production which eliminates the need for imports is tolerated. At all events the dichotomy, exports or import substitution, is not valid. Both policies are necessary at the same time, and the calculation of the net domestic cost of the foreign exchange earned or saved indicates the proportions which should be maintained between investments aimed at one or the other of these targets.

None of these procedures is perfect. The risks of bureaucratization and corruption are great, as is the danger of alienating the foreign trade sector, once it has become a government within the government. But all this is not sufficient reason to favor the automatic interplay of market forces and thus to deliver oneself up to the mercy of international free trade.

The planner should, on the contrary, seek formulas for introducing some stability into foreign trade. Hence the interest in developing the international organization of markets, which unfortunately comes up against the ill will of the great and powerful, despite U.N.C.T.A.D. Hence the need for effective cooperation between the countries of the Third World, who would gain by presenting a program of positive action instead of contenting themselves with the defensive attitude of demanding measures of assistance from the rich countries.

For all these political reasons, and influenced by the example of the European Common Market, many countries of the Third World indulge in inordinate hopes for regional integration along European lines, that is to say, obtained by gradually opening up markets. In my opinion, this is barking up the wrong tree, for the reduction of tariffs primarily serves the expansion of multinational enterprises, established within common markets and more powerful and better prepared to grasp new opportunities. Moreover, this approach obliges the member countries to concentrate the bulk of their efforts and their resources on the consolidation and the modernization of already existing enterprises, threatened by competition. In underdeveloped countries, however, funds available for investment should be allocated for setting up new industries, which can transform economic and social structures, rather than for the rationalization of already existing industries. And this is all the more so in that most of the time, the latter would quite simply have to be closed down, with all the consequences which would follow for the labor market. In short, there is a danger that the cure would be more harmful than the disease. The model of integration for the countries of the Third World should turn away from the European example and focus on the setting up of new industries, on the basis of an overall plan. As it is difficult to create supranational enterprises and to obtain the cooperation of governments with changing and sometimes divergent policies, the most acceptable compromise arrangement, to prepare the way for cooperation, would undoubtedly be to negotiate groups of long-term contracts by which the contracting countries would be sure of deliveries of certain products while obtaining market guarantees for others, in such a way that both sides would benefit from economies of scale in the selective implantation of new industries. This would be a realistic way of tackling the problem of setting up capital goods industries where they hardly yet exist.

Redemption through Science?
Human resources have been neglected in economic calculations since the period of blind faith in machines. Traditional culture, on the contrary, attached a great deal of importance to the qualifications of the craftsman; in a society where machines still counted for little, technique was not distinguished from the skill acquired through apprenticeship.

But for many countries of the Third World, contact with capitalism began with the relentless destruction of the traditional crafts activities, followed by an obscurantist cultural and educational policy designed by the colonial authorities. There is therefore something hypocritical in the zeal with which those countries are urged today to concentrate on the economic value of human resources, especially when this advice neglects the basic fact that the promotion of human capital alone is not of much use if it does not go hand in hand with the transformation of the economic structures themselves. In the light of certain historical experiences, one might be tempted to say that whenever it is proclaimed that man is the most precious form of capital, it means that he is about to be destroyed.

The rediscovery by economic science of the role of people in production has been accompanied by dangerous exaggerations, which consist in quantifying the impact of education and technology on output. This is only one step away from claiming that investment in education, health, or research has a greater profit-earning capacity than the construction of a dam or of a factory. Such comparisons do not make much sense, not only because they are based on a dubious theory,[13] but above all because they neglect the elementary fact that it is impossible to escape from the complementarity of the means and the agents of production.

Furthermore, this excessive quantification pushes into the background the far more complex qualitative problems of educational and scientific policy. It is not enough to have such and such a number of specialists for each 10,000 people; no one would dream, after all, of making the same calculation for poets![14] It is still mandatory that they represent specialities which are necessary to the economy and that their education have consisted of more than cramming. To develop agriculture, agronomists are required, not lawyers. And for dealing with the agricultural problems of the tropics, in countries where there is a plentiful supply of manpower, knowledge of the mechanized cultivation of grains in the American Midwest is not much help.

However, under the influence of certain American economists, a whole school of thought has been created, advocating that planning for skilled manpower should precede and even take the place of economic planning in the Third World. This school makes use of highly elegant quantitative methods, based on correlations between the growth rate of national income and the needs for manpower, but which in reality are founded on the quite crude idea that the process of development is unilinear.[15] A country bent on exploiting its mineral resources needs geologists; on the other hand, the expansion of tourism will not be achieved without the help of hotel managers. Manpower planning can therefore be only an extension of economic planning.

The problem becomes more complicated when we broaden our field of interest to take in education and culture in general, which are too frequently judged merely from the point of view of their supposed impact on productivity. They are, however, really targets of development and not production costs. Without overlooking the complex relations between the cultural and the economic spheres, the promotion of education and culture cannot be considered solely from the instrumental point of view. In this field, strategy should aim at a compromise between the immediate needs of the economy and the possibilities of committing resources for the promotion of culture and education, considered as basic human rights.

Moreover, are not such educational and cultural campaigns an outstanding area for human investment? They could be carried on by an appeal to the voluntary contribution of those who already possess some education, in particular high school graduates. But it is important above all that the content of such instruction not become a factor of alienation; the Third World will certainly not be able to do without an original effort, a total reform of educational curricula at all levels, including that of adult and professional education and all the mixed forms of work-study which are destined to play an increasing role if the pioneering efforts of China in this field prove to be fruitful.

Another compromise is called for in the controversial field of science policies, the last born of development policies. On the one hand, it is unthinkable to aspire today to scientific autarky. This path, which is open to a few big countries, can only be very costly. But, on the other hand, the seemingly attractive approach of relying on the conquests of world science and technology (and of abandoning all efforts of one's own in these fields) conceals very grave dangers. The domination of the industrial economies over those of the Third World becomes greater as a result, for the real cost of technology transfer is high, if one allows for certain hidden components, such as the inflated price of imported equipment and intermediate products. Moreover, the transferred technology does not, most of the time, adapt easily to the natural conditions and to the scale of production called for in the Third World; its implantation merely serves to exaggerate the distortions of the underdeveloped economy. The effects are even more disastrous in the cultural and political spheres. In the long run, the mimetic transfer of knowledge and technologies creates an imposed culture, a falsified scale of values. Beneath the appearances of modernity, a condition of dependence is established which stands in the way of any serious effort toward development.

It is therefore necessary to adopt an intermediate path and to take care in choosing areas for mimetic transfer, those where an effort of adaptation is required, and last, those where an autonomous research effort will be concentrated. Whereas ordinarily importation of technology is organized at present according to the will of the exporter, the ability to make these choices would call for setting up a coherent system of research, education, industrial and technological information, industrial design, engineering, and a regulatory agency overseeing imports of technology.

It is the creation of these facilities and the promotion of research neglected by world science (because it deals with problems specific to underdeveloped areas), which should be accorded priority by Third World countries if they want science and technology to cease being factors of subjection and to become factors of advancement. The first steps will perhaps be costly. They are nevertheless necessary; to the more or less universally accepted principle of protection for infant industries, there should be added, within reasonable limits, protection of the infant science and technology of the Third World.

Not, of course, that I believe in some sort of redemption through science, or in the possibility of replacing social change by scientific revolution. I repeat that they must assume complementary roles, and that the economy must still make full use of the possibilities opened up by science. This entails directing basic and applied research to the real problems of the country and promoting the choice of technologies to the position of a national policy. In fact, it is only by preventing excessive mechanization where there is no call for it (for instance, in the building industry, public works, certain services, and agriculture) that one can hope to reestablish a little of the equilibrium, at present disturbed, between growth and creating jobs. Since flexibility in the output mix is limited by the structure of demand to areas where substitutions are possible, it is on the choice of technologies itself that influence should be brought to bear.

Theoretically such a choice will not pose any major problems in the public sector, where it is possible to do cost-benefit analyses, using shadow prices for factors of production to express the planner's preferences. But influencing the choices of the private sector requires a certain number of administrative controls and a fiscal, financial, and social policy which makes it possible to act upon the real structure of the entrepreneur's costs and profits. The present functioning of market mechanisms causes entrepreneurs to make decisions which are contrary to the public interest. This touches on one of the most difficult and inadequately studied aspects of planning in an underdeveloped mixed economy.[16]

Demographic Policy
That the population explosion aggravates all the problems of the Third

World is beyond any doubt. The increase in production, the jobs thus created, the places available in schools and hospitals and new apartments must be shared among a number of applicants which increases with the rate of demographic growth. For a given pattern of income distribution, growth would create a more substantial improvement in the standard of living if it were possible to reduce the population boom. The population explosion, in conjunction with rural poverty, is at the basis of the most incurable problem of the Third World—the inordinate expansion of the cities and the hideous shantytowns, which is a veritable cancer on the economic fabric of countries too poor to afford the luxury of a modern urban economy. Most of the Third World countries have consequently decided at last to consider seriously a policy of birth control, although it cannot be claimed it will be successful in the next ten or fifteen years, or therefore will have any effect on the labor market before the beginning of the twenty-first century.

Too many difficulties of a technical nature, too many social or religious beliefs, must be overcome (not to mention the still inadequately studied consequences of some of the methods proposed) before effective action can rapidly change demographic trends in the rural areas of the Third World. Sexual abstinence, advocated by those in power in China, is merely a restatement of one of Gandhi's obscurantist ideas and is in flagrant contradiction with the ethical postulates of human liberation which is supposed to be at the basis of Marxist thought itself.

But if it is legitimate, if it is necessary, to make the I.U.D., the pill, or celibacy an element of national policy, one must categorically reject straightaway three common interpretations of the demographic problem of the Third World.

The first uses the population boom to explain the wretched conditions in the Third World, thus going against the most obvious historical evidence. This is an ideological maneuver which is agreeable to public opinion in the rich countries: by presenting an objective and material cause for the Third World's backwardness, it makes it possible to avoid bothersome questions concerning the colonial past, the consequences of domination, and the relationship between the poverty of one group of people and the wealth of another.

The second, following the same line of thought, makes birth control policy the substitute—and not the complement—of an energetic action to increase output, which is the only conceivable basis for the economic and social advancement of the Third World.

The third, finally, advocates neo-Malthusianism on a planetary scale, claiming that the resources of the globe are far too limited to allow the whole of mankind, and more especially the rapidly multiplying population of the Third World, to gain access to the benefits of industrialization without damaging the prospects of those who had the good fortune to be the first beneficiaries of modern material progress. It is therefore necessary on the one hand to limit the population growth of the Third World as soon as possible and on the other to turn it away from industrialization.[17] Rarely has pseudoscience—the alarmist views of the neo-Malthusians not being justified by the use that we have only begun to make of the biosphere—been placed in the service of such a monstruous scheme. This is neither more nor less than reducing the majority of humanity to a subhuman condition to preserve the privileged position of the minority of rich countries.

Notes to Chapter 13

1. The expression is C. Bobrowski's.

2. See Gunnar Myrdal, *Asian Drama* (New York, 1968), vol. 2, chapt. 20, pp. 937-958.

3. Despite a few resounding political failures, Nicholas Kaldor's concepts deserve special attention; see, for instance, *Essays on Economic Policy* (London, 1964), vol. 1, part 3: "The Problem of Tax Reform," pp. 203-293.

4. Thus, for instance, in the work inspired by Kalecki in India, unrefined sugar was considered to be an essential commodity, but the difference in price between raw and refined sugar to be subject to tax.

5. This was one of Kalecki's suggestions to the Indian government at the time

that India's third five-year plan was being prepared. See his article in *The Economic Weekly,* 9 (July 1960).

6. For a more elaborate analysis, I refer the reader to my work, *Patterns of Public Sector in Underdeveloped Economies* (Bombay, 1964).

7. See M. Kalecki, "Problems of Financing Economic Development in a Mixed Economy," in *Essays on Planning and Economic Development,* vol. 2 (Warsaw, 1965), pp. 37-50, and my study "Levels of Satiety and Rates of Growth," in *Problems of Economic Dynamics and Planning. Essays in Honour of Michal Kalecki* (Warsaw, 1964), pp. 343-363.

8. This, at least, is the opinion of many specialists such as R. Dumont. It would certainly be premature to revise it in the light of the early exponents of the green revolution. A world indicative plan for agricultural development, drawn up by the Food and Agriculture Organization of the U.N., postulates a gross average annual growth in value of agricultural output of 3.7 percent, while conceding the difficulty of this task, since over the last decade the rate was only 2.7 percent. According to the F.A.O., a growth rate of 3.7 percent would provide the developing countries with sufficient basic foodstuffs—in terms of calories—but would not guarantee adequate distribution to individuals or even regions (United Nations, Food and Agriculture and Agriculture Organization, *A Strategy for Plenty;* Rome, 1970).

9. This is a point which Ragnar Nurkse did not sufficiently take into account in *Problems of Capital Formation in Underdeveloped Countries* (New York, 1957).

10. Thus, for instance, an expert of the F.A.O. foresees that protein consumption in India will meet only one third of the real requirements of the population in 1975, and two thirds in 1985. Eleven African countries, in the south of the Sahara, with a total population of 63 million inhabitants, will still not be able to meet domestic demand in this area in 1975. The protein deficiency will not be met in 1985, in nine other countries, with 68 million inhabitants. (F.A.O., press comminiqué 70/72).

11. For an interesting attempt to compare the agrarian situation in developed countries and underdeveloped countries, see the two volumes compiled under the editorship of H. Mendras and Y. Tavernier, *Terre, paysans et politique* (Paris, 1969 and 1970).

12. In other words, I do not think that small-scale mercantile production is bound to create capitalists, as Lenin claimed.

13. I am thinking of Cobb-Douglas functions and of the approach advocated by E. F. Denison, in *The Residual Factor and Economic Growth* (Paris, 1964). For a critique of this concept, see, for instance, T. Balogh and P. Streeten, "The

Coefficient of Ignorance," *Bulletin of the Oxford University Institute of Statistics,* 25 (May 1963) and T. Balogh and N. Kaldor in *The Residual Factor.*

14. The remark is N. Calders, from *Technopolis: Social Control of the Uses of Science* (London, 1970).

15. See F. M. Harbison and C. A. Myers, *Education, Manpower and Economic Growth* (New York, 1964).

16. I have devoted a long study to this problem entitled "Selection of Techniques. Problems and Policies for Latin America," *Economic Bulletin for Latin America* (Santiago), 25.1 (1970).

17. I refer the reader to Ehrlich's view cited in Chapter 11.

The operational theory of development which I have described deals especially with factors internal to the countries of the Third World. This is because a country's development potential depends on three essential factors: the political will to become developed and the ability to make autonomous decisions; structures of production capable of physically reproducing themselves or of meeting increased demands for imports; intellectual structures capable of innovating in the Schumpeterian sense of the word, that is to say, of inventing, of copying, of adapting solutions to the problems of production and management.[1]

Now the first of these factors, which is by far the most important, can arise only from within; the two others are affected by external conditions, but not decisively in the long run, except in particularly unfavorable conditions or countries which are very small. Natural resources cannot be overlooked, but the example of Japan is there to warn us against any strict geographical determinism; moreover, the very concept of resources is, in the last analysis, cultural; it is human ingenuity which transforms nature into a source of materials and useful products.[2]

In short, the development of Third World countries will depend on their own efforts; international aid can be only a supplementary contribution. Moreover, it is enough to look at the figures: the Third World, despite unfavorable international conditions, is growing as a whole at rates higher than those formerly attained by capitalism.[3]

I am not saying this to set consciences at rest or to display a facile optimism, the growth rates and the distribution of gains being highly unsatisfactory in the face of accumulated poverty and the population boom. Above all, I do not think that the capitalist route which Europe took in the nineteenth century is an ideal to be emulated. Sunkel is right to say that the present development of Third World countries leads in reality to the disintegration of their economies and their societies, scarcely a fraction of which come to form part of the world capitalist economy.[4]

But it is useful to recognize that aid from the rich countries cannot be the mainspring of Third World strategy, and for that to be recognized on both sides, in order for the underdeveloped countries to liberate themselves from their inferiority complex and for the rich countries to shed some of their arrogance, which is particularly out of place since the difficulties of the Third World stem more from an excess than a lack of foreign interference in their affairs. What is at stake, ultimately, is not the development or the nondevelopment of the Third World, but the way in which it will be achieved, and at what price and in what international climate. If the rich countries understand the situation in time, it is still possible to conceive of this development within a harmonious world order. If they persist in their blindness and in the pursuit of short-term advantage, the countries of the Third World—some of them, at least—will develop in violent opposition to the international order founded on privilege; they will have no alternative other than to attempt to destroy that order—the catastrophe hypothesis—or to break up the world order and to isolate themselves—the least dramatic hypothesis, and also the least likely, so long as effective negotiations for a rational world economic order are not instituted under the auspices of the United Nations.

The impotence of U.N.C.T.A.D. is not a good sign for the future, although the very fact that it has been founded is evidence, despite appearances and changing trends, of a profound change in the balance of power to the disadvantage of the old international regime which should cause even the conservative governments of the Third World from time to time to take up a position against the beneficiaries of the present system. The contradictions will appear in the full light of day at the first sign of a serious deterioration in the international economic situation. Up to now, the high growth rates of the rich countries over the last twenty years have made it possible to allay the impact of the structural crisis of the traditional division of labor between industrialized countries and underdeveloped producers of raw materials.

That this crisis exists, no one doubts. In world trade, as we have seen, the Third World is becoming truly marginalized by change in structures of production in developed countries and technological progress.[5] Apart from petroleum and a few raw materials, the countries of the Third World are experiencing greater and greater difficulty in selling their traditional exports to finance their purchases abroad. As the net transfer of resources in the form of aid is insignificant (if one discounts direct investments of private capital and allows for losses from the deterioration of the balance of trade),[6] the only possible consequence is that the Third World gets further and further into debt more and more rapidly. This debt is today attaining such proportions that it is increasingly curbing new financing as a larger and larger part of aid is absorbed by the servicing of the debt.[7]

How can this vicious circle be broken? Either the flow of grants must be increased considerably, or else the countries of the Third World must be helped to increase their exports rapidly. The first solution is unthinkable in the present circumstances. This leaves the expansion of certain nontraditional exports from the Third World. A few measures have been taken in this direction, but up to now their effects have been negligible, and prospects are gloomy.

The hostile attitude toward any serious program of trade concessions to Third World countries are summed up in a recent article by George W. Ball with the revealing title "Neither Trade nor Aid."[8] The former American Undersecretary of State leaves no room for any hope of disinterested measures in favor of the Third World or of limiting the protectionism of the rich countries. On the other hand, it is very revealing of the ways in which the givers of aid are able to blackmail the beneficiaries.

In view of this, it is hardly surprising that feelings of lassitude, of disillusion, and even of irritation have taken hold of public opinion in the Third World, disappointed by the amount and quality of aid provided by international organizations and the industrialized countries. Bilateral (reciprocal) aid, which is predominant by far, is almost always governed by political considerations which are more or less embarassing for the receiving countries, since the obligation to use the credit on the market of the supplying country is explicitly stated. The attempt by the Americans and the Russians to outbid each other, for reasons which have little to do with generosity, undoubtedly is the sole positive element in the present situation, the appearance on the scene of the U.S.S.R. around 1955 having obliged the industrialized countries of the West to adopt a more flexible attitude.

The problem of aid to the Third World should be urgently reexamined in its fundamental principles. Two recent reports,[9] commissioned respectively by the President of the World Bank and the Secretary-General of the United Nations, are not of a nature to allay one's fears. The first contains not one new proposal and preaches the virtues of direct investment of foreign capital; the second limits itself to considering administrative reforms within the United Nations bureaucracy. However, by all the evidence, it is not at the level of operational details that reform is needed. The basic problems must be discussed. Let us again go to the root of the problem.

The England of yesteryear became industrialized by carving out for itself a colonial empire and by imposing an international division of labor to suit its own ends; this was the source of its wealth and power, and then an obstacle to the modernization of its industries. Most of the other industrialized countries of Europe, the United States, and Japan also benefited, at the time of their industrial revolutions, from more or less favorable external conditions.[10] The U.S.S.R., the only world power to become industrialized by overcoming very unfavorable external conditions, possessed, however, the advantage of a vast territory, rich in natural resources—though this did not exempt it from paying an enormous price for the autarky of the Stalinist period. The regrettable effects of transposing the economic model of the U.S.S.R. to Eastern Europe, immediately after the Second World War, are in fact to be explained by the fact that this model reflected the exceptional conditions of development of a continental nation, struggling against the blockade and the hostility of the surrounding world.

There was a relentless effort to make this model the rule for small countries possessing, despite the Cold War, a few opportunities for foreign trade, if only among themselves. The smaller and the more developed at the outset these countries were, the more they suffered in the process, Czechoslovakia probably having paid the highest price.

The role that fell to the Third World countries in the capitalist division of labor is well known. They became suppliers of raw materials and outlets for the industrial products of the developed countries. But Rosa Luxemburg's thesis should not be taken literally. Capitalism, in order to develop, does not need to annex noncapitalist territories continually; when external markets are necessary to maintain a high level of demand, it is able to create them artificially. The extraordinary expansion of trade among the industrialized countries, moreover, reduces the importance of the markets of the Third World for the industries of the developed countries, and changes in the structure of production make the economy of the developed countries less and less vulnerable to the lack of raw materials from the Third World—except, perhaps, petroleum. The 1967 war between Israel and the Arab countries and the subsequent closing of the Suez Canal have proved the capacity of the world capitalist system to adapt itself to changing conditions affecting supplies, for at least as long as the crisis is not general and it remains possible to choose suppliers and even to play on the rivalries between underdeveloped countries possessing parallel structures of production, or to substitute one channel of communication for another; orders for giant tankers made Japan's fortune.

To the countries of the Third World, the situation is characterized by an increasing asymmetry. They are tied to the international division of labor and dependent on it and, far from being able to transform it to benefit their development, they are forced to accept it as a stifling constraint. In spite of the implantation of many industries in several Third World countries over the last twenty years, their export structure remains practically unchanged and increasingly out of phase in relation to the structure of production. If one agrees to consider the relative share of industrial products in exports as a measure of progress, it is possible to make this lag almost an index of underdevelopment. Furthermore, an increasingly large proportion of these industries are owned by branches of the major multinational enterprises.[11]

A limited group of producers of petroleum and a few other industrial raw materials benefit from flexible outlets for their traditional exports; they can gear their strategy to a better use of earned foreign exchange and, if the political conditions are favorable, start a gradual change in structures of production, spread out over a sufficiently long period not to be rushed. (It is of course necessary for per capita exports to be high: all the oil in the Arab world would not be enough to generate growth in a country as heavily populated as India.)

But for most of the countries of the Third World, traditional exports, measured on a per capita basis, are stagnating, declining, or increasing at a rate which is far from sufficient to allow reasonable growth without a drastic reduction of the coefficient of imports in national income. For these countries, the debate on the respective advantages and disadvantages of substituting local production for imports, or, on the contrary, of an outward-looking economic model, does not make much sense; either they replace imports and develop at a reasonable rate or they stagnate, except in the case where imports do not have to be covered by exports, that is to say, they amount to gifts, or are paid for with credit on terms sufficiently generous not to pose any problems. In other words, these countries will be helped in their development if their foreign exchange is increased and then judiciously spent.

Shortage of foreign exchange is, in my opinion, the sole justification for having recourse to aid, since technical aid usually consists of services which can also be purchased on the market if one can afford to pay the price.[12] Of course, *ceteris paribus,* aid also increases savings, but the *ceteris paribus* is highly doubtful, as is shown by experience. The expectation of aid often causes a decrease in internal savings. It is as though internal savings were replaced by external savings, since aid serves ultimately to finance increased consumption, even when it comes in the form of machines. At all events, it should be possible to mobilize the financial resources for development normally through tax policy, while the lack of foreign exchange appears as an absolute obstacle, once the country has done everything necessary to promote viable exports and to bar superfluous imports.

It is therefore understandable that many countries of the Third World should seek international aid, especially if they think they can obtain it on financially advantageous conditions and without excessive political cost. But how can one explain the solicitude of the developed countries providing this aid, in contrast with their obvious reluctance in the field of commerce itself?

Here we touch on one of the most complicated aspects of international policy, one which has been deliberately confused. Demystification should begin with an analysis of the terms "aid," "assistance," and "cooperation." They are part of the vocabulary Myrdal describes,[13] which turned the "backward" countries of the prewar years into the "underdeveloped" countries of the postwar years, then into the "less developed" countries and, finally, the "developing" countries: diplomats came up with new euphemisms as the number of Third World countries acquiring independence, and therefore seats in the United Nations, increased. In fact, assistance and cooperation designate a large variety of operations, ranging from purely commercial agreements to philanthropic aid for people stricken by calamities.

Under these headings, for instance, come direct investments of foreign capital which, naturally, are intended to be profitable for the investor, sufficiently attractive even to compensate for the risk of political uncertainties. Their aim is not to grant favors to the countries concerned. No one would dream of saying that American companies seek to "aid" the Common Market countries by establishing themselves there, so why should it be any different in the case of the Andean Group, for instance? As for medium- and long-term credit, it is granted under a great variety of financial conditions: a small proportion consists of fifty-year loans with a nominal rate of interest; most of the time, the conditions are those of the international financial market. Sometimes the rates and commissions are exorbitant.

The amount of aid to the Third World, in strictly financial terms, should be calculated as the difference between the real cost of these loans and the cost which would be normal under current market conditions. We would then see it undergo a singular reduction. But even resorting to such a drastic calculation would not eliminate the *indirect* costs of aid: the inflated prices paid for supplies which have to be purchased in the countries providing aid; or the more or less superfluous purchases which would not have been made without apparently attractive terms of credit and which swell imports beyond what is necessary;[14] or the total disruption of development priorities, due to the suggestions or the demands of those providing funds.

However, it is sometimes very awkward to refuse these gifts (only a clear-sighted and courageous government, sure of popular support, can afford to do so), even when they have the disadvantage of prejudicing certain decisions within the planning framework and entailing additional and often considerable expenditure, drawn from the national budget.

In fact, through the mechanisms of aid the rich countries obtain substantial benefits for themselves. First of all, they possess, or think they possess, a means of bringing pressure to bear on the economic and consequently the political decisions of the recipient countries; and this is undoubtedly the chief motive behind bilateral aid programs, predominant by far both on the Western side and on the Russian side (this remark also applies to cases where the motives for applying pressure are not selfish ones, and are even inspired by the desire to really aid the recipient countries).

From this point of view, the geographical distribution of the aid provided by the major powers is very instructive. It is not dictated by the urgency of social and economic needs in this or that country of the Third World. The poorest countries are often granted the smallest amounts per capita, and China has been totally deprived of aid since it broke with the U.S.S.R. Nor is the distribution of aid dictated by the effectiveness or the diligence of the governments which receive it, the most corrupt governments often being accorded exceptional favors. Nor is aid acquired through docility, as many Latin-American governments have learned over the last twenty years. In fact, the country has to be in an important geopolitical position in the eyes of one of these major powers, particularly the United States or the U.S.S.R. Thus, from both sides, funds go preferentially to countries occupying a decisive position on the strategic map of each of these systems, which confront each other and struggle for possession of the soul of the Third World; to actual or potential turncoats; and finally, to countries which, deemed too vulnerable to the influence of the opposing party, have the right to special consideration. This allowed Egypt, up to 1967, and India, from 1954 to the present, to benefit from considerable aid, both from America and Russia. Of course, the points of interest shift as the international situation evolves.

Thus the United States was induced to launch the Alliance for Progress immediately after the victory of the Cuban revolution, although for more than ten years it had turned a deaf ear to the insistent requests for a Marshall Plan for Latin America. And this plan was practically abandoned as soon as the danger of new revolutions like the Cuban was considered to be no longer imminent. Having apparently judged the political profit from aid to the Third World to be too small, the United States is in the process of cutting down on the commitments, although the sums allocated for economic aid represent but a minute fraction of the cost of the war in Vietnam or of the race to the moon.[15]

On their side, the Russians also seem to have given up all claim to exercising any serious influence on the course of events in the Third World through what are in fact very small loans, amounting to the purchase price of key factories and to supplies of arms, undoubtedly overpriced when they are used Soviet army material. Coming onto the scene around 1955 initially gave them a considerable advantage. The monopoly of the West on supplies of heavily machinery was broken. India was able to launch its program to expand its steel industry by means of Soviet aid, especially since the agreement for the building of the Bhilai factory was immediately followed by similar commitments on the part of Great Britain and West Germany. Egypt managed to stand up to American blackmail and still build the Aswan dam. Soviet loans, repayment of which was spread over ten or twelve years at an interest rate of 2 to 3 percent, brought about a real revolution on the long-term capital market. But the amount of loans actually used turned out to be relatively small. The very low level of Soviet trade with the nonsocialist world was a barrier difficult to remove in a short time;[16] the equipment was not always adapted to climatic conditions very different from those to which the Russian technicians were accustomed; and the state of advancement of Soviet technology sometimes left something to be desired in relation to comparable Western equipment.[17] All these factors caused misunderstandings. The disappointment was mutual, in Africa especially, and in the U.S.S.R. Then came the downfall in Indonesia, after the weapons provided by the Russians had been used for the extermination of the Indonesian Communist Party. The only efforts which had appreciable political results were those in Cuba and the Middle East, but it is hard to say whether it was Russian aid or American blundering which should be held responsible. At all events, as far as the Arab countries are concerned, military aid has clearly taken the upper hand over economic aid. In short, in the United States as in the U.S.S.R., it is a time of skepticism: doubt has been cast on the role of aid to the Third World as an instrument of competition between the two systems. This is perhaps a long-term advantage for the countries needing aid, for it will be easier for them at last to pose seriously the problem of multilateral aid.

As for the economic advantages that the granting of aid affords to the countries which provide it, they are far from negligible. In any case, they justify a skeptical view of all that is usually said concerning the cost of aid for industrialized countries. Moreover, the problem is different for the U.S.S.R. and the people's democracies of Eastern Europe on the one hand and the industrialized West on the other.

For as long as the development plans of the East European countries ensure the full utilization of their capacities of production (which is in no way certain in practice), all long-term credit constitutes for them a reduction in available income, either for investments or for consumption. A material sacrifice thus becomes necessary, which can be justified in moral terms (principles of international solidarity), or in political terms (influence), or again as the price of putting of equipment produced in the U.S.S.R. and in the people's democracies on nonsocialist markets, an operation which could be economically advantageous if it made it possible in the long run to buy goods from the Third World with highly profitable exports. It would seem, indeed, that the net domestic cost of a unit of foreign exchange earned by exporting machines is, for the socialist countries, relatively low in relations to other possible exports, even allowing for the cost of the loan calculated at a discount rate considerably higher than the interest collected (the result of the calculation depends on the choice of this rate, and the views of economists are divided on this point). With regard, finally, to military aid, the real cost of the weapons provided is, as I have already said, very low, since often the equipment involved has been discarded as obsolete by the Soviet army; and the structure of prices on the world market is moreover so advantageous for the arms dealer that partial payment in cash, at the time of delivery, sometimes is in itself good business, even if the rest of the payment, financed by credit, is late.

Let us now move on to aid from the capitalist countries. This must be considered from two different points of view, that of the suppliers of products financed by aid and that of public finance.

For the former there are contracts identical to any other governmental order, usually financially attractive to the suppliers since the granting of credit places the seller in an advantageous position for negotiations. It should be stressed in this connection that the

implementation of projects financed by public aid is to a large extent
entrusted to private enterprise, even when the aid is multilateral, since
the United Nations has not yet thought of creating special machinery
to implement this kind of program. In the last analysis, then, the aid
granted to the countries of the Third World consists in offering outlets
for domestic enterprises. This is automatic for bilateral aid; as for un-
restricted and multilateral aid, the use of a few engineering consulting
firms which have a monopoly on the international market frequently
leads to the same results: the contracts are made with the major
American or West European enterprises. On the other hand, the economic potential of the countries of the Third World is seldom relied
upon for the implementation of such aid projects, even when there are
unused capacities of production. The experience of India and of several other Latin-American countries which have attained a certain degree of industrial development could, however, prove more useful to the
other underdeveloped countries than the mimetic transfer of solutions
formulated in highly industrialized countries.

I must digress here to the subject of American assistance in grain.
In selling off a substantial part of agricultural surplus within the framework of a policy of support for domestic farming, the United States
government does not incur any additional expenses. Moreover, under
the terms of its contracts with the Third World countries, the equivalent of the value of the grain in local currency is deposited in a special
account. A part of these funds serves to finance the many activities of
American embassies; another part is loaned to American or local private enterprises dealing with the United States. All in all, it amounts
to selling a part—approximately one third—of the grain. The remainder
represents a real contribution to the development of the countries at
the receiving end, insofar as imports of grain are really indispensable.

The argument that grain cannot finance development thus falls flat,
if one thinks of the possible uses of the exchange saved in this way
which normally would have been allocated for the importing of foodstuffs. On the other hand, one cannot deny the harmful effects, for

domestic farming, of the sale at low prices of the grain received from
the United States. Governments seek by this operation an easy popularity and short-term anti-inflationist effects, but they seriously compromise the chance of an expansion of local agriculture which would
otherwise, in the long run, be important.

But the most debatable aspect of American aid in foodstuffs, as
regulated by Public Law 480, is certainly the obligation under which
the beneficiaries are placed, that of consulting the United States before
releasing the counterpart funds in local currency. For the real economic effect of this assistance in kind makes itself felt the moment the government of the recipient country sells the grain: it thereby increases
its income while reducing purchasing power. Clearly, this operation
helps reduce inflationist pressure. However, the subsequent use of this
income should be the strict responsibility of the government. The release of equivalent funds is not aid in any sense (to consider it such would
be to count the grain twice) and, in economic terms, it is identical to
creating purchasing power by deficit financing. Still, the established
procedure practically gives to the United States government a right of
codecision concerning the use of a substantial part of the public investment funds of the recipient country.

But, it will be asked, in these conditions what is there to prevent the
leaders of the recipient countries from accumulating increasingly large
sums in the counterpart account and deciding not to release them,
since budgetary deficits could compensate perfectly well for their with-
holding? The answer, which is very simple, throws a revealing light on
the motives behind the aid administered according to Public Law 480:
in practice, the condition of negotiating new contracts for grain is the
release of accumulated counterpart funds and their use for purposes
jointly determined by the government of the recipient country and the
American authorities.[18]

I shall now return to the effects that aid may have on the economies of capitalist industrialized countries. As long as their capacities
of production are underemployed, public expenditure in the form of

aid will trigger the multiplier effect and the income finally produced will exceed the income which would have been produced without the allocation of aid. The aid granted finances itself, so to speak, at least within certain limits, which will not be reached for some time. There is obviously a danger of overfueling, producing inflationary pressure, since a part of the demand induced by aid contracts with the Third World may affect sectors of the economy with inelastic supply. But since in any case, in the American economy, public expenditure for armaments and space research is several times greater than the funds allocated for aid to the Third World, there is every reason to consider the latter as a valid substitute for military expenditure, within the unfortunately highly unlikely framework of a reconversion of the American economy to peaceful ends.

If my argument is correct, the following conclusions may be drawn.

First of all, the whole concept of aid to the Third World as a sacrifice for the taxpayers of rich countries is challenged. There is sacrifice only inasmuch as the funds earmarked for aid could be set aside for social programs in the donor country. The cutting down of military expenditure and of ill-conceived attempts to maintain international prestige could, in any case, open up possibilities of a simultaneous increase in aid and domestic social expenditure, although the problems of reconversion should not be oversimplified.

Under these circumstances, it is possible to conceive of a very ambitious program of aid from the industrialized countries to the countries of the Third World affording advantages to both sides and making it possible to speed up the growth rates of all parties.

But it would be pointless to expect such a program to help reduce, in terms of national per capita income, the differential between the two groups of countries, since acceleration would occur on both sides. This is shown in tables 5 and 6, with projections of the disparity in per capita income between the rich countries and the countries of the Third World for the years 1980 and 2000.

Table 5. Projection of Differential in Per Capita Income of Third World Countries and Rich Countries: 1980

Growth Rate of Per Capita Income in Rich Countries	Growth Rate of Per Capita Income in Third World Countries			
	2.0%	2.5%	3.0%	3.5%
2.0%	8.1	7.4	6.7	6.1
2.5%	9.0	8.1	7.4	6.7
3.0%	9.9	9.0	8.1	7.4
3.5%	10.9	9.9	9.0	8.1

The differentials are measured in multiples of the income of Third World countries. The base figure 8.1 was calculated for 1960, from data supplied by the United Nations, corrected for parity of purchasing power using the coefficients calculated by P. N. Rosenstein-Rodan.

Table 6. Projection of Differential in the Per Capita Income of Third World Countries and Rich Countries: 2000

Growth Rate of Per Capita Income in Rich Countries	Growth Rate of Per Capita Income in Third World Countries			
	2.0%	2.5%	3.0%	3.5%
2.0%	8.1	6.7	6.7	6.1
2.5%	9.9	8.1	7.4	6.7
3.0%	12.0	9.9	8.1	7.4
3.5%	14.6	12.0	9.0	8.1

The idea that an increase in aid necessarily produces a reduction in the growth rate of the donor country and an acceleration of that of the recipient country is based on a very simplified view of the arithmetic of national income and the impact of aid. This view has unfortunately taken root in public opinion. By adopting it themselves and by insisting on the fallacious postulate of reducing the gap (whereas in reality all that counts is accelerating the rate of development of the Third World), the politicians of the underdeveloped countries fall in with the opponents of cooperation in the rich countries.

And the misconceptions go on accumulating, accentuated by the hypocrisy which accompanies public discussion. It is indeed impossible for the governments of the rich countries to present aid both as an expression of their magnanimity toward the poor countries and as good business, or at the very least an operation from which a considerable political advantage is expected (to say so would not be politic). And this is all the more true in that there is sincere feeling in favor of aid to the Third World with moral motivation ranging from Christian charity to a feeling of responsibility for the still visible misdeeds of colonialism.

As for public opinion in the recipient countries, one must first of all distinguish the groups deriving personal advantage from cooperation in its present form and who do their best to present it in a better light. Then come the fairly large number of politicians who enjoy the illusion that the aid granted, as inadequate as it may be, is always better than nothing at all and who are content to count their blessings. Last, there are the increasingly large number of disappointed people who, having understood the real mechanisms of aid, denounce the disparity between the stated intentions and the real results. Their frankness is not of a kind to please public opinion in the rich countries, who accuse them in turn of ingratitude and criticize the so-called waste which would result from aid to Third World countries. Cartierism is gaining points, and the phenomenon is not exclusively French: it is also to be seen in the United States and in the U.S.S.R. Governments conclude that it is a good time to cut down on aid, which can only aggravate the indignation of the Third World, including governments normally inclined to co-operate with the major powers. Thus we find ourselves faced with an upsurge of mutual mistrust.

The United Nations naturally bears the repercussions of this, the two opposing parties having their reasons for criticizing the unwieldi-ness and the impotence of the international organizations set up after the Second World War. The rich countries want to reduce their finan-cial commitments, for the United Nations is increasingly getting out of their control, except for the World Bank (which explains the publicity given to the Pearson report and the favorable reception accorded to the Jackson report, both of which agree that the Bank should be given greater powers and made the center of aid operations). The underde-veloped countries are becoming increasingly aware of the limitations of the nonpartisan assistance which they can count on getting.

In view of this, it seems to me that, in order to establish a system of aid which would give the word its real meaning, the following princi-ples should be borne in mind:

1. Aid should be depersonalized, placed as far as possible outside the framework within which governments and corporations have interests at stake, and therefore conveyed entirely by way of nonpartisan channels. The receiving countries should be free to use it as they please, the right of *bona fide* error in decision making being recognized and charged to the cost of learning the difficult art of governing.

2. Since, however, *mala fide* errors and abuses are possible, guaran-tees would need to be considered.

Aid would be granted for periods of six years, the first installment being divided among the countries of the Third World according to a quantitative criterion, proportional to their population and inversely proportional to their per capita income (more complicated arithmetic may of course be considered). The situation would be re-examined every three years and the amount of aid already determined for the next three years could be reviewed, in light of how the resources al-ready distributed have been used.

To this end, two reports would be independently prepared by the government of the country concerned and by a group of experts, chosen from a list approved by all the governments of the Third World. These reports should show how the aid has been devoted to increasing the development potential of the country. More particularly, they should say what has been accomplished with it which would not have been possible without it. Since development potential is not directly measurable by growth rates of national income, worked out over a short period, the analysis should not content itself with a discussion of growth rates. It should try to ascertain what bottlenecks have been eased by the use of aid and what domestic resources have been mobilized by means of it. In the light of these reports (which, in the event of conflicting opinions, could be submitted to arbitration), the allocation of aid would be increased or reduced.

The recipient countries would solemnly promise not to use the aid received for military or paramilitary purposes. Since this suggestion may appear even more naive than the others, I should like to point out that, so far as I know, there exist no more effective means of preventing resources from being diverted to unlawful ends; in any case I assume an international moral standard different from that of today.

Finally, governments guilty of a serious violation of the human rights listed in the United Nations Charter could exceptionally, and for a limited period, be deprived of the right to aid.

3. In order to be truly effective, aid should be able to draw on resources several times greater than the sums committed to it at present. For this it would be necessary for the United Nations to have an independent income at its disposal, in addition to endowments provided by the rich member countries, according to a quantitative criterion proportional to their population and their per capita income. This independent income, which might go so far as to get rid of the very concept of the donor country, could be obtained by means of royalties paid for the exploitation of natural resources considered as a common heritage, such as the rich deposits in the ocean floor.[19] In addition to

their cash payments, the rich countries would be encouraged to contribute to a World Technology Fund, the patents and technical processes of which would be placed at the disposal of public enterprises in the Third World, against the payment of nominal fees and under a procedure guaranteeing that they are effectively used.

4. Without any question as to the right of the recipient countries to spend the aid received in the way which they deem best, the United Nations should be equipped with operational machinery enabling it to assume, at the request of the country concerned, the burden of certain planning operations for which it would be paid back at cost. Among other advantages, this would at last make it possible to obtain reliable information about the costs of this type of operation and, in the long run, to reduce the very substantial profit margins which are enjoyed today on the highly monopolized market of consulting, the building of factories, and public works. Furthermore, the United Nations should possess databanks in all the important fields of technology and management, be in a position to advise interested countries on the best sources of expertise and equipment and, in particular, establish a network of information and of scientific, technological, and economic cooperation among the countries of the Third World. There are good reasons to believe that north-south relations will continue to be maintained by the interest and the effort of the rich countries; on the other hand, practically everything remains to be done in the field of south-south relations, beginning by convincing the countries of the Third World of their real usefulness and of the decisive political importance that their mutual collaboration could have.

The proposals which I have just put forward have no real chance of being implemented in the immediate future. Granted the optimistic hypothesis that they would be well received, they would still need to be refined in the light of experience. It would therefore be good to be able to begin with a pilot project. And I think that the one most suited to such purposes is in the field of scientific and technological aid.

I think this first of all because no one has any doubt about its urgency and importance. Secondly, as science policy has only recently been inaugurated, it still eludes established frameworks and routine practices. Furthermore, the subject has fairly precise natural limits, and experience in this field should lend itself to widespread application in the larger sphere of economic aid. Last, certain scientific and technological aid projects have been under study recently, and they seem to be going in an opposite direction to that which I advocate. What they in fact suggest is that 5 percent of the sums intended for civil research in the rich countries, a very large sum in relation to the scientific effort of the Third World, be earmarked for research on themes of interest to the Third World. If this were the beginning of an overall plan to build up research on technologies suited to Third World countries and to create such technologies, as is suggested by an English research team,[20] I would see only one inconvenience: the insufficient emphasis given to the necessity of immediately placing certain resources at the free disposal of those concerned, even if this means allowing for considerable wastage. Such wastage could after all be ultimately salutary if, at this price, the countries of the Third World were to acquire greater skill in managing research and education. It is unfortunately not inconceivable that this policy could become a pretext for reinforcing the present mechanisms of domination, by making mimetic transfer of finished intellectual products the cornerstone of the strategy of economic growth in poor countries and by giving to the rich countries, through the workings of the market, the advantages of sales of patents and of expertise. If this happened, it could put an end for a long time to the chances of development in the Third World. It is therefore advisable to discuss scientific and technological policy in terms of a diametrically opposed point of view.

For my part, I should like assistance in the field of science and technology (S&T) to be made through the agency of the United Nations, in the form of an allowance for a period of six years originally calculated as a percentage of the national S&T budget, taking into account the real national income per capita. The aid would be reviewed at the end of three years, according to the general rule described above. The recipient country would be free to spend the funds obtained as it wished, but should be able to obtain the backing of various services placed at its disposal by the United Nations, and in particular to be able to make use of databanks and specialists capable of providing it with expert opinion, programs, and advice on equipment and of providing information on the real possibilities of cooperation with other countries of the Third World. It would be useful to make a special effort so that research workers from the Third World could travel for rapid consultation whenever they need to. Would it not be possible, for instance, to alter airline regulations so that the seats which have not been sold an hour before departure may be placed at the disposal of research workers, at a very reduced fare, as part of an international program? Last, the United Nations should create a certain number of advanced research and educational institutes, located in the Third World and designed as places where the research workers of the Third World and their colleagues from the developed countries can meet with each other. These institutions would be involved in basic research, directed at both the needs of the Third World and its possibilities (that is to say, not calling for too great a concentration of financial and human resources to attain a minimum level of efficiency). They would be involved also in applied research in areas hitherto neglected by world science, such as tropical farming, techniques of industrial production not requiring large amounts of capital, building methods for low-cost housing programs and so on. They would organize, for the research workers of the Third World, courses enabling them to keep abreast with what is taking place on the frontiers of world science and to be in a position to train a certain number of high-level specialists. These institutions could be federated in a World Development University, which should of course comprise centers specializing in the social sciences. This University's mission would be to promote interdisciplinary research on development problems and to train the necessary research teams.[21]

Having reached this point, the reader has the right to raise two questions: what is the sense in formulating a set of utopian proposals, in contrast with the pessimism of all the analyses in this book? What chances are there that a program of this kind may one day be accepted?

My reply will be very simple. It is because we are at such a complete dead-end, because there is a risk of disaster, that I think that the time has come to propose an international aid system defined in *opposition* to the present system, instead of continuing to discuss detail while avoiding the substance of the debate. As for its chances of being accepted, I must say that to appeal to what is noble and reasonable in human nature implies a profession of faith on the part of the author and his confidence in the fundamental values of Enlightenment philosophy. Moreover, it is not so much the Third World's chances of development which are at stake as the price which it will have to pay for its progress and which the rest of the world will also have to pay. I am not so optimistic as to believe that reason will prevail before it is imposed on us by a few violent object lessons which could have been avoided.

Notes to Chapter 14

1. I developed this idea in my essay: "L'indépendance du Tiers Monde: Structures de production et structures intellectuelles," in *La liberté et l'ordre social* (Boudry-Neuchatel, 1969), pp. 113-128.

2. See, among others, H. J. Barnett and Charles Morse, *Scarcity and Growth: The Economics of Natural Resource Availability* (Baltimore, 1963).

3. As L. B. Pearson has written in his report entitled *Vers une action commune pour le développement du Tiers Monde* (Paris, 1969), 41 countries of the Third World have managed since 1955 to maintain a growth rate of per capita income of 2 percent yearly or more, which is equivalent to the growth rates of Western Europe and North America during the latter half of the nineteenth century and the early half of the twentieth (see also the article by the same author, "A New Strategy for Global Development," in *Unesco Courier,* February 1970, pp. 4-10).

According to S. J. Patel, per capita income went up, for the developed countries, at the rate of 1.8 percent yearly from 1850 to 1960; see S. J. Patel, "The Economic Distance between Nations, Its Origins, Measurement and Outlook," *The Economic Journal* (March 1964). As the rate of population growth in Third World countries is very much higher than that in nineteenth-century Europe, it follows that the growth rate of national income in Third World countries is higher than the level attained in the past by the industrialized countries.

4. O. Sunkel, "Capitalismo transnacional y desintegración nacional en la América Latina," in *El Trimestre Economico*, vol. 38 (2), no. 150, pp. 571-621.

5. The recovery of the last two years cannot disguise the fact that the participation of underdeveloped countries in world trade in constantly decreasing to the benefit of trade within the group of industrial countries which, in 1969, represented in themselves more than half of world exports (see *International Trade, 1970*, General Agreement on Tariffs and Trade; Geneva, 1970). Whereas, in 1953, the share of the countries of the Third World in world trade was 27 percent, in 1968 it had gone down to 18.3 percent.

6. In a calculation for 1950-1961, which caused a great deal of stir, Raul Prebisch has evaluated the losses resulting from deterioration in the balance of trade of the developing countries at $13.1 billion, compared with inputs of foreign capital of $40.7 billion and $20.9 billion in external payments for the servicing of foreign investments. The data, for Latin America, for the same period, are the following: losses resulting from the deterioration in trade, $10.1 billion, servicing of foreign investments and the foreign debt, $13.4 billion (Raul Prebish, *Towards a New Trade Policy for Development;* Paris, 1964). According to more recent estimates, the annual servicing of the public debt of the Third World countries amounted in 1969 to $5 billion and payments in the way of profits and interest on private investments to some $4 billion. The $9 billion thus paid out represented 70 percent of the total contributions received in the same year from the developed capitalist countries. In fact, according to the O.E.C.D., net financial aid in 1969 rose to $13.297 billion, of which scarcely $7.248 was for the public sector (quoted by A. Angelopoulos, "L'aide aux pays pauvres les écrase de dettes," *Le Monde,* August 11, 1970).

7. According to A. Angelopoulos, ibid., in 1977 the amount for merely servicing the foreign debt will increase to $9.2 billion dollars. It will therefore have doubled. After one adds interest and profits on loans and private investments, the total sum of the service will be very much higher than that of the new loans. In other words, a few years from now, it will be the poor countries who will be aiding the rich countries.

8. Here are the important passages: "Stated explicitly or otherwise, the underlying assumption of most prophets of development is that, with outside assistance,

the poorer countries can sooner or later achieve 'takeoff' by producing not merely agricultural and raw materials but by developing the less sophisticated types of
manufacture. Concurrently, the economically advanced countries are expected
to shift the use of their resources up the spectrum of sophistication toward intensive production requiring elaborate machinery and complex technology. What
this formula for growth has overlooked, of course, is that there are entrenched
forces in the advanced countries that stand firmly against this process, and their
effectiveness is enhanced by the hard fact that, in any democratic society, political power is concentrated in the labor-intensive industries. Because those industries have more workers per unit of output, they necessarily represent more
votes—it is as simple as that. Add to this that the textile industry has not yet
been fully rationalized and still comprises a large number of relatively small but
geographically dispersed units and one can understand why it wields more political clout than the more glamorous computer and automobile industries. What
all this adds up to, of course, is that, as the Northern Hemisphere nations tire of
providing foreign aid—whether out of boredom, disappointment, or the deflec-
tion of their interest to local matters—the developing countries should brace
themselves against major disillusion. For if the virus of protectionism should run
rampant among the giants, it would be the vulnerable emerging countries who
would fall first victim—and the carnage would not be pleasant to see" (*News-
week,* international edition, August 3, 1970).

9. R. G. A. Jackson, *A Study of the Capacity of the United Nations Development System* (Geneva, 1969), vol. 1.

10. In this sense Rosa Luxemburg, *Accumulation of Capital* (New York, 1964)
was probably right to insist on the importance of the foreign market for the development of capitalism. Her thesis remains true if one agrees with Kalecki
to consider the munitions industry as the substitute for a foreign market (M.
Kalecki, "The Marxian Equations of Reproduction and Modern Economics,"
in *Marx et la pensée scientifique contemporaine,* Paris and The Hague, 1969,
p. 321). It is to be pointed out that Rosa Luxemburg devotes one of the chapters of her work to militarism as a field of accumulation (vol. 2, pp. 118-130).

11. According to recent estimates, subsidiaries of American enterprises controlled in 1966 a third of the industrial production of Latin America, 11 percent
of its imports and 35 percent of its exports. These figures quoted by O. Sunkel
(see note 4 above) should be compared with the data on the world position of
these 10,000 subsidiaries of 187 giant North American conglomerates studied by
an American economist, Raymond Vernon. Their production in 1968 reached
$130 billion, which makes them the third industrial power of the world. This
figure represents, roughly speaking, four times the total of North American
exports.

12. This is the famous "foreign exchange gap," in contrast with the "savings gap." See in this connection my study: "The Significance of the Foreign Trade Sector and the Strategy of Foreign Trade Planning," in United Nations, *Planning the External Sector: Techniques, Problems and Policies,* Report on the First Interregional Seminar on Development Planning, Ankara, September 1965.

13. Gunnar Myrdal, *Asian Drama* (New York, 1968), vol. 3, appendix 1, pp. 1839-1842.

14. See I. M. D. Little's contribution to *Towards a Strategy for Development Cooperation with Special Reference to Asia* (Rotterdam, 1968), pp. 54-70. In the article already quoted, Angelopoulos estimates at 20 percent the additional cost of imports financed through restricted loans. Angelopoulos, "L'aide aux pays pauvres."

15. Robert S. McNamara, the former American Secretary of Defense, at this writing the President of the World Bank, pointed out, at the 1970 meeting of the Bank governors, that at the present time aid represents less than 1 percent of the budget of the United States and less than 0.3 percent of the gross national product, which places the United States in eleventh position among O.E.C.D. members providing aid. He pointed out that military expenditure is more than 20 times higher than expenditure on aid and on the basis of his long experience, he even declared that it should be easy to direct the equivalent of 5 percent of military expenditure toward aid to the Third World, by simply cutting down on waste. (See R. S. McNamara, *Address to the Board of Governors,* Copenhagen, September 1970, p. 23.) Who would cast doubt on the opinion of such an expert?

16. According to data from UNCTAD, trade between socialist countries and the countries of the Third World constituted only 2.6 percent of the latters' trade in 1955, increasing to 7.2 percent in 1965 and decreasing to 6.9 percent in 1968, which represented scarcely 2.56 percent of world exports. ("L'aide des pays socialistes au Tiers Monde," in *Problèmes économiques,* October 29, 1970, p. 19).

17. In his book *Les Guérilleros au pouvoir. L'Itinéraire politique de la révolution cubaine* (1970), K. S. Karol describes the setbacks experienced by the Cuban economy on account of the technological backwardness of some of the machinery imported from Eastern Europe (p. 225).

18. In this connection, see the study, already cited, by M. Kalecki and Ignacy Sachs, "Forms of Foreign Aid: An Economic Analysis," *Information sur les sciences sociales,* March 1966.

19. This last idea was at the time of writing a topic of discussion in the United States.

20. United Nations, "World Plan of Action for the Application of Science and

Technology to Development," draft of introductory statement prepared for Advisory Committee on the Application of Science and Technology to Development, Document E/AC.52/L.68, October 19, 1969.

21. I have taken up again and expanded here certain ideas which I presented with H. Marcovich to the Eleventh Pugwash Symposium: *Que peuvent faire les savants pour le développement?* Stanford, September 1970.

Conclusion: The Stakes

In the course of this work I have not hesitated to take positions which are sometimes peremptory and undoubtedly subjective. This stems from the uncertainties presently inherent in any attempt to take an all-encompassing view in the social sciences and from the impossibility of completely eliminating one's ideological preferences. But I also have an emotional commitment, which must be explained autobiographically.

Fourteen years in Brazil and three in India—the countries where I was educated—along with many shorter journeys to Asia, Africa, and Latin America allowed me to discover the Third World for myself. I was all the more open to it because being a Pole of Jewish origin—for which I was exiled twice, in 1939 and 1968—made me sensitive to the problem of ethnocentrisms. I have come up against the real and imaginary frontiers between nations, cultures, races, and social classes since my childhood, and in my profession I naturally tended toward an interdisciplinary approach.

Here, then, despite appearances, is a very personal book which attempts to bridge the gap before it is too late. The urgency of a radical change in attitudes toward the problems of the Third World is therefore the theme of this conclusion.

After Bandoeng and the spectacular arrival of independent India on the world scene, Gandhi came into fashion. The spiritual and political leaders of the oppressed throughout the world and certain statesmen in countries that were achieving independence, in Asia and Africa, inclined toward his philosophy of action based on *ahimsa* (nonviolence) and hoped to derive from it a technique of mass action, and even a philosophy of government.

They were forgetting the charismatic power of this frail man with a prophet's vocation, and the part that it played—forgetting his skill in translating the ideal of independence into a series of limited actions, chosen in terms of changing circumstances, in such a way that each time they were understandable in their concrete reality to the masses of the faithful. They were also forgetting his skill in mixing the sacred and the profane, in combining political goals with the preaching of ethics and patriotic ardor with the religiosity in which Indian culture is steeped. He had the genius to project the political struggle onto a symbolic plane, by imposing on the other side rules which the English would not have been able to break except, if worst came to worst, by drowning India in an ocean of blood and violence which would have made the most barbaric exploits of the Europeans pale into insignificance—no small achievement. Moreover, the continental dimensions of India, the world war, and the way in which Gandhi was able to arrange a way out for the English through compromise, counted for a great deal. But Gandhi's social and economic program, founded on a retrogressive agrarian utopia and sustained by a banal solidarist philosophy, lost its hold on the reality of India and, *a fortiori,* of any other country, once the tasks of construction took precedence over those of combat. It was a symbolic program, designed to make people reject colonizing industrialism, not to ensure them of material prosperity. The Indian masses today aspire to live better without denying their cultural tradition—material well-being having become a universal value, which does not mean an exclusive one.

Today it is Fanon, the prophet of the Third World's redemption through violence, and the Chinese who have come to serve as an inspiration. In their dogged attempt to build a new society, founded on Communist ideals which they have purified, they believe, through criticizing the bureaucratic degeneration of Soviet socialism and which they hold up as a model for the underdeveloped countries of Asia, Africa, and Latin America, the Chinese have never neglected preparedness for a life-and-death armed struggle, which they think will be started by the world counterrevolution when it has abandoned all hope of stemming the irresitible tide of revolution by other means.

It is easy to criticize the Manichean vision of a world in which cities and rural areas, set up as symbols of the oppressors and the oppressed, are seen in opposition to each other, and it is easy to reject the rhetorical device of projecting on the world scale the Marxian model of capitalist society, reduced to two antagonistic classes—the bourgeoisie and the proletariat.

But it would be presuming a very great deal to believe in the real virtue of intellectual analyses. It is, on the contrary, misconceptions that possess the faculty of unsettling the masses, provided that they are presented in a simple, coherent and apparently logical form that can claim to provide an explanation for everything and offer an immediate path of action. A correlation raised to the status of an explanatory law often serves the purpose. This is the way in which racism may be used to explain the contradictions of our world and the antagonism which sets the affluent world of the whites against the impoverished colored world. By a curious working of history, the most reactionary ideology there has ever been, the very ideology which served to justify the worst colonialist excesses and genocides, is now being turned back on its perpetrators. It is placed in the service of the most radical of liberation movements, immediately then to be seized on by the supporters of the old system. It can always serve their purpose provided the terms of opposition are inverted and they are ready to direct their wrath against the yellow peril threatening to engulf the U.S.S.R., which has been promoted to the role of an advanced stronghold of Euro-American civilization; against the American blacks; against the foreign workers who have come to Europe to earn a living; against the native peoples of South Africa and elsewhere. The extreme left and the reactionary right thus find themselves agreeing to wage war on the same field where ethnocentric prejudice, the disfigured image of the other, takes precedence over reason.

Of course the symmetry is not absolute. It is impossible to overlook the historical sequence which has brought us to the present point as well as the high correlation coefficient which, in spite of all I have just said, links skin color and oppression for an American black, a European "metic," and lastly a Vietnamese, fighting against the American invader. Then, apart from the impact of recent events, there is still the living weight of the past, the persistence of stereotypes which have become part of culture and which have been accentuated by an ideological, mystifying, and myth-creating history. The heritage of hatred and mistrust may live on for much longer than the deeds which were the cause of it, not to mention the fact that the Manichean view of the world in terms of racial opposition naturally tends to act as a spur to all kinds of ethnocentrism and to revive all forms of national, tribal, and religious animosity. In the end, this heritage divides men more than it brings them together from either side.

What is at stake is the future of mankind. The discovery of the Third World makes it necessary to reconsider every aspect of our position, our attitudes, our images of the other, and our obligations, and then to move on to action.

Europocentrism must be attacked at the level of its intellectual and cultural manifestations, be they apparent or hidden, virulent or endemic; but it is above all the economic basis of the Europocentric world order which must be challenged. The countries of the Third World will take it upon themselves to do this sooner or later, at a lesser or greater price, with us or against us, within the framework of a harmonious international order or beneath the banner of a militant and even destructive Europophobia.

To the cynics, I say: In the name of self-interest we must take an active part in the emancipation of the Third World, if only as a long-term safety measure. To those who have not forgotten the humanist tradition of European culture, that tradition which, in spite of all that has occurred throughout history, we have the right to share with all men, I cry: It is our dignity that is at stake.

And our freedom too, which will be measured by our capacity to rid ourselves of the domination of *things* and of the inequalities which it creates, and by our ability to conceive and bring to fruition blueprints for society and contracts based on respect for other people. Will the discovery of the Third World be a turning point on this path?

JACKSON LIBRARY – LANDER UNIV.
HC59.7 .S24913   CIRC
The discovery of the Third World /

3 6289 000759172

220425

HC
59.7   Sachs, Ignacy
.S24913
                The discovery of
                the Third world

DATE DUE

FEB 4 1986			
FEB 2 5 1986			

CARD REMOVED